WALES, THE MERCANTILE MARINE AND THE FIRST WORLD WAR

WALES, THE MERCANTILE MARINE AND THE FIRST WORLD WAR

M. D. MATTHEWS

UNIVERSITY OF WALES PRESS
CARDIFF
2025

© M. D. Matthews, 2025

All rights reserved. No part of this book may be reproduced in any material form (including photocopying or storing it in any medium by electronic means and whether or not transiently or incidentally to some other use of this publication) without the written permission of the copyright owner except in accordance with the provisions of the Copyright, Designs and Patents Act 1988. Applications for the copyright owner's written permission to reproduce any part of this publication should be addressed to the University of Wales Press, University Registry, King Edward VII Avenue, Cardiff CF10 3NS.

www.uwp.co.uk

British Library Cataloguing-in-Publication Data
A catalogue record for this book is available from the British Library.

ISBN   978-1-83772-201-3
eISBN   978-1-83772-202-0

The right of Mark Matthews to be identified as author of this work has been asserted in accordance with sections 77 and 79 of the Copyright, Designs and Patents Act 1988.

The University of Wales Press acknowledges the financial support of the Welsh Books Council.

Typeset by Marie Doherty
Printed and bound by CPI Group (UK) Ltd, Croydon, CR0 4YY

Contents

	Acknowledgements	vii
	List of Illustrations	ix
	Notes on Sources and Conventions	xi
	Introduction	1
1	The Normal Run of Business	11
2	Pay and Conditions	31
3	The Outbreak of War	55
4	Alternative Lenses: Women, Small Communities and the International Nature of Crewing	81
5	1915: Mines, U-boats and Close Calls	111
6	1915: Captured by U-boats and Sunk	129
7	Changing the Rules: Unrestricted Submarine Warfare 1915; Convoys 1917–18	157
8	Courage, Compensation and Commemoration 1916–18	179
	Bibliography	203
	Index	209

Acknowledgements

There are many people who have helped in steering my course towards the realisation of this book. I would like to express my particular thanks to the late Professor John Armstrong, who facilitated my first opportunity to give a paper on Welsh maritime history at a European conference in the 1990s; and to both Robin Evans, whose untimely death robbed us of one of the finest Welsh-language writers of maritime history, and the late Ken Lloyd Gruffydd, the foremost writer on maritime Wales during the Middle Ages – all of whose encouragement and support are sorely missed.

I would like to acknowledge all those involved in the creation of the National Maritime Museum's 'Crew Lists of the British Merchant Navy – 1915' website and 'Welsh Newspapers' online at the National Library of Wales, without which this book would have been considerably more difficult to complete.

My thanks are also due to Dr Jamie Davies of the Arts and Humanities Research Council for his suggestions on an earlier draft, to the anonymous reader whose insightful comments have helped make this a much better book, and to staff at the University of Wales Press. Finally, I would like to thank my wife, the writer Jo Mazelis, for her unfailing interest in matters maritime and her generous forbearance of mine.

List of Illustrations

Figure 1	Cardiff docks c. 1911, courtesy of the George Grantham Bain Collection, Library of Congress	11
Figure 2	Crew of the *Edernian* at Santa Fe, River Plate, July 1914, courtesy of the Roberts family of Edern and Rhiw.com	31
Figure 3	Postcard of the LNWR's Irish mail steamer *Cambria* at Holyhead pre-1914	55
Figure 4	The barque *Jordan Hill*, courtesy of the State Library of South Australia, A. D. Edwardes Collection	81
Figure 5	Some of the crew of the *Hopemount* at Cardiff, 1915, courtesy of the Glamorgan Record Office	92
Figure 6	Postcard of German minelayer c. 1915	111
Figure 7	U-boats at Kiel, 1914, courtesy of the George Grantham Bain Collection, Library of Congress	111
Figure 8	'Sinking of the Linda Blanche' ('Kaperung und Versenkung des englischen Handelsdampfer') by W. Stöwer, in the German magazine *Illustrirte Zeitung*, 1915	129
Figure 9	Port Talbot Docks 1915, courtesy Llyfrgell Genedlaethol Cymru/National Library of Wales	157
Figure 10	*Llandovery Castle* Victory Bond poster, Library of Congress	179

Note on Sources and Conventions

Extensive use of online sources has been made in the preparation of this work, and those from which material is frequently drawn are referenced only in the first instance. Much of this material is contained in the following online sources:

- The National Maritime Museum's 'Crew Lists of the British Merchant Navy – 1915' has proved an invaluable resource; available at *http://1915crewlists.rmg.co.uk*
- 'Crewlist', the excellent online resource created and run by Peter and Jan Owens, who were heavily involved in the National Maritime Museum project, has proved particularly useful for access to the scans of the 1915 Merchant Navy Lists; available at *www.crewlist.org.uk*
- 'Wrecksite'; available at *www.wrecksite.eu*
- Mercantile Marine Memorial online; available at *www.londonremembers.com/memorials/mercantile-marine-memorial-ww1*
- *British Vessels Lost at Sea* (HMSO, 1919); available updated online at *www.naval-history.net*
- 'Welsh Newspapers' online; available at *http://newspapers.library.wales/*. For the period of the First World War, this resource has twenty-four English-language and eighteen Welsh-language newspapers, both daily and weekly titles
- An online version of TNA MT 9/1238 'List of Merchant Seamen and Fishermen detained as Prisoners of War in Germany, Austria-Hungary and Turkey, Board of Trade Printed List 31st May 1918' is available at *https://spw-surrey.com/MT9/26-2/*

Despite the utility and ease of access to online resources, they are also subject to degradation in varying ways – a matter that seems to have garnered little discussion to date within the historical profession. The main such resources used here appear to be as secure and permanent as can be hoped for.

Welsh place names in the main text are, in general, those in current usage; in quoted materials they are as they originally appeared. Counties are referred to by their pre-1974 names, with Monmouthshire treated as a Welsh county. Where not stated in the text, Newport is generally used to indicate Newport, Monmouthshire. U-boats are prefixed SM (His Majesties) throughout. In general, on the first mention of a specific vessel on which crew members from Wales were present, the gross registered tonnage (GRT) and date that the vessel was built is given. In a few instances (usually smaller sailing craft) only net tonnages are available from the Merchant Navy Lists. On some occasions the official number for the vessel is also given, to provide clarity about the particular vessel referred to; for example, in instances of very common names or where ships' names have been changed by the owners.

Numbers up to ninety-nine are written, though exceptions have been made in some cases, such as tonnages, percentages and monetary amounts. This does not apply to quotations where original conventions apply. Only approximate positions are given for the sites of wrecks – readers who wish to know exact locations should consult 'Wrecksite' or similar online resources.

For those who are interested in a comprehensive list of all the Welsh merchant mariners who lost their lives, see B. C. Jones, *Book of Remembrance Seafarers from Wales of the Mercantile Marine & Fishing Fleets who lost their lives during World War One 1914–1918* (2014).

Introduction

At midday on Monday 3 August 1914, across most of Wales the temperature was pleasantly in the mid-60s Fahrenheit, and while there was some cloud about, there was much sunshine and blue sky. It was the start of the longest bank holiday in British history, occasioned by the financial turmoil enveloping Europe in the wake of the Austrian ultimatum to Serbia. The banks would remain closed until Friday. The newspapers were full of talk of war, even among the usually anodyne public notices. In the *Cambria Daily Leader*, a broadly liberal newspaper circulating in the populous south and southwest of Wales, an order for the mobilisation of the Austro-Hungarian army sat uneasily next to announcements concerning the Skewen and district summer show and the sailing times for Ilfracombe on the paddle-steamer *Brighton*.[1] At ports and railway stations across the country those making a last-minute dash from the continent crossed paths with foreign nationals answering the various calls to arms and seeking passage in the opposite direction.

At Swansea, a group of Breton onion men were photographed on their way to the railway station and thence for their regiments in France. Arriving from the other direction later that day, was the headmaster of Terrace Road School with his wife and a party of children, whose study trip to Paris had been suddenly curtailed, and a woman who had been holidaying in the Rhineland when the sudden notice for foreigners to leave had been issued.[2] Their accounts of the chaos descending on the continent would be in the next day's edition. Though war was not yet officially declared, enthusiastic crowds had watched the recalled naval reservists departing on the Sunday evening and reports were already circulating of merchant shipping being seized at German ports. By the time the extended bank holiday was over, a long and frequently perilous ordeal for merchant mariners had commenced.

The following account of the experiences, contribution and sacrifice made by the merchant seamen (and women) of Wales during the First World War forms an important strand of our understanding of civilian participation in the conflict. For Wales, although there are some published materials relevant to the topic, they are scattered widely and tend to contain the civilian maritime experience of the First World War within the regional histories of ports and shipping or the histories of shipping companies; there has been no thorough-going examination of the subject. There have been few recent general studies of the mercantile marine,[3] with Richard Woodman's multi-volume history a welcome addition. Further, the monumental nature of the major works concerning the merchant service during the First World War published in the 1920s, probably account for the dearth of subsequent work.[4] Recently, there has been some renewed interest in the subject, for example, by P. Lyon, while the experiences of the fishermen and trawlers during the conflict have been explored by D. d'Enno.[5]

This study is primarily concerned with Welsh participation in the mercantile marine from the outbreak of the war until the end of 1915. This period is of particular interest as it was prior to a number of interventions that would alter the nature of normal maritime commercial operations. In response to the failure to properly co-ordinate merchant shipping as a national asset in the early phase of the war, 1916 saw the appointment of a Shipping Controller, the creation of the Ministry of Shipping and the formation of the Mercantile Marine Reserve, all of which impacted on normal working.[6] Another feature of this early period was that despite the introduction of press censorship at the outbreak of the war, merchant shipping movements continued to be published as normal. The reportage of such and related matters contained in newspapers represents largely unmediated journalism, the veracity of which was generally reliable. Given the paucity of official records and the lack of any Welsh focus in the official published accounts of the mercantile marine for this period, the newspapers of Wales provide one of the few sources for detailed information on this subject. The examples of such journalism used in the following narrative have been selected to represent the full range of realities attendant with such service and to further demonstrate the widespread dispersal of Welsh mariners within the British merchant fleet.

During this period there are no separate figures for the total number of those employed in maritime matters in Wales. The occupational breakdown for England and Wales provided by the 1911 census shows 99,804 'Merchant seamen, pilots, boatmen on seas' (though only those available for enumeration) and 28,197 bargemen, lightermen and boatmen (for whom the figure is probably more representative).[7] A further 5,232 persons were added for navigation services on shore to make a total for England and Wales 'on seas rivers and canals' of 133,233. The total for the whole United Kingdom was 164,605, which included some 1,254 women.[8] Work by Burton on the enumeration of the floating population and the Published Records of the Registry of British Seamen further explores the problems of accounting for merchant seamen at this time.[9] In 1911 there were 25,239 fishermen enumerated for England and Wales either on shore or on vessels that were in port on census night, or that arrived there the following morning. In addition to the 25,239 fishermen classed as such, 2,500 seamen on fishing boats were enumerated, as well as 1,618 other males definitely engaged in the industry. It was noted that a complete statement of the numbers actually engaged in fishing could not be obtained by means of the ordinary census, due to the prolonged absence from home of the crews of many of the fishing vessels. According to estimates made by Officers of Customs, the number of men and boys regularly employed in 1911 on sea-fishing boats registered in ports in England and Wales was 37,224; and the number of persons occasionally employed was 7,057.[10] The total given for the United Kingdom was 63,176, and included some 457 women.[11]

Out of a total *occupied male* population for England and Wales aged over ten years in 1911, of some 14.3 million, 158,000 were recorded as being either on seas, rivers and canals or as engaged in fishing. Roughly speaking, then, those who were engaged in maritime matters comprised slightly more than 1 per cent of the total workforce.[12] For England and Wales about 57 per cent of the *total* population were occupied, and if this percentage is translated across to the Welsh experience, where the total population in 1911 was around 2.5 million, then we might expect some 14,000 to be engaged in maritime occupations in Wales. In Scotland and Ireland in 1911 (for which there are separate figures), which had similar total populations (3.7 and 3.5 million, respectively) and similar numbers of occupied men (1.5 million and 1.4 million), the number of men engaged on 'seas rivers and canals' was markedly different, some 21,000 in Scotland but only 9,500 in Ireland. For fishing, the numbers were 28,000 and 8,500, respectively. Some of the difficulty in having accurate figures stems from the fact that the registration of seamen had been abandoned between 1857 and 1913, with the crew lists (for which no index of names was kept) proving the only central record of serving merchant seamen. In 1910, the Advisory Committee on Merchant Shipping proposed to the Board of Trade that a Central Index Register of merchant seamen should again be created. The Central Index Register was started in October 1913; however, virtually all the CR1 and CR2 index cards for the period 1913–17 have been destroyed.[13]

There are various estimates of the size of the British merchant fleet at this time, for example in 1913 Lloyd's register gives us an idea of the overall make-up of British shipping, which then comprised some 10,466 merchant vessels, totalling 22.5 million gross registered tons. The vast majority of this was made up of iron or steel steamers, with less than 1.5 million tons being sailing vessels. The introduction of oil-fuelled engines had not yet had much of an impact on British merchant shipping. In 1913 there were only twelve such vessels classed by Lloyds, though another twenty-five were under construction.[14] Another source giving figures for 1 July 1914, suggests that the merchant fleet comprised some 8,587 steamers and 653 sailing vessels (these figures do not include vessels under 100 tons net).[15] According to a third estimate, Woodman states that Britain entered the war with a fleet of about 9,500 vessels with a further 1,500 registered in the dominions, chiefly Canada.[16] One survey of the numbers of men in the mercantile marine at this time gives the total number of seamen at 193,500 not including fishermen or lascars. This figure was made up of around 24,000 deck officers, 37,200 cooks and stewards, 106,500 petty officers, sailors and firemen, and 20,600 engineers.[17] Writing in 1922, Archibald Hurd reckoned the numbers of men serving in the merchant fleet at the outbreak of war to be 170,000 British merchant seamen and 100,000 fishermen. Out of these 18,000 were Royal Navy Reservists. A more recent estimate shows 212,640 British seamen, 31,396 'foreign sailors' and 51,616 lascars, giving a total of 295,652 seamen employed on UK-registered merchant ships in 1914. Of these, 14,094 were employed on sailing vessels and 281,558 on steam.[18] In 1914 the Royal Navy comprised 147,000 men, but by 1918 this had increased by around 200,000. The overall increase in numbers (including wastage of some 80,000), were men drawn mainly from the mercantile marine and fishing fleets.[19] The Admiralty Naval Estimates for 1919–20 shows the strength of the Royal Navy at the date of the Armistice as being 415,612, though this figure included the men of the Mercantile Marine Reserve. Some 2,479 merchant ships were lost to the enemy between 1914 and 1918, more than 9 million tons.[20] The Mercantile Marine Memorial at Tower Hill, London, unveiled in December 1928, records the names of the 12,210 seamen who have no other grave than the sea, out of a total of some 17,000 who lost their lives in the merchant and fishing fleets during the First World War. The information provided by the memorial allied with information from the Commonwealth War Graves Commission, while useful, is not easily searchable in a way that will distinguish Welsh mariners.[21] By its nature, the memorial sheds no light on those whose bodies were recovered and buried ashore, or those whose lives were lost under other circumstances such as accident or illness, those injured and those who survived.

Thus, the recent digitisation of 39,000 crew agreements for 1915 by the National Maritime Museum at Greenwich provides an invaluable resource.[22] Crew lists are frequently laid out in the first instance in the following fashion: first, above deck, starting with master, then mates, bosun, carpenters and seamen; then below deck (on steam vessels), the engineering officers, then the donkeymen, firemen and trimmers. Merchant seamen are entered on the crew agreements in a number of different ways. They can be found signed on as sailor, seaman, ordinary seaman or able seaman. An ordinary seaman was the lowest rating on a British ship. An able seaman was by the old definition someone able to 'hand', 'reef' and 'steer', but in an age of steamers this was replaced by the knowledge of the day-to-day working of a ship, leaving aside the specialist skills of navigation and engineering.

Ships' cooks are found on all but the smallest of vessels, and on passenger vessels there were stewards and stewardesses, as well as a plethora of kitchen and related staff.[23] These agreements include all crew who served during the period of the agreement, thus there are frequently more recorded in total than the crewing required, as crew often discharged part way through an agreement, some fell ill, some failed to join ship, some deserted, and replacements were taken on as needed. In some instances, the records of those joining and leaving gives us a partial view of the progress of each voyage. As these crew lists were filed in 1915, among them are agreements for foreign-going vessels that begin earlier than 1915 as voyages could be for up to three years' duration. The focus of this examination of the evidence is set squarely on the matter of merchant seamen going about their normal business, and therefore, although many merchant seamen would serve in the Mercantile Marine Reserve or as Royal Navy Reservists, their particular story is not addressed here. British merchant crews were not expected to enlist (though many did) as the Board of Trade considered that 'the efficient maintenance of our mercantile marine is of vital national interest, and captains, officers, engineers, and their crews will be doing as good service for their country by continuing to man British ships as by joining the Army'.[24]

The activities of the fishing fleets and their use as minesweepers has been discussed elsewhere,[25] and those who crewed the armed merchant cruisers, submarine decoy vessels (also known as Q-ships), troopships, hospital ships and other auxiliary requisitioned craft are not the central feature in the following survey.[26] The Mercantile Marine Reserve came into existence purely through wartime expediency. Mercantile Fleet Auxiliaries – that is, merchantmen on government service (as opposed to the small number of support vessels of the Royal Fleet Auxiliary owned by the Admiralty and flying the Blue Ensign) – were classed in one of two ways. First, there were those that were non-commissioned that were on time-charter on government accounts with their crews remaining subject to the usual civilian legislation of the Board of Trade: the Merchant Shipping Acts. These vessels, flying the Red Ensign of the civilian fleet, shifted men and materiel as normal. Second, there were the commissioned Merchant Fleet Auxiliaries. These were operated in a different manner, their owners having little to do with them while in this state and these were in fact classed as naval auxiliaries, flying the White Ensign. They took roles such as armed merchant cruisers, fleet store ships and ammunition ships. Instead of commercial articles, officers and men of these commissioned auxiliaries signed T.124 forms, binding them to the Naval Discipline Act. At the outset, with the war not expected to last long, seamen signing T.124 forms were only liable to serve six months on board a specified vessel. Problems with this soon led to the agreements being re-drafted so that men were signed on for the duration of the war and liable to serve on any ship.[27] In August 1916 to ease the commissioning of merchant ships, the Admiralty made arrangements for the maintenance of a Reserve at the R. N. Barracks, Portsmouth, of the principal ratings required for filling vacancies on commissioned fleet auxiliaries. At the same time, efforts were made to standardise rates of pay, thus ending the varied rates prevalent up to that date. At least some ships' articles for commissioned Merchant Fleet Auxiliaries (early in the war anyway) are to be found within the normal mercantile crew lists. But, apart from those, precious few records relating to the Mercantile Marine Reserve survive. There are a small number of Admiralty Transport Department files dealing with administrative subjects (until this department was subsumed into the newly formed Ministry of Shipping), as well as the two medal rolls for the First World War era.[28] The participation of Welsh women in the merchant service is discussed later when looking at the involvement of passenger ferries, liners and mail ships in the war effort.

Some idea of the level of activity at Welsh ports during this period can be gleaned from the following figures: imports through Welsh ports in 1914 were running at 4.5 million tons, while exports were at 38.8 million tons.[29] The vast majority of this trade was handled at Cardiff, Swansea, Newport,

INTRODUCTION

Penarth, Barry and Port Talbot. At the outbreak of the war, the groups of docks at Cardiff, Penarth and Barry formed the greatest and most progressive coal port in the world.[30] Unsurprisingly, the majority of Cardiff vessels at the outbreak of war were 'tramp' steamers, though this description is somewhat unhelpful, as many of the ships were relatively new, and many sailed on regular routes. In 1913 these types of vessels accounted for 60 per cent of British tonnage, and at that date about 40 per cent of 'tramps' were in the coal trade. In the same year, 57 million tons of coal were raised in south Wales, over half of which was for export.[31] Cardiff-registered vessels accounted for about half the total UK tonnage engaged in the coal trade.[32] At Swansea in 1913 over 5,800 vessels arrived representing 3.3 million tons of registered shipping.[33] Regular reports on the trade of the smaller south Wales ports such as Swansea and Port Talbot were carried in the local press, and these can provide snapshots of the amount of shipping being handled. For example, in November 1915 there were forty-two steam vessels and twenty-eight sailing vessels at Swansea, and fourteen steam and five sail at Port Talbot.[34] In the north, where the slate trade had been in decline for some time, at Port Dinorwic (Y Felinheli) in 1914 some 47,000 tons of slate were shipped, while at Caernarfon the figure was a little over 6,000 tons.[35] In addition, Holyhead and Fishguard had relatively busy ports dealing in the Irish ferry services.

The mercantile marine operated pretty much as usual for the first two years of the war, notwithstanding the requisition of about one-fifth of the fleet for the fulfilment of military tasks. In addition, the government took charge of insurance arrangements. In respect of hulls, they offered an automatic 80 per cent reinsurance for British ships insured by British underwriters that were part of the existing shipowners' associations: this covered nearly three-quarters of the British foreign-going tonnage. There was, however, no War Risk Insurance Association for small coasters throughout the war.[36] For cargo, a State Insurance Office was created in London that offered a flat rate for all merchant voyages on British ships.[37] Then in 1915 'blue book' freight rates (which were lower than those in the open market) were introduced for vessels on government charter. In December 1916, the creation of the Ministry of Shipping brought all merchant activities under full governmental control.[38] Neither shipowners (concerned about delays and attendant cost) nor the Admiralty at this time saw any benefit in the use of a convoy system for the general protection of shipping, and as a result, for much of the war, it was not part of the general experience of merchant seaman.

In a War Committee cabinet meeting in November 1916, various admirals told Lloyd George that convoys presented too large a target and that they doubted the ability of diverse merchant vessels to hold station.[39] Following the dramatic increase in losses after the resumption of unrestricted submarine warfare by Germany in February 1917, this thinking quickly altered, and the introduction of convoys saved much shipping and many lives.[40] Over time most British merchant ships were fitted with medium-calibre guns for self-defence, with reservists as gun crew. While this may have had a positive effect on morale (as was the case with Q-ships), the material results of such measures had a negligible effect on the losses suffered.[41]

The following survey of Welsh involvement in the mercantile marine examines the work, pay and conditions, and varied experiences that resulted from such activities during the First World War. Three particular sets of participation; those of women, of small maritime communities, and of international crew members, are given separate treatment as an aid to understanding different contexts within this maritime experience. The immediate impact of the outbreak of the war on Welsh merchant mariners is considered, followed by a more detailed exploration of the realities of the conflict at sea and of the dangers that mariners faced as the war against commerce developed. Although this study is largely concerned with the events of 1914–15, later developments that would impact on the lives of civilian crews, such as the introduction of convoys in 1917, are considered along with other matters relating to the vital work undertaken by such crews through to the end of the hostilities.

Notes

1   The *Brighton* 566 GRT (1878) was later commissioned as a fleet messenger.
2   *Cambria Daily Leader* (hereafter *CDL*), 3 August 1914, p. 3.
3   It did not become known as the Merchant Navy until after the War.
4   R. Woodman, *More Days, More Dollars: The Universal Bucket Chain 1885–1920* (Stroud, 2010); C. E. Fayle, *Seaborne Trade*, 3 vols (London, 1922–4); A. Hurd, *The Merchant Navy*, 2 vols (London, 1922).
5   P. Lyon, *Merchant Seafaring Through World War 1, 1914–1918* (Leicester, 2016); D. d'Enno, *Fishermen Against the Kaiser: Shockwaves of War, 1914–1915*, vol. 1 (Barnsley, 2010).
6   Woodman, *More Days, More Dollars*, p. 209.
7   *1911 Census of England and Wales General Report with Appendices* (1917–18, xxxv (Cd. 8491) 483).

8   *1911 Census of England and Wales, General Report with Appendices*, Table 9: 'Occupations of Persons (Males and Females) aged 10 years and upwards in the United Kingdom and in its several Divisions at each Census, 1881 to 1911'.
9   V. C. Burton, 'A Floating Population: Vessel Enumeration Returns, 1851–1921', *Local Population Studies*, 38 (Spring 1987), 36–43; and V. C. Burton, 'Counting Seafarers: The Published Records of the Registry of British Seamen, 1849–1913', *Mariner's Mirror*, 71/3 (August 1985), 305–20.
10 *1911 Census of England and Wales General Report with Appendices* (1917–18, xxxv (Cd. 8491) 483).
11 *1911 Census report*, Table 9, Appendix C.
12 *1911 Census report*, Table 9, Appendix C.
13 CR10 cards covering the period 1918–21 are held at Southampton Archives.
14 A. W. Kirkaldy, *British Shipping* (London, 1914), pp. 227–9.
15 Fayle, *Seaborne Trade*, vol. 1, p. 6.
16 Woodman, *More Days, More Dollars*, p. 198.
17 T. D. Lilley, 'Operation of the Tenth Cruiser Squadron: A Challenge for the Royal Navy and its Reserves' (unpublished PhD thesis, University of Greenwich, 2012), p. 105; C. P. Hopkins, *'National Service' of British Merchant Seamen 1914–1919* (London, 1920), pp. 3–4.
18 C. H. Dixon, 'Seamen and the Law: An Examination of the Impact of Legislation on the British Merchant Seaman's Lot, 1558–1918' (unpublished PhD thesis, University College London, 1981), p. 318.
19 Hurd, *The Merchant Navy*, vol. 1, p. 116.
20 Woodman, *More Days, More Dollars*, p. 333.
21 See *www.londonremembers.com/memorials/mercantile-marine-memorial-ww1* (last accessed 3 November 2024).
22 See *http://1915crewlists.rmg.co.uk* (last accessed 3 November 2024).
23 For examinations of the catering personnel at sea during this period, see Sari Mäenpää, 'Catering Personnel on British Passenger Liners, 1860–1935' (unpublished PhD thesis, University of Liverpool, 2002); Sari Mäenpää, 'From Pea Soup to Hors d'oeuvres: The Status of the Cook on British Merchant Ships', *The Northern Mariner/ Le marin du nord*, 11/2 (April 2001), 39–55.
24 *South Wales Weekly Post* (hereafter *SWWP*), 27 November 1915, p. 2.
25 d'Enno, *Fishermen Against the Kaiser*; J. R. Owen, 'The Royal Naval Reserve and Wales: Prelude to the First World War', *Maritime Wales*, 35 (2014), 51–72.
26 For an examination of merchant seamen serving on armed merchant cruisers, see J. Fisher, 'Neither Fish nor Fowl-Mercantile Seamen on Armed Merchant Cruisers in the Great War', *International Journal of Maritime History*, 28/3 (2016), 496–512.
27 Lilley, 'Operation of the Tenth Cruiser Squadron', p. 213.
28 I am indebted to Len Barnett and his excellent online resource for much of this information on the Mercantile Marine Reserve, *www.barnettmaritime.co.uk/reserves.htm* (last accessed 3 November 2024).
29 *Welsh Historical Statistics*, table 8.8.
30 Kirkaldy, *British Shipping*, p. 558.

31 John Graham Jones, *The History of Wales* (Cardiff, 2014), p. 119.
32 J. Geraint Jenkins, 'Cardiff Shipowners', *Maritime Wales*, 5 (1980), 119.
33 Kirkaldy, *British Shipping*, p. 553.
34 *CDL*, 15 November 1915, p. 4.
35 L. Lloyd, *The Port of Caernarfon 1793–1900* (Caernarfon, 1989), p. 268; J. Lindsay, *A History of the North Wales Slate Industry* (Newton Abbot, 1974), pp. 182–4.
36 T. Coppack, *A Lifetime with Ships: The Autobiography of a Coasting Shipowner* (Prescot, 1973), p. 142.
37 L. Lobo-Guerrero, *Insuring War: Sovereignty, Security and Risk* (London, 2012), p. 58.
38 D. Jenkins, *Shipowners of Cardiff: A Class by Themselves* (Cardiff, 1997), pp. 35–6.
39 J. Grigg, *Lloyd George: War Leader, 1916–1918* (London, 2002), pp. 49–53.
40 Woodman, *More Days, More Dollars*, p. 215.
41 Woodman, *More Days, More Dollars*, p. 205.

1 The Normal Run of Business

Figure 1: Cardiff docks c.1911, courtesy of the George Grantham Bain Collection, Library of Congress

One approach to the varying types of work engaged in by the mercantile marine is to consider the various classes of crew agreement that were in use. Agreement forms were of three major types and covered coasting, home-trade and foreign-going vessels. For the smallest vessels, there were the half-yearly 'Official log book and account of voyages and crew of a vessel of less than 80 tons net register exclusively employed upon the coast of the UK'. These agreements covered the plethora of small vessels engaged in coastal traffic and other duties, as well as the lighters, tugs and tenders that are often less visible in the maritime history of the First World War. Many, though not all, of these smallest vessels were sailing craft. Some vessels operated with just a master and mate, for example on the Chester-registered *John and William*, a 69 GRT flat, built at Rhyl in 1870. Working between Connah's Quay, Mostyn, Birkenhead and Liverpool, the master was from Chester and the mate from Connah's Quay.

At Milford Haven, the 29 net tons ketch *Mary Jane Lewis* (1899), built at Pembroke Dock, was trading locally from January to March 1915, both of the crew were Pembroke men, the master Thomas Phillips being the owner. At Newport (Mon.) the locally built, owned and crewed 14 net ton smack *William Williams* (1877) was running regularly back and forth to Lundy. It was not uncommon for such small vessels to be laid up during the winter; for example, at Cardigan the *Annie* (104117), a 45 GRT ketch built in 1895 that had been converted with an auxiliary engine, was laid up from January to April 1915, and then traded mainly between Cardigan, Milford Haven and Swansea before being laid up again at the end of November. Both the master and mate were from St Dogmaels. Also laid up in Cardigan at this time was the 28 net ton sloop *Margaret and Ann*, built in 1877. Commencing in May, this small sloop traded between Milford Haven, Haverfordwest, Porthgain, Tresaith and Swansea, the master and mate were both from Cardiganshire.

Shortages of crew could cause vessels to be laid up, as was the case for the 29 net ton ketch *Thomas and Ann* (21319) of Milford Haven (originally a yawl, built at Scarborough in 1858) between July and December 1915, while the owners of the Beaumaris-registered smack *Elizabeth*, 46 GRT (21268), also built in 1858, noted that the vessel had been laid up from June to December on account of 'high wages and low freights in the slate trade'. Between January and March 1915, the Beaumaris-registered schooner *Mary Edwards*, 64 GRT (1863), had been laid up at Port Dinorwic, then between March and June completed five trips, Port Dinorwic to Runcorn, then to Abersoch, Aberdovey, Bideford and back to Runcorn. With a crew of three, the mate and cook were both from Anglesey, while the master was a seventy-two-year-old Scotsman.

In August 1914, Hugh Shaw of Connah's Quay was master and part-owner of the Barrow-registered schooner *Kate* (70473), 105 GRT (1875). Born in 1881, he had gone to sea as a cook aged ten and worked his way up. The *Kate* had been sheltering at Holyhead when war was declared. Among the crew of three, consisting of a mate, an able-seaman and a cook, were two Naval Reservists who having been mobilised left the schooner. Shaw noted at this time that several vessels at Holyhead had seen their whole crews called up.[1] By November 1914 it was becoming increasingly hard to find crew for the coasting trades and so Shaw's father Humphrey, then aged sixty-eight, came out of retirement to serve as mate. In 1915, the second half-year agreement for the *Kate* allows us to follow the progress of this small forty-year-old schooner. Leaving New Ross on the river Barrow in County Wexford on 2 July, the schooner arrived at Plymouth one week later. After three weeks there, the *Kate* then sailed for Avonmouth, arriving on 2 August. On 14 August the *Kate* left the Bristol Channel for the china clay port of Par on the south coast of Cornwall, arriving there on 21 August. Six days later the *Kate* sailed for Weston Point, just below Runcorn on the river Mersey, arriving there on 2 September 1915. In the early part of the twentieth century, schooners like the *Kate* were a regular sight at Runcorn, bringing in china clay and flints for the potteries. On 15 September 1915 the *Kate* left Runcorn for Truro. Arriving at Truro on 27 September it would appear that there were no freights offering, as five days later the *Kate* left 'light' for Porthoustock on the Lizard peninsula. Originally a fishing hamlet, this small port had been developed to carry the trade of the local quarries. Leaving there on 4 October the *Kate* proceeded for a second time to Par, arriving four days later. Cargo loaded, the *Kate* left Par on 13 October and again sailed for Runcorn, arriving on 22 October. After a month at Runcorn, the *Kate* sailed for Janeville quay on the river Bride, a tributary of the river Blackwater above Youghal, arriving there on 11 December. The final trip made by the *Kate* in 1915 was to Cork. Despite leaving Janeville quay on 30 December, the *Kate* did not arrive at Cork until 12 January 1916. Although these men were working in the coasting trade, during this period none had seen home for six months.

Other small sailing craft, such as the Beaumaris-registered ketch *Elizabeth* (21273), 56 GRT (1859), with a crew from Caernarfon and Bangor and whose master was aged sixty-eight, were trading to Dundalk, Dublin and Wicklow, while the Jersey-registered ketch *Lucy* (76350) of 58 net tons (1879), owned by Hugh Williams of Llanengan, which with an all Welsh crew was trading between Porthmadog, Cardiff, Wexford and Dublin.[2] Some small vessels did little trade in 1915; for example, the Caernarfon-registered schooner *Mary* (27805), 103 GRT (1859), spent most of the year laid up for repairs, first at Bangor, and latterly at Caernarfon, all of the crew recorded were Welsh. Among the smallest steam vessels were the likes of the *Margaret Ham*, 113 GRT (1913), a Tyne-built tug operated by the Cardiff Steam Towing Company,[3] which spent the whole of 1915 towing in the Bristol Channel; the crew of eight were from Cardiff and Newport. At Fishguard, small steam craft ancillary to the operation of Great Western Railway (GWR) ferry services included the *Pen Cw*, 168 GRT (1912), for towing barges and the steam launch *St David's* (118259), 22 GRT (1903), for tendering, both of which had largely Welsh crew members.

Small steamers such as the Liverpool-registered *Dora* (113396) 296 GRT (1900) were engaged in trading along the Welsh coast. Owned by the Aberdovey and Barmouth Steamship Company, the *Dora* was 130 feet long, with a beam of 23 feet and a draft of 9 feet. In 1915, aged forty-nine, David Williams of Morfa Nefyn had been master of the *Dora* for six years. Born in 1866, he had gained his master's certificate at the age of thirty-two in 1898. Throughout 1915, in addition to the master, the crew comprised a mate, an engineer, a fireman and a couple of deckhands, all of whom hailed from coastal areas of north-west Wales, places such as Aberdovey, Aberystwyth, Edern and Barmouth. The *Dora* sailed regularly from Liverpool for Aberdovey every Friday, loading at a berth on the east side of Trafalgar Lock, and would take cargo up to 6 p.m. on the day of sailing. Leaving Liverpool, the *Dora* would call at Porthdinllaen on the north coast of the Llŷn Peninsula before proceeding on to Barmouth and Aberdovey in Cardigan Bay. On occasions, the ship would also stop in Porthmadog. Carrying groceries, animal feed, cement and other such supplies on the outward trip, the *Dora* returned to Liverpool with livestock, wool, timber and also manganese ore from the mines of Caernarfonshire and Merionethshire.

The schedule of stops on the route was very much determined by the tides. The small print on the posters used to advertise the services provided by the *Dora* give some flavour of the vagaries of small coastal steam traders, noting that sailings were subject to weather and other circumstances permitting, with liberty to call at any ports in any order, to sail without pilot and to tow and assist vessels in distress, and to deviate for the purposes of saving life or property. The *Dora* carried passengers as well as cargo and provided a convenient means for people to reach Llŷn especially those arriving in Liverpool on larger vessels from overseas. The *Dora* made a last visit to Porthdinllaen in October 1915 and was then requisitioned by the Admiralty and assigned to the Liverpool to Belfast crossing in November 1915.[4]

The second main type of agreement was for vessels in the 'home trade only' (home trade limits being from Brest to the river Elbe), which were also half-yearly accounts. Some of the vessels so engaged were of modest size. All the crew who worked on the Liverpool-registered but Welsh-owned *Rebecca*, 301 GRT in 1915, were from Porthmadog, Penrhyn or Edern. The

Rebecca had been built in 1895 in Scotland at a cost of £6,000, and was a small steamship trading in general merchandise between Porthmadog, Pwllheli and Liverpool.[5] The crew of the Liverpool-registered *Thomas and Anne* (74503), a 95 GRT (1876) ketch, engaged in the coasting trade were all from Flint and their agreement noted that they were to provide their own rations. At Llanelli the dredger *Lucy*, 430 GRT (1900), was operated under the jurisdiction of Llanelli Harbour Trust, with most of the crew in 1915 being from the locality.

Another class of vessel working in the home-trade in Welsh waters during this period were the Irish ferry services run by London and North Western Railway (LNWR)[6] from Holyhead to Howth, Dublin, Greenore, and Kingstown (Dún Laoghaire), as well as those run by the GWR from Fishguard to Waterford and Rosslare.[7] While these companies returned half-yearly accounts for their fleets, these accounts did not generally specify which particular vessel the men were working on as crew, so they might be required to work on any of the company's vessels.[8] The various services operated by LNWR, employed large numbers of Welsh crew. In 1915, LNWR was operating a total of fifteen steamers from Holyhead engaged in carrying mail, passengers and cattle and goods, and one dredger, the *Pick Me Up*, 170 GRT (1902).[9] On the books for these vessels were 821 people, the vast majority from Anglesey or north Wales. In June 1915, they comprised: thirteen masters; thirteen mates; eight second mates, five third mates, fifty-three stewards; fourteen stewardesses; thirty quartermasters; eighteen cooks; seventeen galley boys (the youngest just thirteen years old); five bosuns; seventeen wireless operators; twenty carpenters; three pursers and one assistant purser; two artificers; thirty deck boys (five of whom had joined the company in 1914 aged fourteen); thirty cabin boys (four of whom joined aged sixteen); four engineer's boys; fifteen first engineers; sixteen second engineers; twenty third engineers; twenty-nine fourth engineers; eighteen leading stokers; 187 firemen; seventy-nine trimmers; and 175 seamen. The oldest on the books, a small proportion of men in their sixties, were mainly found among seamen and firemen.

Five of the LNWR vessels were requisitioned for use by the Admiralty, with their crew being listed by the company as on 'active service'. The *South Stack*, 1066 GRT (1900), had been requisitioned as a troop transport in 1914 but was returned to the company the following year. Four of the LNWR's fastest steamers were also requisitioned. The *Cambria*, 1842 GRT (1897), capable of 24 knots, was requisitioned as an armed boarding steamer in 1914, and then from August 1915 was in use as a hospital ship. Another vessel that would serve as an armed boarding steamer was the *Scotia*, 1872 GRT (1902), initially requisitioned in 1914 and then returned to the company in May 1917 before being requisitioned again later that year as a troop transport operating between Dover and France.[10] The *Hibernia*, 1862 GRT (1900), was requisitioned in 1914 as an armed boarding steamer and renamed HMS *Tara*, with most of the original crew being retained and signed on under T.124 agreements. Initially patrolling in the Irish Sea, the *Tara* was later transferred to similar duties in the Mediterranean.[11] The crew of the *Tara*, who were largely from Holyhead, would endure a harrowing ordeal following the torpedoing of the ship off the Libyan coast in 1915. Another of the LNWR's ships, the *Anglia*, 1862 GRT (1899), was requisitioned as an armed boarding steamer at the outbreak of war and had then worked as a Fleet messenger until April 1915 before being refitted as a hospital ship. The fate of the HMHS *Anglia* is more fully described in the discussion of hospital ships below.

Two of the LNWR's fleet would be lost due to collisions. The *Connemara*, 1106 GRT (1896), collided with the collier *Retriever* in the entrance of Carlingford Lough on 3 November 1916.[12] The crew of thirty-one, all from Holyhead, and fifty-one passengers were lost. On the *Retriever* eight out of the nine crewmen were also lost. In March 1918, the *Slieve Bloom*, 1166 GRT (1908), was lost near South Stack after a collision with the American destroyer USS *Stockton*. On this occasion there was no loss of life, and the crew and passengers were taken to Holyhead by the destroyer. Included in the lost cargo were 370 cattle. The remaining eight vessels served largely without incident. They comprised: the *Galtee More*, 1105 GRT (built 1898, scrapped 1925); the *Greenore*, 1488 GRT (built 1912, scrapped 1926); the *Slieve More*, 1138 GRT (built 1904, scrapped 1932), whose captain, Samuel David Pritchard, was awarded an MBE in 1920 for services during the war; the *Snowdon* (11039), 1110 GRT (built 1902, scrapped 1935); the *Slieve Gallion*, 1166 GRT (built 1908, sold 1923); the *Slieve Bawn*, 1148 GRT (built 1904, scrapped 1935), which in 1917 came to the rescue of the mined White Star liner RMS *Celtic* off the Isle of Man; the *Rosstrevor*, 1094 GRT (built 1895, scrapped 1926), which had a lucky escape after a torpedo fired at the steamer in May 1918 missed; and the *Rathmore*, 1569 GRT (built 1908, scrapped 1932), which was involved in a collision with a troop ship in March 1918 but was safely towed to port and repaired.[13] The LNWR also operated a ferry service from Fleetwood to Belfast jointly with the Lancashire and Yorkshire Railway Company.

For the crews working on the GWR ferries operating out of Fishguard a similar picture is found. Their largest and fastest vessels – the *St David*, 2529 GRT (1906); the *St Patrick*, 2531 GRT (1906); and the *St Andrew*, 2528 GRT (1908) – were requisitioned at the outbreak of war for use as hospital ships, while GWR's smaller vessels – the *Great Western*, 1339 GRT; *Great Southern*, 1339 GRT; and *Waterford*, 1204 GRT (the only GWR vessel to be fitted with quadruple expansion engines) – continued in use on the Fishguard to Waterford and Rosslare routes. Between July 1915 and January 1916 there were some 440 crew on the company's books; fifty-five of whom were Welsh, including two out of the six serving masters, both of whom were from Pembrokeshire.

The third main class of crew agreement was that for foreign-going vessels. These agreements had the term of voyage (crew would sign on for up to three years) and initial destination and the geographical limits for ports of call stated on the front page. Some of these foreign-going vessels were also of modest size; for example, schooners such as those registered at Caernarfon that were at sea when war broke out. Among them were the *Jenny Jones* (92213), 157 GRT (1893), leaving Plymouth on 4 July 1914 to Newfoundland and any ports between 70° North and 40° South. Four of the crew were Welsh; the master was from Harlech, the mate from Barmouth, and a cook/seaman and an ordinary seaman were from Porthmadog. Three of the crew who had signed on were German, and they were taken as prisoners of war on their arrival at Carbonear, Newfoundland, in October. After returning to Bristol in February 1915 the *Jenny Jones* changed ownership and continued for the rest of the year in the home and coasting trade.[14]

Another example of such craft was the three-masted schooner *Mary Annie*, 154 GRT, built in 1893 and owned by John Jones of Porthmadog.[15] Between June 1914 and March 1915 the crew signed on to sail from Poole to Seville then Newfoundland or Barbados, and also in the Mediterranean trade in any rotation between 60° North and 60° South for a period not exceeding two years. Out of the seven men who signed on at Poole, six had joined from other ships, with only the bosun, Daniel Jones (aged thirty-five), who was from Porthmadog, staying on. He was joined by four other Porthmadog men for this agreement: the master G. Jones (aged forty-one); the mate Griffith Jones (aged seventy-one); Robert Roberts (aged sixty-eight); a cook and able seaman; and Victor Williams (aged twenty), a seaman. During the course of the agreement the mate was taken ill and left the ship at Cadiz in July 1914. A third example of such foreign-going sailing vessels is that of the *John Pritchard*, 118 GRT (1906), one of Pritchard Brothers' Caernarfon-registered schooners, which in June 1914 sailed from Porthmadog initially for Copenhagen. The master was from Pentrefelin, Caernarfon, and among the other crew were two seamen, Christmas Owens (aged twenty-five) and Robert Jones (aged twenty-one), from Porthmadog, both of whom left by mutual consent at Copenhagen in October. The cook/seaman aboard, William Jones, from Maentwrog, was fourteen years old and on his first ship.[16] However, the experience of the majority working in the mercantile marine was not of being under sail of any size, or of sailing in the home and coasting trades but of signing on to foreign-going steamers.

The Normal Hazards of Working at Sea

While steam ships were generally less dangerous to work on than sailing vessels, seafaring still had higher mortality rates compared to other occupations. Immediately prior to the war, the disease and mortality rates were 50 per cent greater than that for similar occupational groups ashore.[17] Home Office figures for 1904 recorded a mean death rate for sailors of 64.5 per 10,000 employed; the mean death rate for miners was 12.9.[18] Between 1905 and 1914 deaths among crew working on steamers from wrecks, accidents and disease averaged 7.5 per 1,000 employed per year (on sailing ships the average was 13 per 1,000 employed).[19] In July 1914, the matter of deaths resulting from disease in the mercantile marine was raised in the House of Commons. In the course of the discussion the President of the Board of Trade, Mr John Burns MP informed the House that while the death rate from disease in the Navy had gone down in ten years from 4.7 per 1,000 to 2 per 1,000, in the Army from 9 per 1,000 to 3.6 per 1,000, and in the civil population from 8 per 1,000 to 4.7 per 1,000, the rate in the mercantile marine remained stationary. He argued for the improvement of hygienic conditions on merchant ships and felt that 'It was up to the shipowners to do all in their power to improve conditions, and labour leaders ... might do good work by educating the men to live up to the higher standards'.[20] At this time, men in mercantile marine had 'about twice the chance of death' compared to those in the Navy or Army, with overall mortality rates for 1913–14 (all causes) of 7.79 per 1,000, compared with 3.25 per 1,000 for the Navy and 2.99 per 1,000 for the Army.[21]

Ships other than passenger liners did not carry doctors and such medical knowledge as there might be aboard was limited to the *Ship Captain's*

Medical Guide along with any first-aid training that the officers had undertaken.[22] Any medication aboard was limited, and ill or injured seamen would be put ashore at the first convenient opportunity. Under section 34 of the Merchant Shipping Act 1906, it was the obligation of the owner to defray the cost of 'surgical and medical advice, and attendance and medicine, and … maintenance … until (the seaman) is cured, or dies, or is returned to a proper return port'. As the obligation of the owner ceased when a 'proper home port' had been reached, the operation of the Seamen's National Insurance Society (which administered the Seaman's Pension Fund set up under section 48 of the National Insurance Act 1911) was an essential element in restoring a sick or disabled man to health.[23] *In extremis* in foreign ports, once whatever pay that might have been due was gone, men would be at the mercy of the nearest consulate.[24] For those who had been shipwrecked or otherwise distressed there were provisions made in the Merchant Shipping Act 1906 for the conveying of such seamen home.[25] The Workmen's Compensation Act 1906 offered some relief for disabling accidents, but it was less effective where the cause was not directly work related or when death ensued. By 1913 there were 8,000 disability claims paid each year, with an average compensation settlement of £13 6s., and where compensation was paid for the death of a seaman, it averaged £160.[26]

Under the terms of the Merchant Shipping Act 1906, the sums payable to those *wholly dependent* on the earnings of the deceased was to be equal to three years' earnings or the sum of £150, whichever the greater, but not to exceed £300. The compensation paid into the courts was to be invested on their behalf and an initial payment made with subsequent weekly allowances awarded. In the case of total or partial incapacity, the scale was 50 per cent of the weekly wage in the preceding year. In the case of there being no dependants, the sum was to be paid to the legal representative of the deceased.[27] In 1915 special arrangements were introduced by the Board of Trade in the case of merchant seamen such that:

> compensation will be payable in the case of all persons employed in any capacity on board British merchant ships who may be injured owing to hostilities. A special scheme has been brought into operation to provide for cases which are not already covered by the Workmen's Compensation Act. The arrangement, also applies to fishing vessels insured under the Government scheme.[28]

Tropical diseases such as malaria were a constant threat to the health of foreign-going merchant seamen, particularly those engaged in regular trades to West Africa, as evidenced by the following examples that both occurred on Elder Dempster ships. In March 1915 news reached Borth of the death of Thomas H. Dutton, captain of the *Patani*, 3465 GRT (1905), of malarial fever at Sapele, Nigeria. He had served with Elder Dempster for sixteen years and before that was with the Swansea Copper Ore Company, whose sailing ships traded between Swansea and the west coast of South America.[29] The following month, Joseph Roberts from Llangollen, the butcher and cook aboard the *Akassa*, 3919 GRT (1910), also succumbed to the sleeping sickness and was buried at sea.[30] Both men worked for a company that had strong ties with Wales. In 1884 Alfred Lewis Jones from Carmarthen (who had been apprenticed to the African Steamship Company in Liverpool in 1857 and later joined Elder Dempster as a manager) took control of the company when Alexander Elder and John Dempster retired – Jones was knighted in 1901. Following his death in 1909, the company majority shareholder became Owen Philipps (later 1st Baron Kylsant), a scion of the Philipps family of Picton Castle in Pembrokeshire, and a shipping magnate in his own right who by 1902 was chairman and managing director of the Royal Mail Steam Packet Company.

In October 1914 a telegram had reached Porthmadog announcing the death in Deal Hospital of Thomas Jones the mate on the *Ocean Ranger*. This 280 GRT brigantine built at Appledore in 1875, Fowey-registered and owned at the time by Pritchard Brothers of Porthmadog, was outward bound from Grimsby to Bermuda and had put into Deal to land Jones, who had been taken suddenly ill and who died a few hours later. The newspaper report further noted that the deceased had a wife and three children and that he had been shipwrecked on three occasions during the past three years.[31] There were three other Welshmen aboard who had signed on at Grimsby: the master David Davies of Caernarfon; the cook John Williams from Harlech; and Lewis Williams, an ordinary seaman from Porthmadog. The crew, now reduced to seven men, proceeded to Bermuda without signing on another mate, though it was noted on the bottom of the agreement that one of the men signed on as a seaman had previously sailed in that capacity, but had lost his mate's certificate due to a shipwreck. The *Ocean Ranger* returned to Liverpool in March 1915; the only additional crew member was a Barbadian cook/steward who joined at Jamaica.

Death while aboard ship was a fairly commonplace occurrence. Thomas Williams of Port Dinorwic had joined the three-masted fully rigged ship

Centurion, 1828 GRT (1891), as a seventeen-year-old apprentice at Cardiff in 1910. He completed his term in June 1914 and then served as third mate until he died at sea in January 1915, having received no wages at any time. Over the course of the last agreement on which he served, starting at Dunkirk in August 1913 and sailing initially for Buenos Aires, three men had been left sick at Santos, including one man from Nefyn, one man left through illness at Geelong, two other men had died, and at least nineteen men had deserted at various ports.

Enoch Williams, an able seaman from north Wales joined the Liverpool-registered four-masted iron barque *Crown of India*, 2034 GRT (1885), in Newcastle in September 1914. With a crew of twenty-three this barque had originally sailed the previous October from Liverpool to Sydney. Before Williams joined, the ship's cook had died at sea in January, and the master, an ordinary seaman and a fifteen-year-old apprentice had all died at Valparaiso in August. Williams deserted at Portland, Oregon in December along with two other able seamen, a Swede and a Dane. Another unfortunate instance involved Percy B. Powell, a fourteen-year-old deck boy born in Carmarthen, but living in Aberaeron, who was on his first ship. On 16 November 1915, while aboard the *Beachy Head*, 4274 GRT (1915), Powell died at sea as a result of accident off the coast of New Jersey, Conn.[32] He had only been at sea for six weeks.

Docks were dangerous places and many accidents and deaths occurred while ships were in port. In May 1915 James Sealey, an able seaman from Aberporth died after falling overboard from the *Patricia*, 780 GRT (1913), as the steamer was leaving Swansea's South Dock. He had been hauling in the fender and overbalanced.[33] In July, George Beynon Stevens, aged fifty-seven, mate of the *Abbot*, 264 GRT (1903), died in Swansea Hospital as the result of an injury received on board ship. He had been lowering one of the ship's boats with other men, when the rope slipped in the winch and the boat hit him on the head. He was taken to hospital but later succumbed to septicaemia.[34] Accidents could also result from falling down holds while ships were being loaded, as evidenced in the following example. In December 1914 the Ocean Coal Company found themselves defendants in a case in which they were charged with a breach of coaling regulations. On 31 August 1914 the steamer *Daleham* was being coaled at No. 27 Tip, Barry Docks. As a result of the hatchway being left uncovered and unfenced, John Morgan, a coal-trimmer in the employ of the Ocean Company had fallen into the hold and was killed. John Parry, a coal-trimmer, who was working on the ship at the time of the accident, gave evidence that the hatchways were uncovered and the coamings only about 9 inches high. It was the duty of the company who were coaling the ship to guard the hatchways. For the defence, the company's solicitor argued that it was quite probable that the deceased had fallen into the hold after he had finished his work. Mr Harding HM Inspector of Factories who was prosecuting replied, 'That is not the point. The case is whether the hold was fenced or not'. In the event, the bench found the company liable and was fined £2 with costs.[35]

Foreign docks could be equally dangerous. Reported in the *Barry Dock News* in April 1915 was the following case of a Cadoxton man who met a violent death in Uruguay:

> Robert Lloyd (33) ... has met his death at Monte Video, and from a letter which has been received at Barry Docks by a woman whose husband was a member of the crew of the steamship Robert Adamson, on which ship Lloyd was engaged as fireman, it seems that he was murdered.[36]

On 7 January 1915, Robert Lloyd had been at work loading pit-props at Barry Docks and joined the *Robert Adamson*, 2978 GRT (1895), last-minute as a fireman from the pierhead. While at Montevideo he was apparently kicked to death and thrown into the dock, with his body being been found on 20 February, tied to a post alongside the ship. Lloyd had a wife and three young children and when he did not return from work his wife became anxious. About a fortnight later she learned that her husband had taken a 'pierhead jump', and she later had word from him from Las Palmas before receiving the notice from the Shipping Federation that her husband's body had been found in the dock at Montevideo. The discharge note for Lloyd on the crew agreement merely reports death by drowning.

Falling into the dock while attempting to re-join ship drunk could also claim lives, as shown in the next instance – though it was the lack of care following the incident that seems to have proved fatal in this case. Arthur Climo, of Penarth, a cook on the Runcorn-registered schooner *Truthseeker*, 110 GRT (1879), was the worse for drink when descending the ladder from the quay wall onto the boat, and he fell into the North Dock at Llanelli. His friend and another man got him out, by means of a hook, artificial respiration was given and Climo was taken to his berth in the forecastle, where he remained for four days. The captain eventually sent for a doctor, who ordered Climo's removal to the hospital, but he died on the way. At the inquest into his death held at Llanelli, the coroner stated:

> One is surprised to find the condition of things existing in this case. The man had no bedding to lie on; he had a bed of boards, and his only clothing was a trousers, shirt, coat, and some canvas of an old boat, although he was suffering from pneumonia. He was in a small bunk ... with his temperature at 101, and breathing forty to the minute. One would have thought it was obvious that the man was seriously ill, and, if it was obvious, then it was the unquestionable duty of those around him to take steps to have proper medical attention. In summing up the Coroner said he did not suggest that there should be a verdict of manslaughter, as there was insufficient evidence to show culpable negligence, but he thought, the captain had committed an error of judgment, and that he ought to have made better provision for the deceased's comfort. The Jury returned a verdict of accidental death, and expressed the opinion that the captain should have at least made the man comfortable on board.[37]

At sea, the risk of wreck was ever present. In the year immediately prior to the outbreak of the war, ninety-three British steam vessels and twenty sailing ships (all over 100 tons) were totally lost due to various causes, according to the wreck statistics published by Lloyd's Register of Shipping. This was in the region of about 1.23 per cent of all British vessels.[38] In December 1914, gales resulted in a number of vessels getting into difficulty around Wales. At Bangor it was reported that the Liverpool and Menai Straits Steamship Company's steamer *Christiana*, 281 GRT (1896):

> apparently overpowered by the gale which had been raging on the Welsh coast during the past week, crashed, on Friday night, into the Bangor pier, causing damage estimated at £500. The *Christiana* is stated to have lost her propeller, but is otherwise undamaged. The gale has been so violent that the Menai suspension bridge has been forced six inches out of position, and all traffic is suspended.[39]

Eight out of the crew of ten on the *Christiana* were Welshmen. On the coast of south Wales, the Cardiff-built *Rosaleen*, 409 GRT (1908), went ashore on the Gower peninsula:

> Our Mumbles correspondent, telephoning at 12.30 p.m., states that terrific seas are running, and that a strong south-easterly gale is blowing. A steamer has gone ashore at Oxwich, and the Mumbles lifeboat has been launched and is proceeding down the coast. It is stated that the steamer in distress is the s.s. Rosaline [sic], one of Messrs. Michael Murphy's Dublin steamers ... left Swansea last night for Liverpool with 450 tons of tin. She went ashore at Oxwich in the high seas, but there are no casualties, and it is expected that she will be floated at the next high tide.[40]

The master aboard was Owen Williams (aged sixty-three) from Anglesey, and the bosun was from Port Dinorwic.

On 8 April 1915 the *Cambria Daily Leader* reported the loss of the Italian built barque *Avanti Savoia*, 1292 net tons (1891):

> LOST WITH ALL HANDS.
>
> Lloyd's Lerwick agent telegraphed yesterday: The barque Avanti Savoia, of Newcastle (Australia), from Iquique for the Tyne wrecked at Culswick, near Vaila, west coast of Shetland, presumably on Sunday night or Monday morning. It is supposed that the crew perished ... A quantity of wreckage and seven bodies have been washed ashore.[41]

All eighteen crew were lost. On the last agreement, which ran from December 1914, there were two Welshmen aboard: Stanley A. Jones (aged twenty-two), a seaman; and John Rowlands (aged sixty-two), the mate who was from Beaumaris.

In April 1915 the *Don Hugo*, 2244 GRT (1899), belonging to the Rio Tinto Copper Company, ran ashore on Margam Sands in a heavy fog while laden with a cargo of copper ore. The *Don Hugo*, which was sailing from Huelva, Spain, for Port Talbot had:

> grounded between the breakwater and the Kenfig River ... The Don Hugo was guarded during the day by a patrol boat. When the tide receded, the vessel was left high and dry, and it was decided to discharge part of her cargo. A large number of men were employed during the day in discharging the copper, which was conveyed in carts to the adjoining railway station on the Moors. The cargo is

valued at about £100,000. So far as can be ascertained, no damage has been caused to the vessel.⁴²

The master, Roger Owen was from Dolbenmaen; also aboard at the time were two assistant stewards, one from Neath (who was on his first ship) and one from Port Talbot. The ship was later successfully re-floated. The following month another steamer got into difficulties in thick fog in the Bristol Channel. The West Hartlepool registered *Clutha River*, 4985 GRT (1914), which had left Barry on the night of Saturday 1 May 1915 laden with coal on Admiralty charter, had returned in tow on the following day:

> in a greatly damaged state, with water over one side of her forward deck and in danger of sinking. After remaining in Barry Roads for some time it was decided to beach the steamer on the mud at Cardiff in order to let the water out of the forehold and forepeak, prior to being refloated and discharged for repair. It appears that several hours after leaving Barry the steamer ran into a dense fog, and the weather was so thick that Lundy Island could not be seen when the vessel ran ashore. She was taken in tow by the Cardiff tug Margaret Ham and brought up Channel.⁴³

The master, who had only taken charge on the day that the steamer sailed, was from Newport (Pembs.) and the bosun aboard at time was from Newport (Mon.). In September, the third wreck to occur in a month off St Davids involved the Llanelli trader *Endcliffe*, 368 GRT (1911), which had been sailing:

> laden with 300 tons of scrap iron, from Preston to Llanelly, [and] struck the Sledges Rock, off Porthgain on Sunday in a fog. The captain immediately reversed the engines, and he faced his vessel towards St. David's running her ashore at Porth Milgan, where she now lies on an even keel and on a sandy bottom. On Saturday the crew were busily engaged removing their belongings, as well as other moveable deck fittings. The captain is sanguine the vessel will be able to proceed to Milford after temporary repairs. This is the third vessel wrecked just about the same place with the last month.⁴⁴

The assistant engineer aboard, W. C. Hinkin, was from Mold.

On 10 October 1915, the *Highland Warrior*, 7485 GRT (1911), sailing London for Buenos Aires via Corunna with general cargo, ran ashore off Cape Prior (near Corunna) – the crew, including a seaman from Cardiff and an assistant steward from Llanon (Cards.), and the passengers were all taken safely off the ship.[45] Following a particularly strong north-easterly gale in November, which caused considerable damage to shipping in the Haverfordwest area, three vessels were ashore on Goodwick beach.[46] Two of these vessels were regular Swansea traders: the Bristol-registered coaster *Echo*, 960 GRT (1891), on board which the mate was from Newport and a fireman from Ebbw Vale; and the Caernarfon-registered steamer *Dinorwic*, 276 GRT (1892), whose crew of ten were almost all from north Wales (the one exception, an Exeter man), and five of whom were from Port Dinorwic.

As seen in the fate of the LNWR ferry *Connemara* in 1916, collisions at sea could be attended by great loss of life. However, those who lost their lives in such wartime incidents were part of the normal mortality associated with shipping and are thus not commemorated on the Mercantile Marine Memorial. One such example that claimed the lives of Welsh crew members was the loss of the Cardiff-registered *Penarth*, 3035 GRT (1896), which was wrecked in a gale on the Sheringham Shoal off the Norfolk coast on 18 January 1915. According to a report in the *Abergavenny Chronicle*:

> The Cardiff steamer Penarth foundered on Sunday afternoon and broke in two, and out of a crew of twenty-seven only five were saved ... The Penarth in charge of Captain Wyves, of Caerphilly, was bound from the River Plate to Hull with maize. On Sunday a gale was blowing with frequent storms of snow and rain. The seas were very heavy and frequently swept the vessel from stem to stern. About half-past three, in a blinding snow squall, the steamer struck on the sand about seven miles off Sheringham. Almost at once she began to break up. Her deck fittings were swept away, her plates started, and the maize washed through them. Two boats were smashed. Then the ship's life boat was launched, the captain and crew tried to scramble into it but they were washed overboard and drowned. At length only seven were left, clinging to the upturned keel. One or two of these rolled off, but managed to regain a hold. Later the steam trawler Glenprosen was sighted. The men shouted and their cries were heard. The trawler

came to their rescue, but it was too rough to launch a boat. One man jumped off the upturned boat and swam, but he disappeared beneath the trawler as she rolled. The other six were got aboard. Three were unconscious owing to the effects of exposure, but two were brought round. The third [man], the chief engineer, whose name was Wallis Stephens, was beyond recovery.[47]

A number of Welshmen were lost in this accident and the chief engineer, who was from Cardiff, died shortly after rescue. Among the five survivors was John Gill, bosun, who came from Ystrad in Glamorgan.[48] Another example of Welsh fatalities due to a weather-related loss occurred following a collision on 6 June 1915:

> News was received on Wednesday that eight lives were lost as the result of a collision during a fog between the coasting steamer and the Ellerman liner City of Vienna, off the Irish Coast, on Sunday. The collision is supposed to have occurred south of the Arklow light, The Gertrude, was sunk with the loss of eight lives. A fireman named Moore is the only man saved ... The others who are lost are: Owen Jones, captain, Moelfre, Anglesey, John Owen, mate, of Benllech, Hugh P. Jones, Moelfre, W. R. Jones, Brynhyfryd, and David Jones (the captain's brother), deck hand, M[ac]Dermot, chief engineer ... and the second engineer, believed to be Griffith Hughes ... Most of them are Anglesey men.[49]

The *Gertrude*, 353 GRT (1899), which belonged to J. Monks and Company, Liverpool, was bound from Ellesmere Port for Waterford with a cargo of coal. The fireman later died from his injuries.[50]

Not all collisions were attended by fatalities. The following newspaper report appeared in March 1915:

> The British steamer Glamorgan, with a cargo of coal for Gibraltar, has arrived at Ferrol. The captain ... reports that his ship was run into 60 miles off the Spanish coast by a large steamer. The latter made off at full speed, the Glamorgan's crew observing that the vessel had the colours of the Italian flag painted on her side. The accident occurred during a clear night. The Glamorgan has a huge hole in the port side, and the boats and the upper works are

destroyed. She arrived at Ferrol with great difficulty, due to her water-logged condition.[51]

Among the Welsh crew aboard the *Glamorgan*, 3538 GRT (1906), were: the master, from Aberporth; the bosun, from Porthmadog; seven sailors, five from Cardigan, one from Blaenyrogof, Llandysul, and one from Glamorgan; the second engineer, from Cardiff; the third engineer, from Llandaff; the fourth engineer, from Penarth; and the donkeyman, from Cardiff. One final example concerns the *London Trader*, 684 GRT (1913), which sank with the loss of ten lives, including that of the chief engineer who was from Newport (Mon.), off Penzance in February 1915. The subsequent inquiry determined that the ship had been lost as a result of proceeding to sea incorrectly loaded and then foundering on encountering heavy weather.[52] The above examples are a far from complete catalogue of the normal risks of working in the mercantile marine.

Conversely, despite the foregoing, the period of the First World War saw dramatic improvements in the mortality rates for merchant seamen. The introduction of the Merchant Shipping (Convention) Act in July 1914, which embodied lessons learned from the *Titanic* disaster, saw the introduction of radio equipment on all foreign-going vessels with more than fifty crew, and provision made for a percentage of the crew to hold lifeboat certificates so as to be able to handle small craft after shipwreck. These and other measures had a such an impact that, excluding war casualties, the average number of crew deaths fell from 825 per year (1911–15) to 385 per year (1916–20).[53] Given the normal hazards attendant on going to sea, those who remained so engaged must have accepted and rationalised such risks as a normal part of their occupation. Such then were the normal working environs of Welsh seamen, the varied and heterogeneous nature of the ships on which they sailed, the trades in which they engaged and the intricate patterns of service that they provided.

Notes

1   N. Ayland (ed.), *Schooner Captain* (Truro, 1972), p. 79.
2   Two of the crew had previously been on the *Walter Ulric*, 112 GRT schooner, built in 1875 at Nefyn, which had worked in the Moroccan grain trade. H. Hughes, *Immortal Sails* (Prescot, 1969), p. 65.
3   See *www.tynetugs.co.uk/margaretham1913.html* (last accessed 3 November 2024).

4   See *www.nefyn.com/Stories/SSDoraAndPorthdinllaen.aspx* (last accessed 3 November 2024).
5   E. Hughes and A. Eames, *Porthmadog Ships* (Denbigh, 1975), p. 249.
6   They also ran other Irish services jointly with the Lancashire and Yorkshire Railway, from Fleetwood to Belfast and Derry/Londonderry.
7   Additional information on GWR ships can be found in S. Gittins, *The Great Western Railway in the First World War* (Stroud, 2010).
8   See *http://1915crewlists.rmg.co.uk/document/211951* (last accessed 3 November 2024).
9   The LNWR also operated a hopper, *C* for taking the spoil dredged from the Garston Channel out to dumping grounds in Liverpool Bay.
10 See *https://sites.google.com/site/holyheadwarmemorial19141918/home/hms-scotia* (last accessed 3 November 2024).
11 A. Eames, *Ships and Seamen of Anglesey* (Anglesey, 1973), p. 511.
12 D. Lloyd Hughes and D. M. Williams, *Holyhead: The Story of a Port* (Denbigh, 1981), p. 154. See also *https://www.anglesey.info/s-s-connemara-and-the-coal-carrier-retriever-sinking-in-1916/* (last accessed 3 November 2024).
13 For more information on these vessels, see J. P. Merrigan and I. H. Collard, *Holyhead to Ireland: Stena and its Welsh Heritage* (Stroud, 2009).
14 For some earlier history of the *Jenny Jones*, see Hughes and Eames, *Porthmadog Ships*, pp. 383–5.
15 She was stopped and scuttled SM U 69 off Beachy Head in 1917 while sailing Glasgow to Treport with coal; there were no casualties.
16 This schooner was later captured and by the Austro-Hungarian submarine k.u.k. U 4 in March 1916 off the island of Antipaxos; there were no casualties.
17 Lyon, *Merchant Seafaring through World War 1*, p. 7.
18 Dixon, 'Seamen and the Law', p. 263, footnote 4.
19 Dixon, 'Seamen and the Law', p. 329.
20 *CDL*, 10 July 1914, p. 1.
21 W. E. Home, *Merchant Seamen: Their Diseases and their Welfare Needs* (London, 1922), pp. 70–1.
22 For a fuller discussion of seamen's health, see T. Carter, *Merchant Seamen's Health 1860–1960* (Woodbridge, 2014).
23 Dixon, 'Seamen and the Law', p. 282, footnote 2.
24 Lyon, *Merchant Seafaring through World War 1*, p. 16.
25 Lyon, *Merchant Seafaring through World War 1*, p. 29.
26 Dixon, 'Seamen and the Law', pp. 263, 265; for example, death or disability due to disease was not covered until 1940.
27 *Workmen's Compensation Act 1906* [6 EDW. VII] c. 58, Schedules, section 1, pp. 18–20.
28 *CDL*, 18 February 1915, p. 1.
29 *Cambrian News and Merionethshire Standard* (hereafter *Cambrian News*), 12 March 1915, p. 2.
30 *Llangollen Advertiser*, 30 April 1915, p. 8.
31 *North Wales Chronicle and Advertiser for the Principality* (hereafter *NWC*), 30 October 1914, p. 5.

32 *Cambrian News*, 26 November 1915, p. 6.
33 *CDL*, 12 May 1915, p. 5.
34 *CDL*, 24 July 1915, p. 3.
35 *Barry Docks News* (hereafter *BDN*), 25 December 1914, p. 7.
36 *BDN*, 2 April 1915, p. 6.
37 *CDL*, 21 September 1914, p. 6.
38 *Monmouth Guardian and Bargoed and Caerphilly Observer*, 7 August 1914, p. 6.
39 *Haverfordwest and Milford Haven Telegraph*, 9 December 1914, p. 4.
40 *CDL*, 11 December 1914, p. 5.
41 *CDL*, 8 April 1915, p. 8.
42 *SWWP*, 10 April 1915, p. 3.
43 *CDL*, 3 May 1915, p. 1.
44 *Amman Valley Chronicle and East Carmarthen News*, 10 September 1914, p. 8.
45 *CDL*, 5 October 1915 p. 1.
46 *CDL*, 15 November 1915, p. 4.
47 *Abergavenny Chronicle*, 22 January 1915, p. 6. The captain's name was in fact Pyves and, though living in Caerphilly, he was from North Shields.
48 See https://www.sheringhamhistory.co.uk/wp-content/uploads/2024/02/1915-DISASTERS-compressed.pdf (last accessed 3 November 2024).
49 *NWC*, 11 June 1915, p. 6.
50 See *www.wrecksite.eu/wreck.aspx?200647* (last accessed 3 November 2024).
51 *CDL*, 10 March 1915, p. 3.
52 See Board of Trade Wreck Report, *www.southampton.gov.uk/arts-heritage/southampton-archives/plimsoll/* (last accessed 3 November 2024).
53 Dixon, 'Seamen and the Law', pp. 283–4.

2 Pay and Conditions

Figure 2: Crew of the *Edernian* at Santa Fe, River Plate, July 1914, courtesy of the Roberts family of Edern and Rhiw.com

Although there had been general pay rates for merchant mariners in peacetime, these were not standardised. There had a been a pay increase following the trade union pressure over issues such as a minimum wage, overtime payments and manning levels, which had culminated in the 1911 strike. The outbreak of the First World War brought great instability and there were significant variances in rates, depending on what had been negotiated by unions and even individuals signing on. Rates could also vary port to port depending on the demand for crew. One constant factor was that with few exceptions crew were 'liable to have their pay stopped the moment their ship was sunk'.[1] Indicative basic monthly rates of pay for able seamen on passenger ships over the course of the war were as follows:

	1914	1916	1918
Liverpool	£5 15s.	£8 10s.	£14 10s.
London	£5 15s.	£8 10s.	£14 10s.
Southampton	£5 0s.	£8 10s.	£14 10s.
Glasgow	£5 15s.	£8 10s.	£14 10s.
Avonmouth	£5 5s.	£8 10s.	£14 10s.
Hull	£5 10s.	£9 0s.	£14 10s.
Bristol	£5 10s.	£8 10s.	£14 10s.[2]

The variation in rates of pay for men on cargo ships can be illustrated by looking at some examples of the wages paid to able seamen/seamen and firemen/trimmers,[3] who were often paid at the same rate and who, taken together, made up the greater proportion of crew on steamers. Rates for such crew on the Evan Thomas, Radcliffe steamer *Jane Radcliffe*, 4074 GRT (1897, formerly the *Windsor*), sailing Cardiff to New Orleans on 6 November 1914 were £5 10s. per calendar month. On the next agreement starting in February 1915, bound initially for Mediterranean ports, the rate had climbed to £8 10s. Similar crew on the Field Line's *Winnfield*, 3343 GRT (1901), in November 1914, sailing initially Barry for Rio de Janeiro were signing on for £6 10s. On the next agreement for Newport to Baltimore in March 1915, this had risen to £7 10s. On the T. Lewis-owned *Southport*, 3587 GRT (1900), Liverpool to Brunswick in March 1913, the rate had been £5 per month for able seamen/seamen, and £5 10s. for firemen/trimmers. In December 1914, at Brisbane, firemen/trimmers were signed on the *Southport* for £10 and able seamen for £8. Presumably those rates reflected a shortage of crew available at Brisbane, or the necessity of expediting a full complement and departure. When crew joined at Callao in April 1915, the able seamen were to receive £4 10s. and the firemen/trimmers £5.

In addition to these rates, various terms for the payment of overtime were often added, and following the outbreak of war, for vessels under Admiralty charter a war bonus was paid to the crew.[4] Agreements also commonly included clauses relating to handling coal, cargo and ballast as required, and assisting in the general duties of the ship. Occasionally men might be paid 'for the run', which could be very profitable. For example, in April 1915 the crew bringing the Tatem Steam Navigation Company steamer *Exford*, 4542 GRT (1911), from Surrey Dock, London to Liverpool, a trip that took just six days to complete, received £5 each. Over the course of the war, the basic pay for able seamen on Liverpool passenger ships rose from £5 10s. per month in 1914, to £14 10s. in 1918 – the rate for coal trimmers went from £6 to £15.[5] The rates paid to other classes of crew were similarly varied. While masters' rates were not generally given on the agreements, they are sometimes given in the half-yearly accounts used by vessels in the home trade; for example, the accounts for the London and South Western Railway's vessels to June 1915 record that three of their masters were receiving £4 *per week*, while the masters on the G. & J. Burns Company's *Puma* were receiving £5 10s. per week.

Not all seamen served on steamers during the war. Out of 21.5 million tons of shipping on Lloyd's Register in 1913, around 1.5 million tons were iron or steel sailing ships.[6] One shipping company with roots in Wales but based in Liverpool, which was still operating large iron and steel sailing ships and four-masted barques was owned by William Thomas of Llanrhuddlad.[7] At the start of 1914 there were five such ships on the books, *Metropolis*, 1811 GRT (1887); *Boadicea*, 1938 GRT (1887);[8] *Crocodile*, 2555 GRT (1892); *Rowena*, 1986 GRT (originally built as the *Cluny Castle*, 1883); and *Colony*, 1750 GRT (1886) – all of them had been sold by the end of 1915.[9] The *Colony*, built as a four-masted iron ship, and later re-rigged as a barque, left London in June 1913 on a voyage not exceeding three years' duration, initially for Buenos Aires, and returned to Ipswich in March 1915. The crew was deemed complete with seventeen hands, of whom no fewer than eight were to be sailors. Among them, the ship's carpenter (on his first trip) was from Swansea, an able seaman from Cardiff deserted at Newcastle in New South Wales (NSW) in December, there was also a seaman from Nefyn and a steward from Bangor aboard. Two of the apprentices were Welsh, one from Holyhead who was indentured in 1910 aged fifteen, was made up to third mate at San Francisco in August 1914 on completion of his apprenticeship, the other was from Swansea, aged twenty-one at the time of sailing, but who had been with the ship since 1909, was discharged sick at Buenos Aires in September 1913. The crew was the usual international mix: the sail maker was Russian, the cook German, and among the sailors were Danes, a Finn, a Norwegian, an American and a Canadian, though the master, mate and third mate (later made up to bosun) were all from Island Magee, Ireland. Also aboard was the master's wife, working for a nominal sum as stewardess.[10] 'No spirits allowed' was stamped next to the bill of fare section of the agreement.

In the early years of the war there were still sail training ships being operated to provide crew for these types of vessel. In 1915 the Devitt &

Moore-owned ocean training ship *Medway*, 2599 GRT (1902), arrived at Barry from Bordeaux with a 'run' crew. A steel four-masted barque originally built in 1902 as a Uruguayan training ship and acquired by Devitt & Moore in 1910, the ship then proceeded from Barry to the Cape Verde islands with cement, coal and general cargo. The next time the *Medway* left from south Wales in September 1916 there were twenty-six cadets aboard.[11] Wage rates for able seamen on sailing vessels at this time were as variable as those on steamers. Such men signing on to the Welsh-owned and Liverpool-registered barque *Colony* at London in June 1913 were receiving £4 per month, men joining in September 1913 at Buenos Aires were receiving £3 10s., while those signing on at Newcastle (NSW) in January 1914 and at San Francisco in September 1914 were being offered £5. Over the course of the twenty-one months the *Colony* was at sea, there were a high number of desertions. Out of the initial crew, five of the able seamen deserted at Buenos Aires in September 1913, another three deserted at Newcastle (NSW) between December 1913 and January 1914 and at the same time, the five able seamen who joined at Buenos Aires to replace the deserters, also deserted. Of the men who joined at Newcastle (NSW) to replace these hands, one deserted at Coquimbo, Chile, in March, and a further three at Cruz Grande, Mexico, in April and May, and towards the end of September 1914 another deserted at San Francisco. The German cook was taken off the ship by the naval authorities after the outbreak of the war. After leaving San Francisco, the crew seems to have settled down and the agreement gives no further details of the ship's movements or of any further changes in the crew until the majority of the remainder of the crew signed off at Ipswich in March 1915. A handful of Welsh mariners are to be found on this agreement including a carpenter from Swansea, an able seaman from Cardiff, an ordinary seaman from Nefyn, a second mate from Holyhead, and a steward from Bangor.

Another example, of Welsh crew under sail at this time is provided by the three-masted steel barque *Conway Castle*, 1694 GRT (1883), owned by R. Thomas & Company of Liverpool and Criccieth. Signing on for Hamburg to Santos, Brazil on 23 February 1914, six of the crew were from Wales: John Williams, master, aged forty-six, of Porthmadog; G. Griffiths, second mate, aged fifty-six, of Criccieth; William Jones, steward, aged forty-nine, of Pembroke; Robert Jones, carpenter, aged twenty-six, and W. Williams, sailor, aged nineteen, both from Porthmadog; and W. G. Jones, sailor, aged nineteen, from Chwilog. The master, second mate and steward had all shipped on the *Conway Castle* previously, while the two Welsh seamen joined from other sailing vessels; W. Williams from the much smaller Porthmadog-owned schooner *David Morris*, 161 GRT (1897), and W.G. Jones from the three-masted barque *Penrhyn Castle* 1349 net tons (1890), also owned by R. Thomas & Company. Sailors joining at Hamburg signed on for £4 per month, while those joining at Newcastle (NSW) six months later in September 1914 were receiving £5 per month. Three German nationals had signed on the *Conway Castle*, two seamen and the sail maker, and following the outbreak of war, both of the seamen were detained by the authorities at Newcastle (NSW) in September, though the sail maker, presumably due to his age (fifty), was allowed to remain aboard, and he subsequently discharged at Valparaiso in November. Also, while at Newcastle, seven sailors, mostly Danes and Russian Finns deserted. Out of the eight men who signed on to make the crew complete again, four, all seamen, were from Wales: Thomas E. John, aged thirty-six, of St Dogmaels; James Thompson, aged forty-one, of Caernarfon; H. V. Watkins, aged forty-eight, place of birth given as just 'Wales'; and E. Davies, aged twenty-four, from Criccieth. Of the Welsh men joining the *Conway Castle* in New South Wales, three had joined from steamers and only one, H. V. Watkins, from a sailing vessel, the Dundee-registered barque *Dudhope*, 1930 GRT (1894). At this point, out of a crew of seventeen, ten men were from Wales. On 27 February 1915 the *Conway Castle* homeward bound from Valparaiso with a cargo of barley, was captured by the German light cruiser SMS *Dresden*, and sunk by explosive charges. The crew were transferred to the Peruvian barque *Lorton* and taken back to Valparaiso.[12] Their discharge date on the agreement is accompanied by the note 'captured by enemy', their pay stopped the same day. The *David Morris* survived the war, but the *Penrhyn Castle* was lost with all hands sailing from Bahia Blanca to Freemantle with a cargo of wheat in April 1915 – at least one Welsh crew member was lost, John Hanson, a seaman, who is commemorated on Porthmadog War Memorial.

Variations in the wage rates for able seamen were also found on the smaller sailing vessels. In July 1914 two of the able seamen signing on the Caernarfon-registered three-masted schooner the *William Prichard*, (109740) 170 GRT (1903), for a voyage from Barry to Newfoundland via Cadiz, were to receive £4 per month. In all, five of the crew were Welsh but one of the seamen, from Llangennech near Llanelli, was let go at Indian Harbour Newfoundland in October on account of his being a reservist. In April 1915, two of the able seamen who joined the crew of the Liverpool-registered but Porthmadog-owned *Elizabeth Bennett*, 161 GRT (1884), were paid £6 per month. An example of a sailing vessel engaged in the home-trade with a Welsh crew was the Caernarfon-registered *Cadwalader Jones*; a schooner of 183 GRT built in 1878. Two of the Welsh able seamen signing on at Runcorn in July 1915 received £3 5s. for the run to Porthmadog. Added to this agreement (and frequently added to those of other sailing vessels) were the terms that no crew should seek discharge at either wind bound or ballast ports.

Another feature of the merchant service was the wide age-range of those who went to sea. To volunteer (conscription was not introduced until the beginning of 1916) for the armed forces at the outbreak of hostilities in 1914 you had to be eighteen, or nineteen if serving overseas, though over the course of the First World War some 250,000 lied about their age and served regardless. The upper age limit for service at the outbreak of hostilities was forty-one, though this was raised to fifty-one later in the war. In the Royal Navy, ship's boys on active service could be as young as fifteen (this did not change until after the sinking in 1939 of HMS *Royal Oak* where 100 of the more than 800 casualties were aged between fifteen and seventeen), but in the mercantile marine there was no such restriction; cadets on sail training ships could be younger, and cabin boys could be as young as twelve. At the other end of the scale, 'old hands' could still be working at seventy.

Another way to try to understand working conditions in the mercantile marine during this period is to consider the work history of an individual mariner. Where these do exist, they tend to be the accounts of men who had made it up through the ranks to the position of master.[13] While these may recount their experiences before obtaining their certificates, there is a dearth of accounts written by men who did not obtain that exalted position. Further, with few exceptions, such accounts remain largely fragmentary and unpublished.

Luckily for Wales, local maritime and family historians have made some efforts to preserve other such memoirs for posterity. One such account is provided in the memoirs of Captain Hugh Roberts OBE of Edern. Born in 1895, Roberts had first gone to sea as a mess room steward aged fifteen and in March 1913 he joined the Cardiff-registered *Edernian*, 3358 GRT (1906), as an ordinary seaman. The *Edernian*, named after the village of Edern on the Llŷn Peninsula, was owned by the brothers Owen and Watkin Williams of Pwll Parc. Registered at Cardiff on 8 August 1906, the *Edernian* spent the next eleven years mostly on the South American run, and several Edern and Llŷn men served as crew during this time. Hugh Roberts joined the *Edernian* at Hull on 29 March 1913. The ship then proceeded first to Antwerp and then to London to load general cargo for the Royal Mail Company destined for ports in Brazil. Discharging the outbound cargo at Bahia Rio and Rio Grande the *Edernian* next sailed for the port of Rosario on the river Paraná in Argentina, where maize was loaded for Plymouth, Falmouth and Cardiff. At the end of August having dry-docked at Cardiff, the *Edernian* then proceeded in ballast for Nordenham, Germany, where a full cargo of salt for Wilmington, North Carolina was loaded. Roberts later recalled:

> Approaching the American coast we ran in to heavy weather, two ports, frames and deadlights in our forecastle being driven clean out and flooding us out. We went to sleep after this in the potato locker above the transom aft, and one morning noticing the propeller had stopped, we came out and found that we had nearly run into a derelict American three-masted schooner lying flat on her side, and her keel at sea surface level. On our arrival at Wilmington we were informed she had been run down by a steamer the previous night, all crew saved.

The *Edernian* then loaded cotton for Le Havre. On 14 December 1913, the *Edernian* was at Penarth loading coal for Rio de Janeiro and from this latter port proceeded in ballast to Baltimore to load coal for Savona. From Italy the ship sailed for Barry in ballast.

The following excerpt from Roberts' account of his time at sea on the *Edernian* is reproduced here at some length, as it is a rare example of a first-person narrative of the ordinary work of a seaman aboard a general cargo steamer at this time:

> We arrived Barry Dock on the 18th April 1914 and had nearly completed loading coal for Algiers when it was found that No 1 ballast tank could not be got empty owing to a leak somewhere, which was found by a diver to be due to loose rivets. These were wedged up by the diver and heavy cement boxes were fitted to enable us to sail on the 24th April 1914. Having discharged at Algiers we proceeded to load salt at Cadiz for Buenos Ayres. Having reached B.A. after a slow passage, to save fuel, we discharged our salt and washed out the holds, but no grain cargo could be had after a salt cargo. Whilst waiting for a charter our bunker coal got overheated and about 600 tons had to be removed and placed on the after

deck by the ship's crew. This took some days and when we had all the coal out most of it was condemned as no longer being safe, as it had been badly overheated. Our next loading port was up the River Plate at Santa Fee, and the cargo was Quebrachio wood, a form of swamp timber, very hard, and heavy, used apparently by tanneries. At this time the 1914–18 War commenced. We eventually sailed for New York via St Lucia ... Having discharged at New York we loaded wheat for home, and when off North Ireland we were intercepted by [an] H.M. Destroyer and we were told to proceed to Lough Foyle where we remained some days. As we were routed via Irish Sea and English Channel to go to Hull our Master engaged a Coastal Pilot. He wore a top hat and frockcoat and appeared familiar with all shore objects as far as Belfast Lough, beyond that point he was unable to recognise any shore mark. He informed the Master that he had only taken the job in order to visit his relatives at Hull. We paid off at Hull on the 11th November 1914 and signed on again on the 9th December 1914 and left with a cargo of coal for Rouen, and then on to Barry Dock in ballast. We left Havre Roads in fine weather but ran into a full South Westerly gale off the Lizard, all hands having to work lifting the ceiling boards off No 4 tank top so as to allow flooding of this compartment. We were nearly ashore on the Lizard when we ran the water into the hold. And we were able to crawl off the land, and sideways past the Longships Light House off Land's End soon after dark. At Barry we took in bunkers and stores, and also 600 tons of clay and stone ballast on the upper deck, sailing on 5th January 1915 for Bermuda for orders.

... We passed well south of the Azores and when we had received our orders off South point Bermuda to proceed to Wilmington N.C. we carried on ... After passing Bermuda we had to throw 600 tons of ballast over the side, and this was indeed a back breaking job, but we managed to get rid of the lot before we sighted our destination. At Wilmington we loaded a full cargo of cotton, just over 17,000 bales of it and brought it to Liverpool, paying off on the 20th February 1915. We signed on again on the 7th March 1915 under a new Master, and loaded a full cargo of coal and some naval stores at Barry, and eventually arrived at St Vincent, Cape Verde Islands at the end of March, and remained there until early October when we left for Key West for orders. We could only crawl across the ocean, and eventually made New York, where we loaded wheat, after a 28 day passage from New York in very good weather we arrived at London, and paid off there on 29th November 1915.[14]

On the final crew agreement covered by this narrative, running from March to November 1915, fifteen out of a crew of twenty-eight were Welsh. In addition to Roberts, the other Welsh crew comprised: the master, who was from Edern; the mate, an able seaman and the donkeyman, all from Nefyn; the carpenter/seaman, bosun/lamps, an able seaman and the mess room steward all from Aberaeron; an able seaman and a seaman from Cardiff; the first engineer from Pwllheli; the second engineer from Caernarfon; the third engineer from Merthyr (he left sick with a fireman/trimmer at Cape Verde); and a fireman/trimmer from Bryncroes.

On 30 March 1917, the *Edernian* struck a mine in the English Channel, but managed to reach Dieppe for dry dock and repair. Then, on 20 August 1917, the *Edernian* was torpedoed by SM UB-10, and this time sunk, 6 miles south-east of Southwold while bound from Middlesbrough to Dieppe with a cargo of steel – fourteen lives were lost including Hugh Roberts' younger brother William.[15] Hugh Roberts at this time was serving as second mate on Evan Thomas, Radcliffe's *Llanishen*.

Another example of such a work history can be found in the case of captain Daniel Jenkins of Aberporth, who was master on two of W. & C. T. Jones's vessels, the *Haulwen*, 4032 GRT (1903), and the *Pontwen*, 4796 GRT (1914), during the war. Jenkins had started on sailing smacks in the coastal trade in 1890, and by 1894 was working as an able seaman for Evan Thomas, Radcliffe on the *W. I. Radcliffe*, 1969 GRT (1886). Over the course of the next six years, he worked his way up to master, and spent much of his time sailing in the 'coal out grain home trades' on various Cardiff steamers. The recent publication of his business letters covering the period 1902–11 provides a rare window into the everyday matters of ship management from the master's perspective.[16] The crew agreement for the *Haulwen* covering the period October 1914 to January 1915, lists thirty-three men, including four from Wales. While Jenkins and the *Pontwen* survived the war, the *Haulwen* was torpedoed by SM U-43 while returning from Montreal to Manchester with a cargo of wheat, 250 miles north-west of Fastnet, in June 1917.

A third ship's master, whose work history can be glimpsed at this time, is that of William Rowlands, who is commemorated on the Ambleston War Memorial in Pembrokeshire. Born in Carmarthen, William had followed his father to sea. He had been educated first at Morriston, then at Adamsdown Navigation School, Cardiff. He subsequently worked for Hughes & Company of Menai Bridge, where he rose quickly through the ranks and then joined Evan Thomas, Radcliffe & Company at Cardiff.[17] In 1914 there were three shipping companies with their origins in Cardigan operating out of Cardiff, of these Evan Thomas, Radcliffe was the largest with twenty-eight steamers, the Cambrian Steam Navigation Company had seven and Jenkins Brothers had five: all three companies were involved in the Black Sea trade, carrying coal out from the Tyne or south Wales to western European or Mediterranean ports, then proceeding in ballast to the Black Sea ports to load grain for continental or British ports.[18]

In November 1914, Rowlands the thirty-one-year-old master of the *Aden*, 2482 GRT (built 1905 at Glasgow as *Craigmore* and bought by Radcliffe in 1908, then sold in 1915), left London for Bristol Channel ports. On departure, also aboard was a third mate from Dinas Powys and an apprentice from Cardiff. A third engineer from Anglesey joined the crew in December. In April 1915 the *Aden* was at Barry, and among the other Welsh crew discharging there were an apprentice and a carpenter from Cardiff, and a second mate who was from Dinas Powys. In September 1915 Rowlands was master aboard the *Euston*, 2841 GRT (1910), with four other Welsh crew members aboard; two apprentices, the donkeyman and the mate. In July 1917, Rowlands was master of the *Paddington*, 5084 GRT (built as the *Patagonia* in 1906, renamed *Swindon* in 1913, then changed to *Paddington* in 1917), when returning to Wales from Cartagena with admiralty supplies and passengers it was torpedoed and sunk by SM U-96 with the loss of twenty-nine lives. Rowlands, along with five other Welsh crew are among those commemorated on the Mercantile Marine Memorial: Thomas Williams, the mate, aged forty-three, of Newborough, Anglesey; Archibald Robert Beer, second mate, aged nineteen, born in Cardiff (he had been an apprentice on the *Aden* two years earlier); Gwilym Rees, second engineer, aged twenty-nine, of Aberaeron; Rhys Edward Francis, third engineer, aged twenty-six, born in Merthyr Tydfil; and John Raymond Evans, apprentice, from Newport (Pembs.), aged seventeen.

During the course of the war Evan Thomas, Radcliffe lost twenty vessels, all bar one to enemy action. However, two of these vessels were later sold and put back in use: the *Picton*, 5084 GRT (1906), was caught up in the 1917 Halifax Novia Scotia explosion (some thirty of the crew were killed, including a number of Welshmen) and, damaged, remained there until sold in 1927;

and the *W. I. Radcliffe* built as *Clarissa Radcliffe* 6043 GRT (135204) in 1913 and renamed in 1917, which was torpedoed in the English Channel in March 1918 but made port, was later salvaged and finally sold in 1935. Four ships had been built for the firm during the course of the war, of which one was lost, two were sold in 1917, the remaining ship the *Clarissa Radcliffe* 5754 GRT (1915) (139099), was one of the seven that remained in service at the end of the war.

The conditions aboard a typical tramp steamer were unprepossessing to say the least, and 'coal dust, grease and seawater were constant companions'. Long hours (this could be up to ninety hours per week – four hours on, four hours off) were accompanied by accommodation, usually in the forecastle, which has been described as a 'squalid, ill lit and ill ventilated floating slum' with 'iron framed bunks riveted to the steel plates of the hull so that they were constantly subjected to the ceaseless drumming of the sea'.[19] Washing and sanitary facilities were rudimentary. Conditions aboard passenger liners were little better, one steward on his first trip in 1912 recalled of the crew accommodation:

> it was situated just over the rudder, accommodating forty men, and its berths were two high in long rows so that to get in them one had to climb over the foot of the bunk. The sloping bulkheads were also lined with what berths shipbuilding ingenuity had contrived to cram in. The general atmosphere was of suffocation and congestion.[20]

Even on first-class liners, the conditions of firemen, trimmers and stokers in 1914 were considered appalling. When Cunard's RMS *Caronia* was requisitioned for use as an armed merchant cruiser, the naval officer taking charge noted of the men in the stokehold that they 'made their own rules, lived rough, gambled, and fought among themselves, and remained apart from ... everyone else on board' and further, that there was no love lost between them and the seamen, including the deck officers, who viewed them as being 'little better than animals'.[21]

Another contemporary account by a ship's doctor on board a Cunard liner stated 'I have seen 24 men in the fo'c'sle, 18 trimmers bunked together, and 30 stewards in one "glory hole" ... Damp dirty or drying gear was everywhere. Light was poor and ventilation a joke'.[22]

Other evidence of the conditions aboard ships can be gleaned from various ports' sanitary inspector's reports; for example, at Barry in June 1915:

289 vessels were inspected. Of these, 41 were defective or dirty. Forty-one notices were given to have the nuisances abated ... Three vessels had been disinfected and 57 seamen's beds destroyed. Three samples of water from ship's tanks were taken, and in one instance the water was found to be contaminated. The tank containing this water was emptied and cleansed ... Two seamen and a ship's officer had been removed to the Sanatorium suffering from typhoid fever.[23]

Hugh Roberts would recall of his trip as mate aboard the *Penare*, 3078 GRT (1900), from Gibraltar with a cargo of phosphate rock that 'This was the dirtiest and most hungry ship I was ever on, the rooms being full of bugs'.[24] Given that this overall situation represented some considerable improvement, it is perhaps unsurprising that at the beginning of the twentieth century some 14,000 men deserted from British ships annually.[25]

Despite the grievances over provisioning having been largely addressed by the 1906 Merchant Shipping Act (introduced by then President of the Board of Trade, Lloyd George), the seaman's diet still largely consisted of 'a tedious variation on the themes bread, salt meat, dried peas, rice, ship's biscuit, tea and coffee'.[26] Lobscouse, a long-standing dish of north European sailors, which has been described as 'one of the oldest and most savoury of the forecastle dishes', consisted of salt meat, ship's biscuit, potatoes, onions and spices all minced together and stewed.[27] To make matters worse, independent evidence provided to the Board of Trade in 1906 suggested that cooking at sea (particularly on sailing ships) was 'wholly uncharacterised by skill'.[28] The rules regarding the provisioning of the crew were set out in some detail in Section 25 of the Merchant Shipping Act 1906. The weekly scale of provisions for each of the crew (not including the lime or lemon juice, sugar or other anti-scorbutics required by law) was as follows: 28 quarts of water, 3 pounds (lb) of soft bread, 4 lb of biscuit, 3 lb of salt beef, 2 lb of salt pork, 2.25 lb of preserved meat, 0.75 lb of fish, 6 lb of potatoes, 0.5 lb dried or compressed vegetables , 0.333 pint of green peas, 0.333 pint of cavalanches (chickpeas) or haricots , 2 lb of flour, 0.5 lb of rice, 8 ounces (oz) of oatmeal, 1.75 oz of tea, 4 oz of coffee, 1.75 lb of sugar, 0.5 lb of condensed milk, 0.5 lb of butter, 1 lb of marmalade or jam, 0.5 lb of syrup or molasses, 4 oz of suet, 0.5 pint of pickles, 5 oz of dried fruit, 2 oz of fine salt, 0.25 oz of mustard, 0.25 oz of pepper, 0.25 oz of curry powder, and 3 oz of onions. These provisions were to be reasonably distributed throughout the week.

The issue of soft bread under the scale was not required on a ship of less than 1,000 gross registered tons, or if rough weather rendered the making of the bread impracticable. On ships where soft bread was not issued, an equivalent amount of biscuit was to be issued instead. An equal quantity of fish, up to an amount not exceeding 0.75 lb in any one week, could be substituted for preserved meat under the above scale. The fish issued could be fresh or dried fish, or canned salmon or herrings. Fresh potatoes were to be issued for at least the first eight weeks of the voyage in the case of every ship leaving a port within the home-trade limits at any time between the last day of September and the first day of May, and at any other time when they could be procured at a reasonable cost. When in port, soft bread was to be issued instead of biscuit; and when procurable at a reasonable cost, 1.5 lb of fresh meat and 0.5 lb of fresh vegetables to be issued daily in place of salted and preserved rations. Another condition of the act was the requirement that there be a cook employed on all vessels 1,000 tons and over. The final provision was that stokehold hands were to receive sufficient oatmeal and one quart of water extra daily while under steam.

Not all seamen received the benefits of the 1906 Act, some signed on having to find their own provisions, such as the crew of the Morel Brothers of Cardiff *Westergate*, 1742 GRT (1881), in July 1914, sailing from Bristol to Lisbon via Cardiff. Able seamen/seamen and firemen/trimmers were signing on for £1 15s. per week (by December this had advanced to £2). On smaller vessels engaged in the coasting trade, such arrangements were more usual. On ships where sufficient numbers of the crew were lascar, Indian or others not accustomed to a European diet, there were different scales of provisions supplied. In B. Traven's fictionalised account of his experience as an American seaman serving just after the First World War, he describes the weekly fare on board a tramp steamer:[29]

> For breakfast we had a thick barley soup cooked with prunes. Sometimes the breakfast consisted of black sausage with rice. Then again it was potatoes in their skins with salted herring; another course was beans with smoked fish. Every four days the same dish appeared again, beginning with thick barley soup cooked with prunes. Never before had I known that all such things could be eaten by human beings, and that such strange mixtures could exist anywhere on this earth where ships with steam-engines had been seen. The dinner on Sunday consisted of boiled beef with mustard

sauce or corned beef and a slimy gravy, and sometimes cabbage, but mostly potatoes. Monday dinner was salt meat which no one ever ate, for it was only a sort of meat-crust soaked in salt. Tuesday we had dried salt fish, which was always stinking. Wednesday it was vegetables, and prunes swimming in a paste of potato starch. This paste was called the pudding. Thursday the dinner was again salted meat which nobody could eat.[30]

Traven's account contains considerable detail of the dangers of working in the stokeholds of tramp steamers. The two vessels depicted in his book were a tramp gun-runner and a newish cargo vessel that had been set up for a deliberate insurance job, but these were far from being entirely fictional conceits. For example, the ex-LNWR steamer *Edith*, was arrested by Belgian Authorities in 1913 on suspicion of just such a gun-running charge. The *Edith* had undergone substantial alterations over time, having been a paddle steamer when built originally. Following a sinking in 1875 and subsequent salvage, two years later the *Edith* had been rebuilt as cargo steamer and was further modified in 1892 to screw propulsion. The *Edith* was to have been sold for scrap in 1912 but ended up in Belgian hands. Similarly, 'insurance jobs' of the type described by Traven were not unknown. At Cardiff in the period just prior to the outbreak of the war, the temptation of the increasingly large discrepancies between insured and actual values, and the advent of claims on 'policy proof of interest' type insurances, led to the port acquiring what was described as an 'unenviable reputation for scuttling vessels' – that period saw both changes in the law and the phenomena of shipping companies based there relocating offices and registering their ships in other UK ports to escape the opprobrium and raised premiums.[31]

The spread of steam propulsion leading up to the First World War had brought significant structural changes to the make-up of the crew, particularly on the largest vessels where the numbers of engine room personnel far exceeded those on deck.[32] One description of the conditions on board for engine room crew in the early years of the twentieth century leaves little to the imagination, noting that they were:

indeed Spartan and grim, and on many older ships fireman and trimmers had no designated changing or wash rooms and consequently they brought coal dust and sweaty grime into their accommodation from which few cleaned themselves before rolling exhausted into their bunks. It was extremely difficult to prevent such a space from becoming filthy and squalid. These spaces then took on the all pervading smell of a mixture of body odour, coal fumes, cigarette and pipe tobacco smoke, oil and urine. On ships that carried grain such spaces could become infested with cockroaches and rats.[33]

The following account, compiled by former merchant seamen from Barry, describes the work performed by the men in the stokehold, and although written about those serving during the Second World War it is nonetheless relevant as it provides a rare glimpse of this type of work. That the experience of the 'black gang' (the name arising from their uniform coating of coal dust) had changed little since 1914–18, rested on the longevity of the triple expansion marine steam engine. First introduced commercially in 1881, it continued to be manufactured well into the twentieth century. Despite being outdated, its reliability and low cost saw all the 2,710 Liberty Ships built by the Americans powered by such engines: the first of these being launched some twenty-three years after the Armistice was signed. Further, there were many steamers still in the merchant service in 1939 that had survived the First World War. From the size given for the compliment of firemen and trimmers, the description that follows would relate to a vessel of around 8,000 GRT, the slightly smaller Allan Line steamer *Corinthian*, 7333 GRT (1900), for example, which had a couple of Welsh stewards among the crew in April 1915, had a 'black gang' numbering twenty-nine firemen and trimmers:

> The 'down-below' seamen were responsible for working the boiler rooms and their adjacent coal bunkers. Collectively, they were known as the 'Black Gang', a term that lasted well into the diesel era. Strictly speaking, 'Black Gang' referred to the trimmers and firemen – the men in the stokeholds and the bunkers. 'Stoker' and 'fireman' are two different titles for the same job, but the term 'fireman' is almost exclusively used on ships. The normal 'Black-gang' might consist of six firemen, two trimmers and a 'peggy'; altogether, on a '3-watch' ship, a total of 27 men. 'Trimmers' have always been needed because the firemen require a constant supply of coal. Even lower in social crew status than the men they served, they bunked and messed separately. 'Trimmers' have always had the dirtiest and the most physically demanding jobs on the ship – the

absolute bottom of the engineering hierarchy. Needless to say – they received the lowest pay.

Being a fireman involved much more than shovelling coal and maintaining the fires and this required more skill that they have been given credit for. The fireman would keep a careful eye on the fires, not only through the furnace doors, but through the ash-pit doors as well. There were usually three fires to a boiler – two 'high ones' and a 'low one' … Dark shadows visible beneath the fire-bars indicated the presence of clinkers – hard, fused lumps of coal or non-combustible minerals. These 'clinkers', along with areas laid too thick with green coal, would prevent sufficient air from passing through the fire. Steam output, as well as economy, would suffer if this was allowed to continue unchecked.

… the fireman rarely had the luxury of leaning back on his shovel; once the furnace had been fed, the fire had to be maintained throughout his watch, so that all the coal burned properly and efficiently – with the hottest, cleanest fire possible. This required a lot of work right up close up to the open furnaces. Further; feeding the furnaces, with their insatiable appetite for coal, was a physically demanding and exhausting job.

… While in port, most of the crew could count on 'going ashore' at one time or another – and blow off a little steam. Unfortunately for the trimmers, when the ship is 'bunkering', they had to stow the coal being loaded and trim as the coal was loaded and moved about – with nothing more than a wet rag tied over their face to keep the choking dust out of their lungs. All, of course, under the watchful eye of the chief engineer, who kept a close watch on the ship's 'trim' and made sure she did not develop a list. Back at sea again, their work continued with the same wet rag for protection and only a portable safety lamp hung from the deck beams above to aid their vision as they worked into a dank steel catacomb that pitched and rolled with the motion of the ship. On a long passage, the pace of their work increased as the fuel in the lower bunkers was depleted and it became necessary to move coal from the upper reaches into the lower bunkers.

… Managing the Black Gang required a bit of savvy on the part of the engineering officers on Merchant Ships; the stokers and trimmers were hard men – they had to be – and supervising them required an approach that was neither too lax nor too heavy-handed. Again; while their job was certainly the most unappreciated, it was one of the most vital; without them, the ship simply didn't run. Despite all of the hardships – and their lowly status, they took an enormous amount of pride in their job.[34]

The regulations for discipline in the merchant service provided for fines for a range of six offences: for striking or assaulting anyone on board or belonging to the ship, 5s.; for bringing or having on board intoxicating liquor, 5s.; for drunkenness, 5s. for the first offence, and 10s. for the second; for being in possession of offensive weapons, 5s.; for insolence or contemptuous behaviour towards the officers or disobedience, 5s.; and for absence without leave 5s. per day. The offences listed underline the concerns with safety and discipline as much as a propensity of crew members to drunkenness and violence. Writing in 1911, Henry Moffat, a long-serving mariner who had worked his way up to skipper noted that while he did not wish to unduly disparage 'jacks', in his opinion a large percentage of the crew aboard British ships and steamers were 'drunken, good for nothing men' with 'an endless stock of assurance and impudence'.[35] Such was the prevalence of drunkenness that ships could be delayed from sailing. One such example came to light during an inquest into the drowning of a sailor from the Swansea-registered *Kings Lynn*, 589 GRT (1880), at Drogheda in April 1915. It was reported that the master, R. W. Hopper, in replying to the Drogheda coroner:

> made some remarkable statements. The vessel, he stated, would have sailed to Newcastle upon Tyne on Saturday night, notwithstanding the fact that the whole crew were drunk. That was a dangerous thing to do, but it was a common occurrence. Neither the Customs nor the Board of Trade interfered, and ship masters had no alternative. The foreman of the jury remarked caustically 'No wonder German submarines easily sink British ships.'[36]

Among the crew in question was a Swansea seaman, B. J. Morgan.

Two examples of inquiries into the loss of vessels in which drunkenness was implicated as a contributing factor are to be in found in the Board of Trade Wreck Reports for the *Mikasa*, 255 GRT (1913), and *Socotra*, 6008 GRT (1897), in 1915, both of which had Welsh crew aboard at the time of the incidents.[37] In the first case, drinking rum and falling asleep at the wheel caused the stranding and subsequent loss of the steam trawler *Mikasa* on the Devon coast. In the second case, the master's liquor consumption may have contributed to errors in navigation that caused the stranding and loss of the *Socotra*: over the course of sixteen weeks, the master had requisitioned seventy-two bottles of Irish whiskey from the owners, and a further forty-eight bottles of whisky and six bottles of gin had been supplied to him by the storekeeper, though it was stated that this whisky was used mainly for entertaining in hot-weather ports. One has only to peruse the court sections of the contemporary local newspapers to see the regularity of drunk and disorderly or assault charges brought against merchant seamen. Firemen and trimmers had an even worse reputation.

While entries on the 1915 crew agreements for failure to join and desertion were relatively common, few such offences are to be found reported in the Welsh papers concerning Welsh crew. Some idea of the scale of the problem can be seen from figures for 1908, which show that 21,000 men deserted (largely abroad) and 16,000 failed to join (largely at home).[38] Following the introduction of the Defence of the Realm Act on 8 August 1914, disobedience could have more serious consequences for crew than the mandatory 5s. fine, however, and the penalties for those brought to court on charges of desertion, or failure to join resulting in delayed sailing (particularly on Admiralty chartered vessels), or of imperilling ships were more severe. A number of prosecutions for 'failing to join' hired military transports were reported in 1915 in the *Barry Dock News*, with the men so charged facing sentences of up to two months' imprisonment with hard labour.[39] Penalties for failing to join ships that were not requisitioned by the Admiralty were less severe; in one case a seaman from Skewen who had failed to join a steamer was fined 30s.[40]

Two Welsh mariners on the *Barranca*, 4124 GRT (1906), returning from Santa Marta, Colombia, to Garston in August 1915 found themselves aboard a ship that had been put in danger due to the refusal of the men in the stokehold to obey the master's orders. It was later reported that:

> Fourteen firemen and trimmers were sentenced at Liverpool on Wednesday to twenty-eight days' hard labour for refusing to work overtime on board the Elders and Fyffes steamer Barranca after the captain had received a wireless message which necessitated putting the vessel at full speed. It was stated that when the captain ordered the men to work a six hours' watch instead of four they

unanimously refused, declaring that their trade union regulations would not allow them to work more than a four-hour watch without extra pay of 9d. an hour. The captain told the court that owing to the men's action he could not get full speed out of his vessel, and the men had imperilled not only their own lives but those of other members of the crew and of two passengers. One elderly fireman complained that the men were fatigued by the work already done. 'If there had been sixty submarines,' he said, 'and my home had been in danger I could not have done what I was asked to do.'[41]

In another example, a wireless operator from Wrexham was aboard the Union-Castle mail steamer *Cluny Castle* 5152 GRT (1903), in May 1915, when the actions of some of the firemen and trimmers similarly imperilled the vessel. Thirteen firemen and trimmers were subsequently charged with refusing to obey the lawful command of the master. It was stated at the Thames Police Court that:

> their conduct exposed the vessel to grave danger from submarines. Mr. Paley Scott, who prosecuted, said that when the vessel was ready to leave Plymouth for London a deputation, representing the firemen and trimmers, told the captain that they declined to work the ship unless he undertook not to penalise a man who had gone ashore without leave. The captain refused to give the undertaking, and ordered the men to return to duty. The speed of the vessel afterwards decreased owing to the refusal of the men to keep up steam. The ship was in imminent danger of being driven on a breakwater, and the anchor had to be dropped. The captain ordered the men to return to duty, but they refused, and he signalled for assistance. Two destroyers answered the call, and a naval lieutenant persuaded the men to return to their work.

The charges against five of the men were dismissed, but the remaining nine were sentenced to fourteen days' hard labour.[42]

In a case which combined both anti-Welsh language and unpatriotic attitudes, a seaman from Aberavon who was in court for breaking nine panes of glass while drunk at the Red Lion Hotel, Port Talbot, stated that he had objected to men in the bar talking Welsh and had smashed the windows.[43] When he was charged the defendant said, 'It will be safer to be in gaol than going to sea, because you might be torpedoed'. However, in place of a custodial sentence he was ordered to pay a 20s. fine, 30s. in damages, and advocate's fee, totalling £3 11s.[44] The man in question had just signed off from the Swansea-registered *Nigaristan*, 4344 GRT (1913), which had been brought from Barry to Port Talbot on 28 April 1915. He had been paid £2 2s.7d for the run. This was almost half a month's wages for a day's work, which probably accounted for his drunkenness. In June he joined the *Aldersgate*, 3687 GRT (1906), for the river Plate but left the ship with the master's consent at New York in September 1915.

While the foregoing opinions regarding both the prejudices and sobriety of seamen might be widely held (and perhaps well founded), there were voices that recognised the other side of the character of those who went to sea in the merchant service. Addressing the annual meeting of the Barry Missions to Seamen in 1915, the Right Rev. Bishop Crossley stated:

'There was one characteristic about a sailor which was very remarkable. They would best understand if they travelled by the Barry line with coaltrimmers. On no occasion would a coaltrimmer part with his shovel. This shovel was a trimmer's treasure, which was polished and kept as though it were part of himself. The sailor was exactly opposite. He would part with anything, except his tatoo [sic] marks. A sailor would give with all his personality and his purse ... Our security also rests with our mercantile service,' the speaker added, amidst applause. 'Have we heard of any cowards? Are there any sailors who wanted to stay behind because there were submarines about? No ... The sailor was not afraid of danger, and faced death very often.'[45]

Pay and working conditions at this time varied enormously, from ship to ship and from trade to trade. There were worlds of difference between the experience of an apprentice on a fully rigged sailing ship and a trimmer on a steamer, or between the master of a passenger liner and the cook on a coastal trading schooner. All existed in what was a very fluid workforce where many crew changed ship regularly, and overall accommodation and welfare for the majority was barely adequate. While varying from trade to trade, the widespread presence of 'foreign' crew on British merchant ships was not a particularly unusual feature of the workforce, although they may be slightly over-represented in the crew agreements considered here.

PAY AND CONDITIONS

Following the outbreak of war, the Royal Navy had immediately called up some 56,000 reservists and thereafter began to draw a large number of seamen from their usual occupations, one result of which was a higher incidence of 'foreign' seamen signing on British vessels. This aspect of the composition of crews on ships will be discussed more fully in a later examination of the broader societal and cultural attitudes relating to the participation of international crew at this time.

Improvements had been implemented with regard to seamen's diet and to the amount of space allowed for the accommodation of crew. The provisions of the 1906 Act saw an increase from 72 cubic feet to 125 cubic feet for each seaman, though this also took into account shared facilities such as mess rooms, bathrooms and washing facilities. The legislation did not, however, apply to vessels built before that date (or under construction on 1 January 1907) or to vessels under 300 tons burden, or to fishing vessels. All crew were subject to ship-board hierarchies, whether on deck or in the stokehold with discipline largely mediated by financial penalties either by fines or demotion. The introduction of the Defence of the Realm Act brought more serious consequences for those failing to join, and those serving on T124 agreements would be bound by naval discipline. Discrepancies in the rates of pay between merchant seamen and Navy ratings for identical duties on auxiliary vessels, hired transports and suchlike led to moves towards standardised rates, though such comparisons did not reflect the much higher level of welfare provision made by the Royal Navy, which to some extent ameliorated lower rates of pay. Wages for all classes of mercantile crew rose during the war, partly due to labour shortages but also due to the increased risks faced by crews that were recognised by the payment of war bonuses.

Notes

1. Woodman, *More Days, More Dollars*, p. 205.
2. Lilley, 'Operation of the Tenth Cruiser Squadron', p. 211, figure 49.
3. Men in these classes signed on under a variety of descriptions, able seamen and seamen were usually paid at the same rate, whereas ordinary seamen were paid less. 'Fireman and trimmer' is the most common designation in the stokehold, though there are also instances of men signing on as just 'fireman' or 'trimmer'.
4. This was not always across the board – some agreements specified which members of the crew were eligible.
5. Lilley, 'Operation of the Tenth Cruiser Squadron', p. 212, figure 50.

6   Kirkaldy, *British Shipping*, p. 227.
7   For more on William Thomas's shipping interest, see Eames, *Ships and Seamen of Anglesey*, pp. 439ff.
8   This was a three-masted ship.
9   See *www.bruzelius.info/Nautica/Ships/Fourmast_ships/Catalogue.html* (last accessed 3 November 2024).
10   For more on the experiences of women at sea on sailing vessels, though for a slightly earlier period, see, for example, Aled Eames, *The Captain's Wife* (Llanrwst, 2016); and J. Druett, *Hen Frigates: Passion and Peril, Nineteenth-Century Women at Sea* (New York, 1998).
11   Woodman, *More Days, More Dollars*, pp. 67-9.
12   Woodman, *More Days, More Dollars*, p. 250.
13   For an examination of the training and certification of deck officers at this time, see Alston Kennerley, 'Nationally Recognised Qualifications for British Merchant Navy Officers, 1865-1966', *International Journal of Maritime History*, 13/1 (June 2001), 115-35; and Alston Kennerley, 'Aspirant Navigator: Training and Education at Sea during commercial voyages in British Ships c.1850-1950', *The Great Circle*, 30/2 (2008), 41-76.
14   See *www.rhiw.com/y_mor/hugh_roberts/hugh_roberts.htm* (last accessed 3 November 2024).
15   Among them were a number of Welshmen: first mate William Griffith, Nefyn; William Roberts, Edern, and his friend Hugh Griffith Hughes, Nefyn, both ordinary seamen; a seaman from Cardiff; and the carpenter who was from Pwllheli – all are commemorated on the Mercantile Marine Memorial.
16   D. Jenkins (ed.), *'I Hope to have a Good Passage': The Business Letters of Captain Daniel Jenkins, 1902-11* (Newport, 2016).
17   I am grateful to Steve John and his West Wales War Memorial Project for this information. His site, *https://ww1.wales* (last accessed 3 November 2024), has been a useful resource.
18   D. Jenkins, 'Cardiff Tramps, Cardi Crews', *Journal of the Cardiganshire Antiquarian Society*, 10/1-4 (1984-7), 416-17. See also J. Geraint Jenkins, *Evan Thomas Radcliffe: A Cardiff Shipowning Company* (Cardiff, 1982).
19   Jenkins, *Shipowners of Cardiff*, p. 419.
20   R. Hope, *Poor Jack* (London, 2001), p. 295.
21   Woodman, *More Days, More Dollars*, p. 223.
22   Hope, *Poor Jack*, p. 305.
23   *BDN*, 9 July 1915, p. 6.
24   See *www.rhiw.com/y_mor/hugh_roberts/hugh_roberts.htm* (last accessed 3 November 2024).
25   Woodman, *More Days, More Dollars*, p. 109.
26   Jenkins, *Shipowners of Cardiff*, p. 420.
27   W. H. Smyth, *Sailor's Word Book: A Dictionary of Nautical Terms* (London, 1996).
28   Eames, *Ships and Seamen of Anglesey*, p. 485.
29   See the second part of B. Traven, *The Death Ship* (New York, 1991).
30   Traven, *The Death Ship*, pp. 104-5.

31 Jenkins, *Shipowners of Cardiff*, pp. 26–8.
32 A. Kennerley, 'Stoking the Boilers: Firemen and Trimmer in British Merchant Ships 1850–1950', *International Journal of Maritime History*, 20/1 (2008), 191–220.
33 Richard P. de Kerbrech, *Down Amongst the Black Gang: The World and Workplace of RMS Titanic's Stokers* (Stroud, 2014).
34 This description is taken from the work of David Simpson et al. and the original can be found at *www.barrymerchantseamen.org.uk/articles/BMSfiretrim.html* (last accessed 3 November 2024).
35 Woodman, *More Days, More Dollars*, p. 19; H. Y. Moffat, *From Ship's Boy to Skipper* (Paisley, 1911).
36 *CDL*, 21 April 1915, p. 3.
37 These can be found at *www.southampton.gov.uk/arts-heritage/southampton-archives/plimsoll/* (last accessed 3 November 2024).
38 Dixon, 'Seamen and the Law', p. 326.
39 See, for example, *BDN*, 9 July, p. 6; and 16 July 1915, p. 7.
40 *SWWP*, 5 August 1916, p. 6.
41 *Herald of Wales and Monmouthshire Recorder*, 18 September 1915, p. 11.
42 *CDL*, 21 May 1915, p. 6.
43 According to the 1911 Census, 43.5 per cent of the population spoke Welsh at this time.
44 *CDL*, 30 April 1915, p. 4.
45 *BDN*, 26 November 1915, p. 5.

3 The Outbreak of War

Figure 3: Postcard of the LNWR's Irish mail steamer *Cambria* (right) at Holyhead pre-1914

On the last day of peace, 3 August 1914, due to the lack of an available sea-pilot, the almost brand new British oil-tanker *San Wilfrido*, 6458 GRT (1914), *en route* from Hamburg to Portland in ballast, hit a mine while passing Cuxhaven at the mouth of the river Elbe and sank in shallow water, becoming the first merchant shipping loss of the war.[1] This incident was witnessed by two Welsh seamen whose ship had sailed immediately prior to the *San Wilfrido* and whose story was later reported in the *Herald of Wales and Monmouthshire Reporter*:

> To be seventy yards away from a ship when she is blown up by German mines, and to escape the same fate by a matter of seconds, is an experience that falls to the lot of few, and so the story of two Swansea men who witnessed the sinking of the s.s. San Wilfrido

on Bank Holiday is of interest. They are Mr. W. C. Simmons, who for some time was local secretary of the Seaman's Union, and who is now second engineer on the s.s. City of Oporto; and Mr. A. Hall, a fireman on the same vessel. 'We left Hamburg on Sunday afternoon, the day before Bank Holiday, and we were the last boat to leave before war was declared by England,' they said. 'The San Wilfrido was following us, and when we got off Cuxhaven we took aboard the last mine pilot left there. We were then in the neighbourhood of mines, and the pilot immediately had the ship's helm put to starboard. The San Wilfrido, who was following us, went to port, and was immediately struck by a mine on the starboard bow. In answer to the whistle of a German tug she tried to go astern, but the tide was too strong, and two mines struck her amid-ships, and another on the port quarter, going right through her, and sinking her in about twenty minutes. We were not more than 70 yards away, and if the San Wilfrido had got the pilot first we would certainly have gone on to the mines ... We are very lucky indeed to get back safely.'[2]

All forty-one crew were taken off by a German tug, most of these men were from the Tyne and they would soon all be imprisoned for the duration at the Ruhleben internment camp.[3]

On the following day, 4 August 1914, seventy-three British steamers and three sailing vessels were detained in German ports.[4] Their crews comprised 155 British merchant ship's officers and 888 ratings who all found themselves interned in Germany; most of whom ended up at Ruhleben. Some of the crews were roughly treated and initially they were held in hulks on the river Elbe. By 1918 the number of British seamen held in the camp would rise to 2,752.[5] Ruhleben was some 10 kilometres west of Berlin and the main camp for civilian detainees (those living, studying or working in Germany at the outbreak of the war) and included seamen and trawler-men captured in the early months of the war. During the war, between 4,000 and 5,000 mostly British prisoners were held there.[6]

Most of the ships detained in Germany at the start of August were taken on the river Elbe with some sixty-two vessels recorded as being seized at Hamburg and another two at Harburg just to the south.[7] Among them was the Cardiff-registered *Dartwen*, 4793 GRT (1913), owned by the W. & C. T. Jones shipping company, with sixteen men out of a crew of thirty from Wales. Herbert Arnold Jones of Cardiff, the chief officer of the *Dartwen* was released from Ruhleben in January 1917 having been the subject of Foreign Office correspondence regarding the continued detention of British seamen aged over fifty-five.[8] At almost the other end of the spectrum of the types of shipping in use by the mercantile marine in 1914 was the *George Casson*, a 154 GRT (1863) schooner, owned by Pritchard Brothers of Caernarfon and sailing regularly in the slate trade, which was seized at Harburg. The crew of five – a master, a mate and three seamen all from North Wales – were imprisoned at Ruhleben.[9]

The Cardiff-based Hain Steam Ship Company, with thirty-four ships at the start of the war, had two of their St Ives-registered vessels seized on the river Wesser: one at Brake, the *Trevider*, 4260 GRT (1913); and further up the river at Bremen, the *Treglisson*, 4265 GRT (1912), which had been discharging grain brought from Taganrog in Russia. Both ships had Welsh crew members: on the *Trevider*, the first engineer was from Cardiff; the mess room steward from Barry Docks; and the carpenter from Aberaeron. On the *Treglisson*, ten of the crew were from Wales: the carpenter was from Aberporth; the third engineer from Abercanaid; three firemen, a donkeyman, two apprentices and a sailor were from Cardiff; and an ordinary seaman from Llanarth.

Welsh crew were also present on some of the other British shipping that was seized on the Elbe: there were six men on the *Saxon*, 495 GRT (1898), owned by the West of England SS Company Ltd – four of them from Amlwch including the mate, an engineer and the cook, while the master, Rowland Humphreys, though living in Liverpool, was also an Amlwch man.[10] There were fifteen Welsh crew on board the Bristol-registered *Scarsdale*, 3714 GRT (1912), among them eight men from Barry, including the cook, bosun and fourth engineer, and four men from Cardiff including the master and chief officer. There were also three Swansea men on the Dublin-registered *City of Cadiz*, 780 GRT (1862).

An account of the conditions endured by such interned men was reported in the *North Wales Chronicle and Advertiser* in December 1915:

EXPERIENCES OF AN 'INTERNED' WELSHMAN – STORIES OF GERMAN CRUELTY
A young Pwllheli sailor, named Richard Jones, was among the 85 British prisoners released from the German internment camp the other day. Jones and many of his comrades formed the crew of a vessel which was in port at Hamburg when the war broke out.

They were kept on the ship for three months under a threat that an attempt at escape would be visited by condign punishment. From the ship they were transferred to a shed at Minister Jaager, where the conditions were not particularly inviting. The place was infested with rats, the bed clothing was scanty, and the food was inadequate as well as indifferent in quality. Dinner consisted of a kind of broth, made of turnips or carrots, without any meat or fat, but with an occasional bit of uncooked herring. They were treated with the utmost contempt and called 'English dogs' and other choice epithets ... Any prisoner found smoking was tied to the public lamp-post and made all object of derision to the passers-by. The whole camp was deprived of bread because a Belgian prisoner was detected smoking. When the Camp was moved to Ruhleben during January last, the conditions improved considerably. The food was the same, but it was rendered more palatable because the prisoners became their own cooks. Games such as football and golf were also introduced, together with living pictures. Smoking was allowed, and permission to receive parcels from the homeland.[11]

Another report concerning interment at Ruhleben was given by William Adams, seaman, shortly after his return home to Barry in January 1916. Adams had spent nearly eighteen months as a prisoner of war in Germany and was released due to being over fifty years old and therefore unsuitable for active service. Adams had been aboard the London-registered *Rubens*, 3587 GRT (1906), which had called at Hamburg on the way home from Rangoon. Adams told the *Barry Dock News* that:

There were about thirty seamen amongst the crew ... and the captain, Mr. French, had his wife on board, as it was his last trip before retiring from the sea. Some of the captain's friends succeeded in getting his wife away, but [he] dropped dead whilst playing draughts in captivity at Ruhleben sometime later. Asked how they learnt that war had been declared, Adams replied that German soldiers came aboard their ship ... and they were hustled on board two hulks, where they were kept under terrible conditions for six weeks. They were then removed to Ruhleben in cattle trucks, and although the journey occupied seventeen hours, they were not given food or drink of any description. On reaching their destination they were served with a meal of dry bread and water, the only food they had since they began the journey.[12]

At the time of Adams release there were some 1,600 British prisoners at Ruhleben, and Adams told reporters that on the whole they 'were cheerful enough, but the food was poor and insufficient, and the confinement very trying'. Adams believed that without the 35,000 parcels that arrived from Britain every month the prisoners would have starved, as food at the camp consisted of dry bread and coffee for breakfast, with just a vegetable soup for dinner. Adams also praised the work of the women of the Dutch Red Cross for the way in which they provided clothing and food for the seamen prior to their embarking for home.

More than a few of the other interred crew from the *Rubens* were either Welsh or living in Wales: A. C. Butcher, engineer's steward, A. Cranza, able seaman, J. Kirwan, seaman, and H. Tolin, bosun, gave Barry as their home address; A. A. Glen, chief engineer, H. Sampson, fourth engineer, and D. I. Salmon, apprentice, gave Cardiff; E. Owens, carpenter, Aberporth; W. J. Evans, chief officer, Aberystwyth; and J. Egan, able seaman, Cadoxton. Of these, Tolin was released in January 1915 and Kirwan in January 1916.[13] Some of the Welsh crew who would be imprisoned at Ruhleben had been taken further afield. At Memel in East Prussia, now Lithuania, the Cardiff-registered *Glyndwr*, 2425 GRT (1904), a steel twin-screw steamer (originally built as the *Craigronald*), was seized and then converted to use as auxiliary seaplane carrier.[14] Two of the *Glyndwr*'s crew were from Cardiff. Out of the forty-five crew on the Glasgow-registered *City of Khios*, 3496 GRT (1878), which was detained in Turkish waters at Smyrna, ten were from Wales, nine of them from Newport.[15]

In October 1914, an agreement was reached for the mutual repatriation of clergy, civil medical practitioners, women, children and men under the age of seventeen and over fifty-five. In August 1915, Germany agreed to the repatriation of invalid civilians of any age, but this was not the case for merchant seamen, who the German Government insisted on regarding as a separate class. In 1915 the repatriation of ships' boys under the age of seventeen was agreed to, and in 1916 it was further agreed that seamen over fifty-five years of age (and on reaching fifty-five) should also be repatriated. No satisfactory arrangement was ever reached regarding the repatriation of invalid merchant seamen. The position was further complicated when Germany insisted on treating crews of defensively armed merchant ships as combatants. In 1917, a further agreement was made to repatriate all interned civilians over forty-five years of age (with some exceptions), which included the crews (but not the officers) of merchant ships.

During the course of the war the Board of Trade would print a series of lists of all merchant seamen held prisoner and their locations. This information was shared with a number of interested parties including government departments, shipowners, unions and such like associations. In all, eight lists are known to have been produced. In April 1918, a letter detailing the numbers captured and interned over the course of the war listed a total of 3,228 merchant seamen. Of these men, thirty-nine had died, one was executed, 515 were released or repatriated, with 2,673 remaining in captivity at that date.[16] The final Board of Trade list, dated 31 May 1918, contains the names of 3,252 men. Of these, 214 were from Wales, with half of those men hailing from Cardiff. The vast majority of Welsh seamen, who found themselves in such circumstances, remained interned for the duration.

From the start of the war, shipping companies around Wales needed to make arrangements to adjust their operations in the face of rapidly changing circumstances. In August 1914 the Amlwch shipbuilders William Thomas & Sons were engaged in, among other activities, the ownership and management of a handful of sailing vessels. Three days after the outbreak of war, William Thomas wrote to his insurers seeking permission for the schooners *Emily Millington*, 110 GRT (1896), to sail from King's Lynn to the English Channel, and for the *Meyric*, 198 GRT (1904), to proceed from Plymouth for either the Bristol Channel or the Mersey. He further sought reassurances that another two schooners, the *Kate* (63917), 129 GRT (1872), and the *Winifred*, 123 GRT (1890), then at sea, were still covered until arrival at their ports of destination. Thomas also wrote to the captains of the *Emily Millington* and the *Meyric* that they might have to lay off the crews and lay up the vessels until the situation was clearer. In the event, however, both captains fixed freights and sailed instead.

There were a number of Welshmen aboard these vessels: the master of the *Emily Millington* was from Porthmadog; on the *Meyric*, the master was from Amlwch, the mate was from Cardigan and the cook from Anglesey; aboard the *Kate* (63917), the master was from Port Dinorwic and the mate from Moelfre. Another concern for Thomas was the Beaumaris-registered Barkantine *Gaelic*, 223 GRT (1898), then at Runcorn, whose master William Griffith was from Llanbedr, Merionethshire. Thomas wrote to advise him that it would not be prudent to fix a cargo for anywhere under the prevailing conditions. When Thomas was informed on 18 September 1914 that the captain had accepted a freight for Grimsby, he was keen to remind Griffith of the great risk attending going to the Humber (the steamer s.s. *Runo* had recently struck a mine in that vicinity with the loss of twenty-nine lives), and that all the east-coast light-ships were extinguished. After the safe arrival at Grimsby, the insurers declined to cover the *Gaelic* to any Channel ports unless first towed to Harwich. This was to ensure that the vessel kept to shipping lanes that had been cleared of mines. As the cost of such a proposition was prohibitive and as the vessel could not be kept at Grimsby indefinitely, the insurance was transferred to a company, which, for an increased premium, did not insist on the tow. When the *Gaelic* arrived at the Downs on 30 September 1914, the North Sea had been closed to sailing vessels.[17] By the time William Thomas had sat down to write to his insurers and captains, Welsh vessels and crew were already caught up in the conflict at sea. On 6 August 1914 the Liverpool-registered steamer *Drumcliffe*, 4073 GRT (1905), sailing from Buenos Aires to Trinidad for bunkers before proceeding for New York had a lucky escape. Stopped off the north-east coast of Brazil by the German light cruiser SMS *Dresden*, Captain Thomas John Evans of Criccieth who had his wife and two young daughters aboard, convinced the Germans that he knew nothing of the outbreak of hostilities having left port before war was declared. He was able to secure the release of the *Drumcliffe* conditional on receipt of the parole of the master and crew that they would not serve during the war and would be subject to summary execution should they be found so engaged.[18] The *Drumcliffe* was then allowed to proceed having had its radio equipment disabled.[19]

The Caernarfon-registered three-masted topsail schooner *Frau Minna Petersen*, 176 GRT (1878), was not so lucky. Sailing from Porthmadog with a cargo of slate before war was declared; the schooner was captured by a German torpedo-boat on 7 August 1914 near the mouth of the river Ems and taken into Emden. It is not known what became of the crew, but most likely they were taken to Ruhleben. At the outbreak of hostilities, both surface commerce raiders and U-boats observed prize or cruiser rules. Under such rules enemy merchant ships, or neutral vessels that could be carrying cargo for the enemy and that could be judged 'war contraband', would be stopped. In the event of such a vessel being deemed a legitimate target – the crew, who were allowed to abandon ship (as they were non-combatants going about their everyday work), were to be removed to 'a place of safety' before the raider either sank or seized the prize.[20]

The first U-boat attacks on merchant ships started in October 1914. There was, however, no concerted plan against allied merchant shipping at this time, and only four British merchant ships had been captured and sunk by U-boats up to the end of January 1915.[21] One of these vessels, the Glasgow-registered *Malachite*, 718 GRT (1902), was a well-known local trader at Llanelli whose demise at the hands of SM U-21 on 23 November 1914 off the Seine estuary was reported in the *Llanelly Star*.[22] On 30 January 1915 the first three British merchant vessels to be torpedoed without warning were attacked by SM U-20 and thereafter U-boat tactics rapidly abandoned any attempt to conform to international law.[23] What followed was a period of undeclared unrestricted submarine warfare that soon hardened into policy, and that was only fully halted in April 1916 following a number of 'sinking without warning' incidents including the *Lusitania*, 31550 GRT, on 7 May 1915, the *Arabic*, 15801 GRT (1903), on 9 August, and the Italian passenger liner *Ancona* on 8 November 1915 (flying the Austro-Hungarian flag), all of which had Americans on board.[24]

When unrestricted submarine warfare was resumed in February 1917, the United States severed relations with Germany and this ultimately brought America into the war. At the outbreak of the war, shipmasters, shipowners and naval officers were all united in their objection to the use of convoys.[25] Although their reasoning proved wrong-headed in light of the developing submarine war against allied commerce, the convoy system was not officially adopted until rapidly mounting losses brought about a change of policy in May 1917. These developments were, however, yet to unfold.

Not 'Over by Christmas' August–December 1914

As early as September 1914 in the western Pacific, Welsh merchant seamen were experiencing the attention and depredations of German commerce raiders. The Cardiff-registered *Southport*, 3588 GRT (1900), had sailed from Auckland on 12 July 1914 to load phosphate at Nauru, which was then one of the German Marshall Islands protectorates. The *Southport* had certified accommodation for thirty-five but was to be considered crewed with twenty hands, not fewer than eight of whom were to be sailors. At Nauru there were other ships waiting and long delays. To save coal while waiting for a signal to return to Nauru, the *Southport* had been in the harbour at Kusaie (now Kosrae), the most easterly of the German Caroline Islands, since 4 August, unaware that war had been declared. On 4 September

1914, the *Southport* was captured by the German raider SMS *Geier*, an unprotected cruiser of the Bussard class that had been built for service in the German overseas colonies. The *Southport*'s engines were disabled and tools taken so that the *Geier* could go off. The crew of the *Southport* managed to rebuild the engines by cannibalising other parts, obtained food and supplies from the local inhabitants, and had sailed on 18 September reaching Brisbane at the end of that month. Two of the engineers aboard were from Wales and both had signed on to the *Southport* in March 1913 for an initial passage from Liverpool to Brunswick. They were W. E. Harris, aged thirty-one, the second engineer who was from Newport and who would sign off at Callao in April 1915; and A. Griffiths, aged twenty-one, the third engineer from Cardiff who discharged at Marseille in July 1915. The *Southport*'s master was a naturalised British subject, originally from France but living in Cardiff.[26]

Two weeks after the *Southport* incident, two Welsh crew members were among those aboard the Liverpool-registered *Ortega*, 7970 GRT (1906), who had a plucky escape from the clutches of the German light cruiser SMS *Dresden*.[27] The *Ortega* was a passenger ship capable of 15 knots, built by Harland & Wolff for the Pacific Steam Navigation Company. There was accommodation for 160 first-class passengers, 128 second-class passengers, 300 third-class passengers and 500 emigrants in the between deck dormitories. The *Ortega* had a large crew, with certified accommodation for 181, and when war was declared the ship was at Montevideo *en route* for Callao. On 16 September 1914 the *Ortega* left Valparaiso for Liverpool carrying around 300 French Reservists. The *Ortega* was chased by the *Dresden* off southern Chile and when ordered to stop on 19 September, it instead headed at full speed into the uncharted Nelson Strait, which forced the *Dresden* to abandon the chase for fear of running aground. The *Ortega*, sometimes led by two lifeboats that were taking depth soundings, proceeded by way of the Smyth Channel through to the Strait of Magellan and was then met by the Chilean warship *Almirante Lynch*.[28] On 29 October 1914, the *Ortega* was back in Liverpool and ready to leave again for Callao. There were six Welsh crew on this trip including two stewardesses: Kate Jones, aged thirty-six, from Porthmadog; and Alice Maguire, aged thirty-seven, from Wrexham. The other Welsh crew were William John, aged fifty-two, a fireman and trimmer from Cardiff; L. W. Roberts, aged thirty, a steward from Holyhead; Griffith T. Williams, aged eighteen, an ordinary seaman from Edern; and Thomas Williams, aged twenty-six, an able seaman from Benllech.[29]

The first Cardiff vessel to be lost was the Reardon Smith-owned and Bideford-registered *Cornish City*, 3816 GRT (1906), which was sailing Barry to Rio Janeiro with 5,500 tons of coal. On 21 September 1914 in the central Atlantic off Brazil this steamer was stopped by the light cruiser SMS *Karlsruhe*. The crew were taken on board one of the *Karlsruhe*'s tenders, the *Rio Negro*, then the *Cornish City*'s sea-cocks were opened, and a scuttling charge was set, though this only blew a small hole in the ship, which took a long time to sink.[30] According to one source, the chief engineer on the *Cornish City*, William Lilley (a son-in-law of William Reardon Smith), was among those taken prisoner,[31] and would join the crews from twelve other British and one neutral vessel (which had all been taken by the *Karlsruhe*) aboard another of the tenders, the former Nord Deutsche Line *Crefeld*, 3973 GRT (1895).

They were not the only Welsh crew members to have fallen foul of the *Karlsruhe*. Arthur Jones from Aberystwyth was the master of the Liverpool-registered Liver Shipping Company's *Lynrowan*, 3384 GRT (1907), when the ship was taken by the *Karlsruhe* on 7 October 1914. The *Lynrowan* had been sailing Buenos Aires for Liverpool with a cargo comprising 5,500 tons of hides, maize, sugar and talc. Jones and the crew were put aboard the *Crefeld* and the *Lynrowan* was sunk with bombs. Another Welsh prisoner aboard the *Crefeld* was fourth officer Stanley Galloway from Wrexham, who had been on the Liverpool-registered *Indrani*, 5706 GRT (1912). The *Indrani* had been twelve days out from Norfolk (Va.) with a cargo of American coal for Rio de Janeiro when overhauled and captured on 17 September 1914.[32] There may have been more Welsh crew confined on board the *Crefeld*, as a number of the other vessels captured by the *Karlsruhe* at this time had been either outward or homeward bound to Liverpool and one had been outward bound from Barry with coal. By mid-October there were 419 captured crewmen on board the *Crefeld* and the conditions were cramped and rations short. The captain of the *Karlsruhe* decided to send what had effectively become a prison ship to neutral Tenerife to rid himself of the captives and they were no doubt all relieved to be landed safely at Santa Cruz on 22 October 1914.[33] Arthur Jones would later serve on another Liver Shipping Company ship, the *Lynrota*, 3684 GRT (1902), which sailed from Boston in April 1915 carrying food for starving Belgians – on this agreement were also B. Robertson, a second mate from Aberaeron, and J. Williams, a fireman/trimmer from Penarth.

Other examples of Welsh crew taken prisoner by German surface raiders in the South Atlantic in October/November 1914 are provided by the steamers *Hurstdale*, *North Wales* and *Exford*. On 23 October 1914, the day after the crew of the *Cornish City* had been freed, the Liverpool-registered *Hurstdale*, 2752 GRT (1902), which had left Swansea some three months earlier, was sailing Rosario to Bristol with a cargo of maize when seized by the *Karlsruhe* 205 miles south-west of St Paul's Rocks. The *Hurstdale* was then sunk and the crew, along with those from two other vessels that had been taken (the *Glanton* and *Vandyck*), were put aboard another of the *Karlsruhe*'s tenders, the Hamburg-Süd-Amerika liner *Asuncion*, and taken to Para (Belem) in north-western Brazil, where they were released on 2 November 1914. The master of the *Hurstdale* was J. Williams of Swansea.[34]

On 16 November 1914, the Newcastle-registered *North Wales*, 3691 GRT (1905), belonging to the North Shipping Company (Hugh Roberts & Sons), was under Admiralty charter at the Falkland Islands. Carrying coal in support of the naval squadron operating in the southern Atlantic, the *North Wales* was seized and sunk by the SMS *Dresden*. The crew were put aboard the Kosmos liner *Rhokotis* (then in company with the *Dresden*) and were later landed at Callao.[35] The *North Wales* was captained by Griffith Owen, aged forty-three, of Erw Goch, Morfa Nefyn, Llŷn, and the majority of the twenty-seven captured crewmen were Welsh. They comprised the mate, Thomas Evans, aged fifty-two, the first engineer David Roberts, aged forty, and the second engineer, Morris Owen, aged twenty-nine, all from Porthmadog; the second mate R. H. Parry, aged forty-one, from Bethesda; the steward, D. Williams, aged forty-one, from Caernarfon, an able seaman; D. A. Jones, aged twenty-one, from Aberaeron; three sailors, John Evans, aged twenty-seven, from Caernarfon, and J. Rees Wilson, aged seventeen, and Hugh D. Owens, aged twenty-one, who were both from Nefyn, as were the mess room steward, Hugh Roberts, aged sixteen, the carpenter, William Williams, aged twenty-seven, the bosun and lamps, Griffith Williams, aged forty-eight, and the donkeyman Richard Hughes, aged thirty-three. The final Welsh crew member aboard was a fireman/trimmer, J. M. Evans, aged forty-one, from Carmarthen. All had signed on the *North Wales* at Cardiff on 28 August 1914. Captain Owen made his way back to Liverpool and arrived on 16 February 1915, where he filed the ship's papers (which had been saved), and the crew were formally discharged. He was later was given the captaincy of another vessel, coincidentally, of the same name.[36]

The second Cardiff-owned steamer to be lost to enemy action, this time belonging to Tatem's, was captured by a German surface raider on 19 October 1914 in the Indian Ocean. The Cardiff-registered *Exford* (128527),

4542 GRT (1911), was under Admiralty charter and sailing for India with 5,500 tons of Welsh coal when sighted and stopped by the light cruiser SMS *Emden*, the crew taken prisoner and the *Exford* then retained for use as a collier. Two of the men aboard the *Exford* were from Llanelli.[37] Their confinement was in this instance brief, as later that day the Liverpool-registered *Saint Egbert*, 5596 GRT (1914), which had been captured one day earlier was released along with the crews of all seven vessels that had been taken. The *Saint Egbert* arrived at Cochin on the Malabar Coast on the 20 October 1914.[38]

The final example of Welsh crew who were captured at sea by German surface raiders concerns the British Columbia registered four-masted iron barque, *Drummuir*, 1844 GRT (1882). On 2 December 1914 the *Drummuir* was captured by the SMS *Leipzig* 70 miles off Cape Horn near the Wollaston Islands, Chile, while sailing Swansea for San Francisco with coal. The vessel was towed about 70 miles to the north side of Picton Island, Tierra del Fuego, and the coal transferred to colliers for Admiral von Spee's armoured cruiser force. The *Drummuir* was then sunk on 6 December. The crew were taken on board the German auxiliary *Seydlitz* (1902), which two days later was one of only two vessels that managed to escape after the Battle of the Falklands (the other being the SMS *Dresden*). In February 1915 a first-hand account of these events was given to *Cambria Daily Leader* by two young sailors from Burry Port. W. Evan Davies and W. H. Matthews signed on the *Drummuir* at Swansea on 5 September 1914 and two weeks later they had sailed for San Francisco with a cargo of coal:

> On Dec. 2nd ... while beating south, we sighted the German squadron. The cruiser Leipzig came towards us and took us all prisoners. Our ship was taken in tow to a place near Picton Island ... Next day our cargo of coal was taken on board the two transports, and after dismantling the barque a shot from the cruiser sent her to the bottom. All our clothes and effects were lost to us. On Dec. 5th we were taken before the German Admiral on board the Scharnhorst, and he questioned us. We were only four English sailors, and we had to sign a paper that we would not go aboard a ship again. If he met us again aboard any ship he would have us all shot. We were then taken aboard the hospital ship ... On Dec. 6th we saw smoke on the mountain, and the Germans told us that it was the English signalling off the Falkland Islands ... Next day we were

going towards the Falkland Islands, and we were told that the German Fleet were going to bombard the Falkland Islands, and that they had been given orders to sink all English boats. On Dec. 8 we sighted the Falkland Islands, and we saw the smoke of three strange ships. The Germans told us that it was the British Fleet, and they were right, for it was part of Admiral Sturdee's squadron. We saw the fight begin, and saw the Leipzig sink. Then a fog came on. Two of the English cruisers came after us and if the fog had not come down we could have been sunk too. We went round the Horn to the South Pacific coast, and after a short stay came back to the Atlantic again. On December 21st we were taken ashore and placed at an hotel, and eventually sent home.[39]

While these events were taking place in distant waters, there were also dangers present in home waters.

In December 1914 there was a German naval raid on the coastal towns of Hartlepool, Scarborough and Whitby. At Hartlepool two men were killed when the harbour was shelled, two merchant ships were damaged and two fishing vessels sunk. One of the merchant vessels damaged was the Cardiff-registered *Phoebe*, 2754 GRT (1894), belonging to Turnbull Brothers, which had recently arrived at Hartlepool from Archangel. One of the crew remaining aboard when the *Phoebe* left Hull after repairs on 8 January 1915 bound for Buenos Aires, was a mess room steward from Cardiff. Up to this point, and as reflected in the foregoing evidence for Wales, the majority of British merchant vessels lost to enemy action (other than those detained) had been occasioned by German surface ships following prize or cruiser rules. However, the most dangerous threat to the lives of merchant seamen (and fishermen) in the early months of the war was that of German mines.

From August to December 1914 out of sixty-five merchant vessels that were lost, fifteen were lost to mines.[40] Out of these fifteen vessels, five crews suffered fatalities, totalling forty-two dead in all. The fishing fleet fared worse, with at least ninety-one men dead from fourteen crews out of the seventeen fishing vessels that were lost to mines during the period.[41] On 27 November 1914, the London-registered *Khartoum*, 3020 GRT (1893), with a crew of twenty-three sailing Tyne for Oran with 4,000 tons of coal, hit a mine and sank 20 miles off Spurn Head. The survivors, picked up soon afterwards by a trawler were landed at Grimsby. The following account of events sheds some light on the ship's master who was a Cardiganshire man:

The Khartoum a small Cardiff steamer, laden with coal, struck a mine in the North Sea on Thursday, and foundered. The explosion shattered the vessel forward. The crew of twenty-three hands escaped in their lifeboats, and were landed at Grimsby uninjured. Captain J. T. Evans, who resides at Clarence Embankment, Cardiff, is a native of New Quay, and has been master of the ss. Khartoum since December of last year ... The first intimation the captain's wife had of the accident was a wire from her husband, handed in at Grimsby as follows: 'Khartoum struck mine, and landed Grimsby. Crew all safe and well.' Captain Evans was in the China Sea when war broke out between Russia and Japan. He was also at Antwerp with his wife when Germany declared war on Belgium, and his wife had to return to England in a refugee ship, whilst her husband proceeded with his vessel to Rotterdam.[42]

On Christmas Day 1914, while sailing from Mostyn to the Tyne with a cargo of salt cake and salt ash, the Glasgow-registered *Gem*, 461 GRT (1887), struck a mine.[43] Among the ten crew who died was J. E. Williams, an able seaman from Flintshire. In this particular case, we can see some of the impact that his death had on his family, through the operation of the Workman's Compensation Act 1906. The following particulars were reported at Holywell County Court in March 1915:

on Thursday, before his Honour Judge Moss, an application was made for the investment of a sum of £257 14s. 6d. paid into court as compensation ... to Frances Williams, Penrhos ... widow of John Edward Williams, able-bodied seaman on the steamer Gem, which was sunk by a German mine in the North Sea on Christmas Day last ... Mrs. Williams stated that her husband ... earned about £2 a week – his average was £1 13s. od. a week. She was dependant on her husband. Her son, Griffith Thomas Williams, who was now in the Territorials, allowed her 5s. 7d. from his pay. Before joining he earned 10s. a week as a farm labourer. Her daughter, Edith Caroline, aged 16 was in service. Three other children aged 15, 7, and 5 years respectively, were at home and were wholly dependant. She applied for the payment of £20 directly and £4 a month ... His Honour found that the amount paid in was proper compensation in respect of the death of the deceased, and ordered that the sum of £20 be paid out to the applicant forthwith, the balance, less the costs, to be invested in the usual way, and to be paid out for the maintenance of the widow and children at the rate of £3 per month. He considered the applicant ought to manage on that amount, with the 5s. 7d. a week from her son now in the Army. She would have a weekly income of £1 0s. 7d. Many people had to do on less and applicant must try, otherwise the money would be expended before the children were able to earn.[44]

Another vessel that probably fell victim to a mine at this time was the schooner-rigged steamship *Therese Heymann*, 2393 GRT (1890), which had left the Tyne for Savona with a cargo of coal on Christmas Day and was never seen again. Thomas Evans, aged fifty-two, the master, who was from Aberarth, was one of the twenty-one crew who were lost.[45]

Admiralty requisitioning would eventually see as many as one-fifth of merchant vessels pressed into service and many civilian crews found themselves serving on ships that had been re-purposed due to wartime expediency, among them were those that were suitable for the transport of troops and also for the speedy evacuation of the wounded. The following examples give some idea of the scope of this facet of the mercantile marine's involvement in such matters.

Troopships

At Hamburg on 29 April 1914, O. Roberts, aged thirty-eight, of Caernarfon signed on as first engineer on the Liverpool-registered *Knight of the Garter*, 6655 GRT (1902). The original agreement allowed for a period of up to three years, sailing Hamburg to New York via the Bristol Channel. In the event the voyage would terminate in London in March 1915. The majority of the crew were Chinese, and a 'Chinese scale of provisions' was appended to the agreement (the allowances being less, and more limited than the usual scale). In addition, it was stated that 'no member of the Chinese crew will be allowed to land on the continents of America, Australia, South Africa or New Zealand without permission of the master'. Such provisions were common on vessels with crews who were mainly Chinese or lascar, and frequently 'native' cooks were provided.

The crew agreement allows us to see some detail of the movements of the ship prior to being requisitioned as a troop transport. In May and

June 1914 *Knight of the Garter* was at Cardiff, where a new master, who was from Newport (Pembs.), and a second mate, from Cardiff joined. In the third week in September at Adelaide, the ship's carpenter deserted, and in October while at Sydney the Chinese sailors' cook deserted, as did the wireless operator who was from Eccles. At some point after this, the ship was requisitioned as troop transport and sailed for New Zealand. At Wellington in late November and early December a number of additional crew were taken on to assist in the business of serving as troopship HMNZ 15. Troops forming part of the Second Reinforcement New Zealand Expeditionary Force were then embarked and HMNZ 15 sailed on 14 December arriving in Egypt on 28 January 1915.[46] On the next crew agreement the ship was under Admiralty orders with the crew receiving the war bonus of £1 per month. Another ship that served as HMNZ transport was the London-registered *Limerick*, 6825 GRT, built in 1898 as a passenger/refrigerated cargo vessel and owned by the New Zealand Shipping Company. Requisitioned at the start of the war, the *Limerick* sailed as HMNZT 7 in the main body of reinforcements from Wellington in October 1914, arriving at Egypt in December. On this occasion HMNZT 7 was carrying twenty-one officers, 495 men and 348 horses. Between March and September 1915, still on government service, there were a number of Welsh crew, including the cook from Chepstow, stewards from Wrexham and Bassaleg, and assistant stewards from Clydach Vale, Merthyr and Barry.[47]

Among the larger ships requisitioned was the 12552 GRT White Star Lines *Cymric*, which had transported troops to France in 1914.[48] In September 1915 this liner was responsible for the delivery of 17,000 tons of ammunition brought from the United States, one of the largest shipments up to that date. There were a number of Welsh among the crew: a deck steward from Cardigan; three stewards, one each from Pwllheli, Denbigh, and Rhuddlan; the third baker was from Mold; the chief butcher from Bangor; the carpenter from Porthmadog and the carpenter's mate from Anglesey; a storekeeper/able seaman from Anglesey; a quartermaster/able seaman from Porthmadog; two able seamen from Amlwch; an ordinary seaman from Penmaenmawr; the second engineer from Menai Bridge; and two firemen, one from Swansea and one from Cardiff. In May 1916 the *Cymric* was torpedoed and sunk 140 miles west-north-west of Fastnet by SM U-20.

On 4 November 1915, Llewelyn Hughes, a wireless operator from Aberystwyth was hospitalised when the Liverpool-registered troopship *Mercian* was intercepted and shelled by SM U-38 commanded by

Max Valentiner.⁴⁹ The *Mercian*, 6305 GRT (1908), was a cargo vessel with passenger accommodation and was active throughout 1915 transporting troops to and from the eastern Mediterranean. In November 1915 the Lincolnshire Yeomanry embarked at Southampton for Salonica as infantry. Following a rough passage that occasioned having to put in at Gibraltar, on 3 November 1915 the *Mercian* was attacked in the Mediterranean by SM U-38 using a 15-pound gun. After more than an hour of being bombarded, the *Mercian* escaped. However, in that time seventy-eight men were wounded, twenty-three were killed, with a further twenty-two troops and eight crew members missing. Later, thirteen of the Lincolnshire Yeomanry and five crew members were rescued. Having run clear, the *Mercian* made for Oran, Algeria, where the French treated them very kindly. Some thirty men were buried at sea or at Oran, and five days later the troops again set sail, calling at Malta, then proceeding to Alexandria.⁵⁰

After his recovery Llewelyn Hughes would serve on the Elder Dempster-owned *Eloby*, 6545 GRT (1913). By July 1917 the *Eloby* had completed three years of service transporting troops, equipment and supplies between Britain and France and Egypt, and had narrowly avoided being torpedoed in 1916. In a cruel twist of fate on 19 July 1917, while *en route* to Alexandria with French troops and a cargo of explosives, the *Eloby* was torpedoed by SM U-38, still under the command of Max Valentiner and sunk 75 miles off Malta. Llewelyn Hughes, then aged twenty-seven, was among the fifty-six crewmen including the master, who perished along with around 100 of the troops aboard. Another Welshman among the crew killed that day was Albert Wynn Williams, aged forty-seven, the second engineer. Born in Bangor in 1869, Williams was the third son of foundry owner David Wynn Williams and he had attended Garth National School before serving an apprenticeship at his father's foundry. After learning his trade, he moved from Bangor to Birkenhead to work for Cammell Laird, then Lampert and Holt, before joining Elder Dempster.⁵¹

One of the greatest losses of life at sea during the First World War involved the troopship *Royal Edward*, 11117 GRT, built as the *Cairo* in 1907 before being sold to the Canadian Northern Steam Ship Company in 1912 and renamed. Requisitioned at the outbreak of war to bring Canadian troops to Europe before being used as an internment ship off Southend-on-Sea, the *Royal Edward* was the first transport to be lost during the war.⁵² On 28 July 1915 at Avonmouth 1,367 officers and men embarked, the majority of them reinforcements for the 29th Infantry, along with members of the Royal Army

Medical Corps all bound for Gallipoli. On 13 August, while sailing Moudros for Lemnos, the *Royal Edward* was torpedoed by SM U-14 and sank within six minutes: out of the 220 crew and 1,367 troops aboard, 935 lives were lost. Among the crew were eleven men from Wales, four of whom lost their lives: W. J. Williams, aged fifty, a chef from Monmouth; two fireman/trimmers, J. Carney, aged forty-five, from Cardiff, and Griffith Griffiths, aged thirty-one, from Treherbert; and W. Jones, aged fifty, a greaser from Holyhead – all are commemorated on the Mercantile Marine Memorial.

Hospital Ships

As we have already seen, two of the LNWR's Holyhead steamers, the *Anglia* and the *Cambria*, were pressed into service as hospital ships. From August 1915 the HMHS *Cambria* was in use on the Dover to France service. There were forty-one Welshmen listed as serving among the crew of the *Cambria* for the half-year to 31 December 1915: W. Jones, aged fifty-seven, from Anglesey, a leading stoker, had been with the company since 1880; out of eight firemen, five were from Holyhead, two from Anglesey and one from Caernarfon. Out of eight trimmers, seven were from Holyhead and one from Amlwch, one of the cabin boys was from Llanfechan and another from Holyhead. Three of the stewards and a cook were from Holyhead, as were the purser, quartermaster, bosun and the first, third and fourth engineers. The second engineer and a deck boy were from Porthmadog. Of the two carpenters, one was from Amlwch, the other Menai Bridge. Of the eight seamen, three were from Holyhead, one from Anglesey, one from Caernarfon, one from Aberystwyth, one from Llanfair and one from Amlwch. The *Cambria* continued in use as a hospital ship on the Dover-France service until May 1917, and was then transferred to Holyhead to act as a hospital carrier between that port and Dublin. In December 1917 the *Cambria* was converted into an armed transport and resumed service on the Dover-France crossing before returning to the Holyhead-Dublin service in February 1918. At the end of the war the *Cambria* was returned to the company, renamed the *Arvonia* in 1919 and eventually scrapped in 1925.[53]

The other LNWR steamer used as a hospital ship, the *Anglia*, had a less fortunate war. On 17 November 1915 while sailing Boulogne for Dover carrying 390 wounded from the Western Front and nursing staff, HMHS *Anglia* struck a mine a mile off Folkestone Gate and immediately began to sink. In all, 164 lives were lost, including twenty-five of the crew, of whom twenty-three were from Holyhead.[54] They comprised: chief engineer George Edward Williams, aged fifty-seven; Joseph Williams, third engineer, aged thirty-two; Owen Thomas, a stoker, aged fifty-five; six firemen, Robert Stuart, aged thirty-three, John Lewis, aged forty-one, Owen Jones, aged forty-five, Owen Jones, aged twenty-eight, John Jones, aged sixty, and R. Evans, aged forty-three; Robert Pritchard, a trimmer, aged twenty; William Lewis, a quartermaster, aged fifty-six; J. Hughes, a cook, aged twenty-eight; N. J. Campbell, a purser, aged thirty-seven; Richard Roberts, chief steward, aged thirty-seven; Meredith Williams, a second steward, aged twenty-eight; two other stewards, Alfred Wallace, aged thirty-one, and William Henry Calloway, aged twenty-three; a seaman, William Edward Bassett, aged fifty; two cabin boys, Robert Williams, aged twenty, and Albert F. Ashton, aged nineteen; Thomas H. Owen, a galley boy, aged nineteen; Lewis David Hughes, engineer's boy, aged seventeen; and Richard Thomas, a deck boy, aged sixteen. Of the other two crew lost, one was James Redmond, aged twenty-nine, a fireman from Liverpool, and the other was Thomas Richard Parry, aged twenty-five, a seaman from Caernarfon.[55] On the agreement for the second half of 1915, they are all listed as having been 'discharged'.

At the inquest that was later held into the death of chief steward Richard Roberts, the evidence given by three witnesses vividly conveys the terror of the situation in which they found themselves. The principal witness was the captain, L. J. Manning, who recounted the following:

> At 12.30, when we were about three miles off the shore ... there was a very loud explosion, apparently under the port side forward of the bridge. It blew the bridge to smithereens, and I was blown on the lower deck. I ran to stop the engines, which were running, but found the speaking tube and telegraph had been torn away. I ran up to the wireless room to order the 'S.O.S.' call to be sent out, but found the operator coming out with blood on his face. He stated that the instruments had been burst to pieces. Then I went with Chief Officer Horner to help in getting out the boats on the port side, which was the only side available. The vessel had a heavy list, and was down by the head very much. We got the first boat away with about fifty people all safe. As the engines were racing I went to the bridge to stop them from there, but the gear had been destroyed. Chief Officer Horner went down the weather side of the ship to help Dr. Hodson get the wounded up, and I went along the

lee side to do what I could, but the sea was rushing along there. As the ship sank I and the chief officer slid into the sea from the deck. I was unconscious when picked up.

Two Holyhead men who were in the stokehold at the time also recounted their experiences. Edward Williams, a fireman, who had just gone on watch said:

> I heard a tremendous report, caused by the explosion forward. We all rushed from the engine room and stokehold, and when I reached the deck I saw that No. 8 boat had just been lowered, and was leaving the vessel, when she went down. I cannot say what caused the boat to sink, it might have been the result of the suction, or she might have been filled from the rush of water from the condenser. The occupants were swimming about for a little, but I did not see them for long, as I went down to my room for my life-belt. I had no sooner reached the deck again when I found myself in the water, which was icy cold. I swam about for what appeared to me to be hours, and I saw a woman struggling in the water. I swam up to her, and found that she was one of the nurses ... she was fighting for life bravely, and when I reached her she clung to my back, making no struggle, but simply holding on to me. She was crying quietly, but otherwise was wonderfully calm. I swam about, for a little longer, and at last we were picked up by a torpedo-boat's crew.

William Williams, a trimmer, recalled:

> Shortly before the explosion occurred I was in the stokehold, and then, with my mate, Robert Pritchard, we went to the steward's washhouse. He put his head out of the porthole, and then I put my head out and had hardly done so when I heard the noise of the explosion, the force of which jerked my head back. I then ran along the alley way with Pritchard. The latter got into a boat, and he called out to me to join him, but it was too late as the boat had been already lowered. I crawled along the davits, clinging to the ropes. Mr Hugh Thomas, the steward, called me back from there, and I went back, pushing Mr George Bagnall back in case he should fall into the sea. I then went below, and searched for the engineer's

boy, Thomas Hughes, but failed to find any trace of him. For some time afterwards I remained on deck with the wounded, and when the Destroyer came alongside I jumped in.[56]

Among the other surviving crew were Owen Roberts, a leading stoker, a firemen Robert John Jones, Rowland Griffiths, a coal trimmer, and Hugh Thomas, a steward, all from Holyhead; three seamen, Richard Jones from Holyhead, Robert Roberts from Caernarfon and John Roberts from Menai Bridge; John Thomas Hughes, a steward from Bangor; Robert Thomas, a cabin boy from Anglesey; Owen Price, a third mate from Aberffraw; Howell Pierce, second engineer from Porthmadog; Hugh Williams, fourth engineer from Anglesey; George Bagnall, a bosun from Menai Bridge; William Hughes, a carpenter from Port Dinorwic; an Irish steward; a cook from Liverpool; and a wireless operator from Plymouth. The *Anglia*'s master, L. J. Manning, from Hillsborough, would later serve on both the *Cambria* and *Scotia*.

Despite the loss of life, this would not be the worst incident involving a hospital ship with Welsh crew aboard. The Union Castle Line *Llandovery Castle*, 10639 GRT (1914), had been commissioned as a hospital ship in July 1916 and assigned to Canadian forces. In June 1918, HMHS *Llandovery Castle* was torpedoed by SM U-86 and sank within ten minutes, 100 miles off the Irish coast. There were 258 people aboard: 164 crew, eighty members of the Canadian Army Medical Corps and fourteen nurses. This would prove to be one of the war's worst atrocities at sea, and a total of 234 lives were lost. Following the sinking, in an effort to cover up the attack, which had been in contravention of international law and the standing orders of the Imperial German Navy, the U-boat commander proceeded to run down the lifeboats and machine-gun the survivors, ultimately only one boat with twenty-four aboard survived the attack. Among the Welsh crew lost that day were: George Curtiss, a sailor, aged thirty, from Ruthin; John Allan, a fireman, aged thirty, born Newport (Mon.); William John Collier, an ordinary seaman, aged seventeen, from Cardiff; three able seamen, John Jones, aged sixty, from Llandudno, William Owens, aged forty-one, from Llanfair PG, and John Owen, aged twenty-six, from Newborough, Anglesey; Sydney Matthews, a pantry boy, aged fourteen, born in Denbigh; and James Murdoch McIver, a carpenter, aged thirty-one, from Pembroke.

In a similar manner to the requisitioning of the LNWR's vessels, some of the GWR's vessels were put into Admiralty service at the outbreak of war. The surviving crew agreement for GWR vessels for the period June to

December 1915 shows the *St David*, the *St Patrick*, and the *St Andrew* in use as hospital ships (they had been adapted to carry 180 patients each) running between Southampton, Dover and French ports.[57] All three were fitted with triple screws and Parsons turbine engines capable of 20 knots. Windham Thomas Wyndham-Quin, the fourth earl of Dunraven (whose house overlooking the sea at Southerndown in Glamorgan was used during the war as a convalescent hospital for 'Tommies') later recalled being alongside one or other of the GWR 'Saints' at Boulogne in 1915; at this time, he was seventy-five and master of the *Grianaig*, 351 GRT (1904), which he had personally financed to use as a hospital transport.

His involvement had come about following a request from Lady Dudley with help organising transport for the Australian Voluntary Hospital. Initially he had purchased a steam yacht for the purpose, but quickly realised that a larger vessel was more suited to carrying the wounded.[58] Dunraven found himself and his ship at Moudros in the summer of 1915 while the Gallipoli campaign was playing out. His description of conditions there give some idea of the experience of crew who found themselves on hospital ships and hospital transports, and were no doubt familiar to all the Welsh crew who experienced this corner of the Aegean. Dunraven observed that Moudros Bay and Gallipoli were in an 'awful state of confusion' with the Bay containing 'a most extraordinary flotilla of ships and other things that floated – things that looked like Noah's Ark or houseboats, river steamers, country sailing craft with motors stuck into them ... little old trawlers and drifters':

> We arrived at Mudros [*sic*] Bay the first week in June. The conditions were very bad. Wounded were packed like sardines in a tin in the hospital ship that was in the Bay at that time. They lay head to foot so close together there was not room for nurses to move. The few surgeons were exhausted with operating. Of course the difficulties were great. Wounded had to be taken off the Peninsula under fire in boats, flats rafts – anything indeed that could be got alongside, and transferred to tugs, drifters ... and then again to the hospital ship at Lemnos.[59]

Dunraven would be among those who survived the war.

As can be seen, the experiences of those captured overseas by commerce raiders and subsequently released, differed greatly from those who found themselves interned in Germany, the majority of whom were held for the duration. Those who served on troop transports and hospital ships witnessed events from different perspectives but ultimately faced similar risks. The existence of a range of first-hand evidence taken from the accounts of captains, seamen, trimmers, firemen and others, helps with the formation of a more rounded view of their lived experiences. Such accounts also help to leaven anonymous statistics and give voice to the highly particular though essential information provided by the crew agreements.

Notes

1. Woodman, *More Days, More Dollars*, p. 246.
2. *Herald of Wales and Monmouthshire Recorder*, 22 August 1914, p. 3.
3. TNA MT 9/1238, '*List of Merchant Seamen and Fishermen detained as Prisoners of War in Germany, Austria-Hungary and Turkey, Board of Trade Printed List 31st May 1918*'.
4. Fayle, *Seaborne Trade*, vol. 1, p. 54.
5. Woodman, *More Days, More Dollars*, pp. 247, 320.
6. d'Enno, *Fishermen Against the Kaiser*, pp. 116–18; see also Matthew Stibbe, *British Civilian Internees in Germany: The Ruhleben Camp 1914–1918* (Manchester, 2008). A number of accounts of life at the camp have been published.
7. *British Vessels Lost at Sea 1914–1918* (London, 1919).
8. 'Changed conditions in Germany', *The Times*, 29 January 1917, p. 8; TNA FO 383/25.
9. Hughes and Eames, *Porthmadog Ships*, p. 292.
10. Eames, *Ships and Seamen of Anglesey*, p. 506; TNA MT 9/1238, 'List of Merchant Seamen and Fishermen detained as Prisoners of War'.
11. *NWC*, 31 December 1916, p. 3.
12. *BDN*, 7 January 1916, p. 6.
13. TNA MT 9/1238, 'List of Merchant Seamen and Fishermen detained as Prisoners of War'.
14. See https://www.hazegray.org/navhist/carriers/germany.htm#glyn (last accessed 3 November 2024).
15. Note, this vessel was not seized until October 1914, though the crew did all end up in Ruhleben.
16. TNA MT9/1039/M31456.
17. B. D. Hope, *A Commodious Yard: The Story of William Thomas & Sons, Shipbuilders of Amlwch* (Llanwrst, 2005), pp. 200–4.
18. *British Vessels Lost at Sea*; Woodman, *More Days, More Dollars*, p. 248; *Cambrian News*, 17 March 1916, p. 5. The newspaper stated that there were two daughters.
19. Fayle, *Seaborne Trade*, vol. 1, p. 169.
20. For more on this matter, see Woodman, *More Days, More Dollars*, p. 201.
21. The *Glitra* was captured and scuttled in October by SM U 17, the *Malachite* and *Primo* were captured and sunk by gunfire by SM U 21 in November, and the *Durward* captured and sunk by bombs by SM U 19 on 21 January 1915.
22. *Llanelly Star*, 28 November 1914, p. 4.

23 Woodman, *More Days, More Dollars*, p. 262.
24 Anne Cipriano Venzon and Paul L. Miles (eds), *The United States in the First World War: An Encyclopedia* (New York, 1999), p. 54.
25 Woodman, *More Days, More Dollars*, pp. 202, 213–15.
26 See http://1915crewlists.rmg.co.uk/document/189099 (last accessed 3 November 2024); RSS/CL1915/3578/14.
27 They were George Harris, leading fireman from Ruabon, aged sixty-seven, and William Pritchard, second-class bar and storekeeper, aged twenty-eight, from Anglesey.
28 See https://www.theyard.info/ships/ships.asp?entryid=376 (last accessed 3 November 2024).
29 See http://1915crewlists.rmg.co.uk/document/200059 (last accessed 3 November 2024); RSS/CL/1915/3791/13.
30 Fayle, *Seaborne Trade*, vol. 1, p. 255; see also entry in *British Vessels Lost at Sea*.
31 See http://reardonsmithships.co.uk/rslduringww1.pdf (last accessed 3 November 2024).
32 *Flintshire Observer*, 12 November 1914, p. 3.
33 Fayle, *Seaborne Trade*, vol. 1, pp. 255–61.
34 Woodman, *More Days, More Dollars*, p. 251, *South Wales Weekly Post*, 7 November 1914, p. 6.
35 Woodman, *More Days, More Dollars*, p. 250; Eames, *Ships and Seamen of Anglesey*, pp. 507–8; Fayle, *Seaborne Trade*, vol. 1, pp. 340–1.
36 In 1916 the *North Wales*, 4072 GRT, built 1909 (previously SS *Wakefield*) also owned by Roberts & Son and described as an HM Transport on the Mercantile Marine Memorial, was on voyage from Hull to Canada in ballast when torpedoed off the Scillies on the 26 October by SM U 69. Captain Owen and all his crew went down with the ship.
37 *CDL*, 26 October 1914, p. 5.
38 The *Exford* was recaptured by armed merchant cruiser *Empress of Asia*, and arrived at Singapore on 11 December 1914, then renamed *Brendon* later in 1915.
39 *CDL*, 10 February 1915, p. 4.
40 Losses for the fishing fleet are discussed in some detail in d'Enno, *Fishermen Against the Kaiser*, pp. 67 ff.
41 These numbers have been abstracted from www.naval-history.net/WW1NavyBritishShips-Locations10AttackedMNDate.htm (last accessed 3 November 2024), which is based largely on *British Vessels Lost at Sea* – while these figures may not be 100 per cent accurate, they give a clear idea of the threat posed by mines.
42 *Cambrian News*, 4 December 1914, p. 2.
43 The two surviving crew were picked up and taken to Wisbech.
44 *Flintshire Observer*, 15 March 1915, p. 6.
45 West Wales War Memorial Project, Aberarth, see also Board of Trade Wreck Report, www.southampton.gov.uk/arts-heritage/southampton-archives/plimsoll/ (last accessed 3 November 2024).
46 See https://navymuseum.co.nz/explore/by-themes/world-war-one/troopships-departed-nz-ww1/ (last accessed 3 November 2024).

47 Later sunk off Bishop Rock inbound from Sydney with frozen meat and general cargo in 1917.
48 Ray Westlake, *British Battalions in France and Belgium, 1914* (Barnsley, 1997), p. 34.
49 West Wales War Memorial Project, Aberystwyth Alexandria Rd School.
50 See *www.dublin-fusiliers.com/ships/mercian.html* (last accessed 3 November 2024).
51 See *http://historypoints.org/index.php?page=in-memory-of-albert-wynn-williams* (last accessed 3 November 2024).
52 'British Troop Ship Sunk', *The Times*, 18 August 1915, p. 7.
53 See *https://sites.google.com/site/holyheadwarmemorial19141918/home/hms-cambria-1* (last accessed 3 November 2024).
54 Eames, *Ships and Seamen of Anglesey*, p. 515.
55 See *https://sites.google.com/site/holyheadwarmemorial19141918/home/hmhs-anglia* (last accessed 3 November 2024).
56 *NWC*, 26 November 1915, p. 6.
57 See *http://1915crewlists.rmg.co.uk/document/212021* (last accessed 3 November 2024).
58 Earl of Dunraven KP, CMG, *Past Times and Pastimes*, vol. 1 (London, 1922), pp. 231–7.
59 Earl of Dunraven, *Past Times and Pastimes*, p. 244.

4 Alternative Lenses
Women, Small Communities and the International Nature of Crewing

Figure 4: The barque *Jordan Hill* on which Kate Stephens of Briton Ferry served as a stewardess, courtesy of the State Library of South Australia, A. D. Edwardes Collection

Welsh Women at Sea during the First World War

The experiences of women at sea have in recent years begun to attract the attention of both historians and those interested in representations of gender relations and there is now a burgeoning literature that seeks to cover these subjects.[1] As yet, there is little examination of the work of women in the mercantile marine during the First World War. While there were relatively few women working in the mercantile marine at this time, they can be found as matrons and stewardesses on a surprisingly wide variety of vessels. There were no women at sea in the Royal Navy and the activities of the Women's Royal Naval Service from 1917 are not considered here.[2]

A cursory search of the 1915 crew lists for 'stewardess', which was the most common occupation of women at sea (the gendered job titles though uncomfortable to contemporary readers aid in this part of the research), returns nearly 4,000 results. After allowing for the duplications inherent in the data (which have been discussed above) such a search suggests that there would have been somewhere in the region of 1,000 women (a figure that broadly conforms to the figures given by the 1911 census) working in the British mercantile marine at this time. While these were predominantly British, women of many other nationalities can also be found on the agreements. Women who signed on as stewardesses did so in one of two ways. They were either worked for regular wages or they were the wives of the officers (deck or engineering), or pursers, travelling with their husbands (and sometimes other family members), most often as supernumeraries for 1s. per month. Some can also be found working passages. Some seventy or so of the women at sea in 1915 were from Wales and while the majority of them were stewardesses, there are a few in the records working as matrons, some of whom would have been trained nurses. A much fuller account of the experiences of a stewardess who worked on the largest of passenger liners and later served as a nurse on the HMHS *Britannic* can be found in the published memoirs of Violet Jessop.[3]

Two women from Caernarfon have the distinction of having worked aboard some of the world's largest ships – the White Star liners RMS *Adriatic* 24,541 GRT (1906), and RMS *Baltic* 23875 GRT (1903).[4] A. Parry, aged thirty-one, a stewardess from Caernarfon, can be found on two agreements for the *Adriatic* between May and July 1915. The *Adriatic* maintained a passenger service between Britain and America throughout most of the First World War. Despite still being in normal commercial use, among *Adriatic*'s cargo during a voyage from New York in September 1915 was 16,000 tons of cargo consigned to the British government, presumably for the British war effort, including 150 motor trucks and several aeroplanes. The *Adriatic* also served for trooping.[5] In July/August and again in November/December 1915, Ellin R. Roberts, aged forty-three, of Caernarfon, was working as a matron on the RMS *Baltic* on the Liverpool to New York via Queenstown (Cobh since 1922) service. Ten years earlier, this ship had been the largest in the world. The *Baltic* had assisted with evacuation of Americans from Europe and would later be used in transporting the Canadian Expeditionary Force from Halifax,

Nova Scotia, to Britain. Roberts was at this time earning £4 10s. per month, though some of the stewardesses aboard were earning £5 per month.

Two other Welsh women were working as stewardesses on White Star Liners in 1915. In January 1915, J. Parry, aged forty-four, of Anglesey, was on the *Arabic*, 15801 GRT (1903), sailing for New York via Queenstown. Parry was one of four women aboard the *Arabic* (there were three stewardesses and one matron) and she discharged at Liverpool in February. On 19 August 1915 the *Arabic* was sailing Liverpool for New York with eighty-six passengers and general cargo including mails. Some 50 miles off Old Head of Kinsale, the *Arabic* was torpedoed by SM U-24 and sank within fifteen minutes. At the time of the attack the *Arabic* had been zigzagging at 16 knots. Eighteen passengers, including some Americans, were lost, and there were two Welsh among the twenty-six crew who died. The other Welsh stewardess aboard a White Star Liner was C. A. Profit, aged thirty-eight, from Rhuddlan, who was working on the *Cymric*, 13369 GRT (1897), Liverpool to New York in August 1915. Profit was one of four stewardesses aboard, all earning £4 10s. per month. As we have seen, the *Cymric* had been used as a troopship at the beginning of the war. The following year, on 8 May 1916, while returning from New York, *Cymric* was torpedoed 140 miles west-north-west of Fastnet by SM U-20 with the loss of five lives.

For most of 1915, A. Evans, aged thirty-five, from Wrexham was working regularly as a matron for the Glasgow based Allan Lines on their Canadian/North American mail service. Over the course of the year, she worked on at least three of their fleet. On 17 January 1915, Evans discharged at Liverpool from the *Pretorian* (she had signed on in December 1914), which had just completed a month-long passage Glasgow to St John, New Brunswick, via Liverpool and back. Originally built in 1901, the *Pretorian* was 7654 GRT after rebuilding in 1908, with accommodation for 280 second-class passengers and 900 third-class passengers. The *Pretorian* also had certified accommodation for some 180 crew. Leaving aside the deck and engineering complement necessary for the ship's operation, we can see from the agreement that in addition to Evans and five stewardesses, the make-up of the remaining fifty-four crew who were mainly occupied on the passenger side of business comprised: a purser; an assistant purser; a surgeon; a chief steward; a second steward; a saloon steward; twenty-two assistant stewards; a linen-keeper; two bedroom stewards; a barkeeper; a deck/smokeroom steward; a bath and boots steward; a storekeeper; a printer; a second cabin steward; a steerage steward; a salon pantryman; an assistant pantryman; a steerage pantryman; a night watchman; a chief cook; a second cook; a passenger cook; two assistant cooks; a vegetable cook; a chief baker, a second chief baker; a chief butcher, an assistant butcher; a barber; an assistant passenger/ship's cook; and first and second telegraphist/assistant pursers (both on a nominal wage). In addition, there was an officer's steward, an engineer's steward, a ship's cook and an assistant ship's cook. Overall, the majority of the crew were Scots, though there was one Welsh able seaman from Nefyn aboard. On this agreement, early on in the war, a sum of 10s. a month war risk allowance was being paid (excepting officers and engineers). If the ship was carrying 'His Majesty's Mails' there was a further bonus payable of 10s. a month for certain sections of the crew. At this time Evans was receiving £5 per month, while the five stewardesses also on this agreement were receiving £3 10s.

Starting on 23 January 1915, Evans was again working the Liverpool to St John's passage, this time on the *Corsican* (1907) 11419 GRT. There were also three stewardesses on this agreement; one of them was Elizabeth Jones from Bangor.[6] From the start of the war the *Corsican* had been used for transporting troops, in August 1914 between Southampton and Le Havre, then in September to Alexandria and Bombay.[7] On launching, the *Corsican* had provision for 300 first-class passengers, 400 second-class passengers and 1,500 third-class passengers in steerage. Evans then worked the next return passage commencing on 26 February 1915 on the same ship. On this passage, one of the stewardesses was A. McCarthy from Milford Haven.

The *Corsican* was back in Liverpool at the end of March, but Evans does not appear on any crew agreement for the next month or so. In the middle of May her name is listed on agreements for both the *Grampian*, 10187 GRT (1907), and the *Sicilian*, 6224 GRT (built 1899 but 7238 GRT after rebuilding in 1908). It seems most likely that Evans had been transferred from one to the other immediately before sailing and this was probably not that unusual as it occurred again later in the year. Then in August 1915 she was back on the *Corsican*, Liverpool to Montreal and Quebec, the agreement now noting that a war bonus of £2 per month was payable to all ordinary members of the crew. On 10 September 1915 her name is again on the agreement for the *Corsican* but she was transferred before sailing to the *Sicilian*, which had been in service on the Glasgow-Halifax-Boston route since 1912.

In October Evans was back on the *Corsican* Liverpool to Quebec and Montreal, with six stewardesses also aboard. From this agreement we can see in some detail the way that the war 'bonus' was distributed – it was £1 for all crew, except ordinary seamen, deck boys, and bell boys who received 10s., and barbers who received nothing as agreed by the Seafarer's Joint Committee 30 March 1915. In addition to this amount, a further 'special allowance' of 20s. per month was to be paid to all crew with the previous exceptions applying. Also added to the agreement, and a tacit acknowledgement that the *Corsican* was being used for trooping duties, was the provision that should the vessel carry more than 200 troops (combatant) then a further 20s. per month was to paid to the crew (deck and engineering officers excepted) calculated from embarkation of the draft to the arrival at port of disembarkation. The same conditions as above applied to deck boys, bell boys and barbers.

The *Corsican* had certified crew accommodation for 300, though there were a total 326 names entered for the period covered by the agreement (plus one apprentice). Of these, thirteen failed to join at Liverpool, one was transferred to another ship before departure and one was rejected by the ship's master, a further six crew did not join until the ship reached Montreal, presumably taken on following the desertion of ten of the original crew there. Among the other Welsh crew aboard there were four assistant stewards, two from Wrexham, one from Holyhead and one from Prestatyn, an assistant-cook from Holyhead, a second pantry man from Wrexham, a second steward from Welshpool, an able seaman from Swansea, and the surgeon from Barmouth. On her last agreement of the year, starting on 19 November and signing off on 15 December 1915, Evans was again on the Liverpool-Quebec-Montreal run on the *Corsican*, on this trip there were also seven stewardesses aboard, three from Liverpool, one from Bootle, one from Stornoway and one from Kingstown in the Grenadines.

Other Welsh women working on Allan Lines ships in 1915 included S. Riley of Holyhead, matron, who joined the *Corinthian*, 7333 GRT (1900), at Montreal on 5 August 1915 for £7 per month, along with eight stewardesses, one of them from Cardiff. The *Corinthian* had been used for trooping the Canadian Expeditionary Force in 1914. Earlier that year Riley had worked on two of the Canadian Pacific Railway Company's ships on the same route. In March, Riley had been on the maiden voyage of the *Metagama*, 12420 GRT, from Liverpool to St John's earning £5 per month, other stewardesses on this trip were receiving £3. In September Riley was working on the *Missanabie*, 12648 GRT (1914), for £6 per month.[8] Both of these ships were used for trooping duties in 1915, the *Missanabie* had transported the Canadian 23rd Battalion from Halifax, Nova Scotia in February and the *Metagama* brought the Canadian 1st Reinforcing Draft from Montreal in June. Another Welsh stewardess who had worked on the *Missanabie* at the start of 1915 was J. C. Grims, aged forty-five, from Nefyn.

One of the stewardesses also aboard the *Metagama* at the same time as Riley in March 1915 was J. C. Evans, aged forty-five, from Nefyn. Evans had also worked on the Allan Lines *Grampian*, 10187 (1907), which had been under charter to Canadian Pacific Railways from 1912 on the Glasgow/Liverpool to Montreal route. Another Welsh stewardess, L. Lewis, aged twenty-three, from Cardiff, who worked on the *Metagama*, can also be found on agreements during the course of the year for the *Missanabie*, the *Sicilian*, the *Corsican*, the *Corinthian* and the *Grampian*. A. McCarthy, who we have already seen working as a stewardess on the *Corsican* in February, also worked on the *Corinthian* and the *Scandinavian*, 12099 GRT (1899), which were used on the Boston run. In 1917 Allan Lines – which during 1880s had been the largest privately owned shipping company in the world – was taken over by the Canadian Pacific Railway Company.

Elizabeth Jones, who was working on the *Corsican* in January 1915, can also be found on two agreements later in the year for the *Tunisian*, 10576 GRT (1900). The *Tunisian* had been used as a troopship in 1914 for the Canadian Expeditionary Force, and had then been used as a German prisoner-of-war ship for a time at Ryde, Isle of Wight. In 1915, under sealed orders, the *Tunisian* made two trooping voyages. Between March and June, Jones was earning £3 10s. per month plus the £1 war bonus. The *Tunisian* left Barry at the beginning of March and was at Bombay in April, where among other crew joining were three stewardesses working a passage and who arrived at Avonmouth in May before discharging at Cardiff on 22 June 1915. While the *Tunisian* was at Avonmouth, eighteen men deserted, including a waiter from Penarth, an assistant steward from Cadoxton, two fourteen-year-old deck boys, one from Barry and one from Cardiff, a trimmer also from Cardiff, and two assistant stewards, one from Barry and one from Cadoxton.[9] Just four days after arriving at Cardiff, Jones sailed again, first to Devonport, then Malta in July (where a number of Maltese crew deserted), arriving at Alexandria by the middle of August. Returning via Genoa and Marseille, Jones discharged at Liverpool at the end of October.

Irish Sea ferries and packets were frequent employers of Welsh stewardesses. Mary Jane Weaver, aged thirty-six, from Neyland, spent most of 1915 working on GWR vessels on the cross-channel Fishguard, Waterford, Rosslare service, but during that time she also did a two-month transfer and worked instead on the Lancashire Yorkshire London and North West Railway's *Duke of Connaught*, 1562 GRT, running between Fleetwood, Fishguard and Rosslare. Five Welsh stewardesses were working for the Dublin Steam Packet Company, which was then operating four vessels carrying mail and passengers on the Holyhead to Kingstown route: the *Ulster*, (104972) 2641 GRT (1896); *Leinster*, 2646 GRT (1897); *Munster*, 2646 GRT (1897); and *Connaught* 2646 GRT (1897).

The company had 252 crew on the books in 1915, 129 of them Welsh – ninety-five from Holyhead, another twenty-seven from Anglesey and a further seventeen from other parts of north Wales. Out of nine women working for the company, five were Welsh – Jane Parry, aged twenty-two, Louisa Parry, aged twenty-three, and Hannah Owen, aged thirty-three, all from Holyhead; Ellen Cook, second stewardess, born on Anglesey; and May Hughes, aged thirty-eight, chief stewardess from Caernarfon. One of the Dublin Steam Packet Company's other ships, the *Connaught*, was transferred to Admiralty service in April 1915.[10] Louisa Parry and Hannah Owen would both lose their lives when the *Leinster* was torpedoed by SM U-123 just outside Dublin Bay in October 1918. The *Leinster* was carrying nearly 700 passengers, mainly military personnel but there were also around 100 civilians. More than 500 were killed in the largest loss of life in the Irish Sea. Out of the crew of seventy-seven, thirty-seven lost their lives, with around half of those being from Anglesey.

Hannah Owen had left school aged fourteen and gone to London. On returning home to Holyhead, she went into domestic service. Owen subsequently worked at Mill Road Infirmary in Liverpool, at the Home for Incurables, Parliament Street, Liverpool, and New Highfield Hospital, Knotty Ash. Owen then joined the City of Dublin Steam Packet Company, in or around 1905, and had worked on all their ships.[11] Louisa Parry had been educated at Park School, Holyhead. In 1911, when she was fifteen, Parry commenced training as a nurse probationer at Moreton-in-Marsh, Gloucester, and later worked at Mexborough, Yorkshire. Parry started working with the City of Dublin Steam Packet Company as a stewardess in 1914, where her sister Jane was also working.[12]

The LNWR's Holyhead steamers (as we have seen) were also large employers of Welsh maritime labour. On their books in 1915 were fourteen stewardesses, of whom twelve were from Holyhead and one from St Asaph (one was Irish). While it is not possible to see from the agreement exactly which vessels these women were aboard as the agreement is an aggregate covering all of the employees (who could be required to serve on any of the company's vessels), in one case we do know – as it was noted that Elizabeth E. Jones of Holyhead, aged twenty-eight, was serving on the hospital ship HMHS *Anglia* from April to July 1915.

Two stewardesses from north Wales were working for Scottish shipping companies. L. Beasant, born in 1862, from Bangor, worked on the Stranraer-registered *Princess Maud*, 1655 GRT (1904), throughout 1915. This vessel was in service on the Stranraer to Larne route operated by the Port Patrick and Wigtownshire Railway Company. Beasant, then aged fifty-three, was earning 11s. a week. The company was operating three steamers at this time and Beasant had previously worked on another of these, the *Princess Victoria*, 1687 GRT (1912), which was being used for trooping in the second half of 1915. The other stewardess was Helena Edwards, aged thirty-seven, of Connah's Quay. At the end of April 1915, she was working for 12s. a week as a stewardess aboard the Glasgow-registered *Puma*, 1225 GRT (built in 1899 as *Duke of Rothsay*). The *Puma* was one of sixteen vessels operated by the Burns Steamship Company of Glasgow and was employed in the coasting trade carrying mail, passengers and cargo between Glasgow, Greenock, Wemyss Bay or Ardrossian, and Belfast, Dublin, Londonderry, Larne, Liverpool and Manchester. Following the opening of the ship canal in 1894, Manchester had grown to be Britain's third largest port despite being 40 miles inland. Edwards also worked on much larger vessels.

On 3 August 1915 at New York, Edwards joined the Cunarder *Saxonia*, 14297 GRT (1900), for the return passage to Liverpool at £5 per month. Edwards was on the *Saxonia* again in late September, but transferred off after only one week and then joined the Pacific Steam Navigation Company's *Orduna*, 15498 GRT (1913), sailing Liverpool to New York on 11 October 1915. One of four stewardesses aboard, Edwards, along with the others and the matron all discharged at New York in the last week of October. Edwards returned five days later when she and eleven other stewardesses joined the Anchor Line's Glasgow-registered *Tuscania*, 14348 GRT (1914). This was shortly after the *Tuscania* had helped to rescue the passengers and crew from the Greek ship *Athinai*, 6045 GRT, which caught fire on 13 September 1915, a few days out from New York. The cause of the fire was later found to have been an act of deliberate arson by German spies. Also working on a Burns Steamship Company vessel in the home trade was Elizabeth Alice Davis, aged thirty-eight, of Swansea, who in April 1915 was briefly aboard the *Pointer*, 1182 GRT (1896).

One Welsh stewardess was among the unfortunate victims of the most famous example of a passenger ship to be torpedoed without warning when the *Lusitania*, 31550 GRT (launched 1906), was sunk on 7 May 1915. From an account that was published in the *Cork Free Press* we learn that after the ship sank, Mary E. Jones of Llanfairfechan, aged forty-three, finding herself in the water, held on to the right arm of one of the passengers Flor O'Sullivan for support. Jones had grabbed Flor's arm so tightly that she left deep marks on his arm. They drifted in the water for about two hours, striking against lifeless bodies in the water. Mary Jones by this time was losing strength and kept asking if there was any boat in sight. O'Sullivan described her cries as heartrending. At about the time he saw a boat in the distance she died and lost her hold.[13]

Wives and Families at Sea

It was not that uncommon to find Welsh women at sea accompanying their husbands and signed on the books for nominal wages, this could also apply to other family members aboard, though there are a few examples of both wives and other family members being paid normal rates of pay. As we have seen, it was possible to find women at sea during this period aboard the last of the ocean-going sailing ships still plying their trade. Two Welsh examples are Daisy Burgess from Swansea and Kate Stephens from Briton Ferry.

In July 1914, Daisy Burgess, aged thirty-six, was the matron on the Liverpool-registered *Golden Gate* (formerly the *Lord Shaftesbury*) built in 1888. The *Golden Gate* was a 2340 GRT four-masted steel ship (later re-rigged as a barque) sailing Newport (Mon.) to Montevideo. The wife of the master, Daisy was on the agreement for nominal wages. Three ordinary seamen from Newport were also aboard, as was a sail maker from Swansea. On arriving at Montevideo on 13 September 1914 the ship was wrecked on the breakwater and deemed a constructive loss, then condemned and sold in January 1915. The crew presumably all found their way onward, though neither Daisy nor her husband appear on any other agreement filed in 1915. The *Golden Gate* was later bought, repaired and continued to sail until finally scrapped in 1934. Two of the crew who had been aboard the *Golden Gate* when wrecked – William Blakewell, aged twenty-four, an American sailor, and Perce Blackborow, aged nineteen, an ordinary seaman from Newport – stranded by the loss of the *Golden Gate* went to Buenos Aires in search of a ship. There, Blakewell found work on Shackleton's ill-fated *Endurance*,

Blackborow was considered too young for such a voyage, but stowed away regardless.[14]

Months before the outbreak of war, in February 1914, Kate Stephens, aged fifty, from Briton Ferry, was stewardess on the 2290 GRT *Jordan Hill*, a four-masted barque built in 1892, sailing Liverpool to Sydney and Newcastle (NSW). Like Daisy Burgess, she was the master's wife and had signed on for nominal wages. When her husband died suddenly at Talcahuano, Chile, on or about 16 December 1914 she left the ship without signing off. A Scottish master took charge for a month before being superseded by John Roberts of St Davids, Pembrokeshire. There were a handful of other Welsh crew aboard on this agreement – a seventeen-year-old apprentice from Caernarfon, a bosun/able seaman who discharged in Newcastle (NSW) in September, and, while in Chile, a seaman from Anglesey deserted in December, and an ordinary seaman from Cardiff and an able seaman from Holyhead both left with the new master's consent in January 1915.

Far more Welsh women were to be found at sea on various classes of steamers. A. A. Coats, aged thirty-one, from Swansea had joined her first ship the Sydney-registered *Lodorer*, 3207 GRT, in April 1914. The wife of the master, she had signed on for nominal wages outward bound from Hull to New York and would be at sea for some seventeen months in all. There were a number of other Welsh crew aboard – the mate and his two sons; one a nineteen-year-old able seaman and the other a fifteen-year-old midshipman (on a nominal wage) were from Fishguard, as was a sixteen-year-old ordinary seaman. The third engineer was from Cardiff, and a fireman/trimmer was from Swansea. A second engineer who was from Pontypool joined the ship at Algiers in June 1914. The *Lodorer*, which had been originally built as the *Sandyford* in 1904, but renamed in 1909, left Hull in April 1914 and from various entries on the agreement it is possible to see some of the movements of this tramp steamer. Arriving at New York in May 1914, the following month the ship was at Algiers, and then Port Said. Reaching Brisbane in early August, the *Lodorer* then called at a number of Australian ports: Albany and Townsville in July, Sydney in August, then Melbourne and Port Adelaide in September. The agreement contained a clause stating that if working on the Australian Coast the wages would be paid at the current 'Australian coast rate'. In November the *Lodorer* called at the African Cape ports of Port Natal, Cape Town and Durban, and then in December while at Beira (at that time a Portuguese port) in Mozambique, a thirty-six-year-old able seaman died aboard. In 1915 the *Lodorer* was back in the Americas, calling at

Philadelphia in late February 1915, then Colon in March, before proceeding through the Panama Canal to arrive in Honolulu in April. The majority of the crew finally discharged at Liverpool in September 1915. The *Lodorer* was then immediately requisitioned for use as a Q-ship, with the next agreement noting that the ship was operating On His Majesty's Service ('OHMS'). There were a number of Welsh crew aboard for the run from Liverpool via Barry to Portsmouth immediately prior to the ship being commissioned at Devonport in October.

Among other wives at sea before the war broke out was Mary Ellen Williams, aged thirty-six, from Swansea, with her two children, Hedley, aged four, and Eileen, aged three. She joined her husband, the master J. L. Williams, who was from Criccieth, on the Liverpool-registered *Berwindvale*, 5242 GRT, at Cardiff in June 1914. The ship was bound from London to Havana, but Mary and the two children signed off with the master's consent at Newport News, Virginia, in August 1914, they re-joined the ship at Norfolk (Va.) in November and arrived back at Swansea in January 1915. There were other crew from Wales aboard – the fourth engineer, chief steward and second cook were all from Cardiff. A larger family grouping can be found in the example of the Evan Thomas, Radcliffe freighter *Patagonia*, 6011 GRT (1913), which by September 1915 was being used as a Russian Naval transport. On the agreement covering the period May to October 1915, along with the master D. Davies, aged forty-five, were what appears to be his entire family: H. M. Davies, stewardess, aged thirty-seven; Iris Beryl Davies, stewardess, aged seventeen; W. J. Davies, cadet, aged fourteen; and Howard Davies, cabin boy, aged twelve – all of whom were on their first ship. On 15 September 1915 sailing Odessa for Nicolaieff in ballast, the *Patagonia* was torpedoed aft by SM UB-7 (Wilhelm Werner), and sank 10.5 miles north-east of Odessa, Ukraine – all the crew survived.

Two Welsh women who were working in the coasting trade in 1915 were Ada Smith, aged twenty-four and born at Barry Dock, and B. Symons, aged twenty and from Cardiff. Ada was working on the Newport-registered *Uskside*, 2208 GRT (1913). She had joined the ship as a stewardess at Bowness on 30 November 1915 and was receiving £3 per month. This was her first ship and she left the *Uskside* at Leith on 16 December. It seems likely that she was the wife of the first engineer who was already aboard. According to some sources the *Uskside* was requisitioned for use as a Royal Fleet Auxiliary for the duration of the war.[15] Symons worked for one week only on the Penzance-registered *Cloch*, 745 GRT (1883). It seems probable that she was the master's daughter, also on her first ship, and earned 15s. a week. Other Welsh women can be found taking passages for nominal wages as they travelled out to join ships on which their services were required.

The final example of a Welsh woman working at sea considered here is that of a matron from Brecon, Emily McPherson, who was most probably the wife of M. G. McPherson, the first engineer on board the Grimsby-registered *West Marsh*, 1593 GRT (1896), which was working in the home trade. The *West Marsh* was owned by Grimsby paper-makers Peter Dixon and Son. Emily, who joined and left the ship at Hull, was aboard from 22 July to 26 August 1915 and was earning £5 per calendar month. Emily was not the only woman aboard at the time, as rather unusually there were two other women, the master's wife and daughter working as stewardess and assistant stewardess. All three had given their previous ships as the *Cairnisla*, which is what the *West Marsh* had been called before being bought by Dixon in July 1915. While the foregoing provides only the briefest examination of some of the surviving evidence, it is hoped that the existence of such material will

Figure 5: Some of the crew of the *Hopemount* at Cardiff, 1915, courtesy of the Glamorgan Record Office. The *Hopemount* was captured by SM U-35 and sunk by gunfire in the Bristol Channel in June 1915. There were no casualties. Two Welsh sailors were among a crew of twenty-four, which included Scots, Scandinavians, Liverpudlians, a German and a Genoese, with the firemen and trimmers hailing from West African ports in Cape Verde, Nigeria, Sierra Leone and Liberia, as well as St Lucia in the Caribbean

further encourage those interested in the working lives of Welsh women and their place in the narratives concerning Welsh involvement in the momentous events of the First World War.

Small Communities

Llangrannog, 7 miles south of New Quay, was a busy little coastal community with a long-standing maritime tradition. At the end of the nineteenth century, it has been estimated that as many as 90 per cent of the male inhabitants were occupied in shipping and related activities. By the outbreak of the war shipping from small ports such as this had gone into steep decline, in no small part due to competition from the arrival of the railways. Nonetheless, the tradition of going to sea remained strong in this community, as will be seen. When the 1911 census was taken, the parish of Llangrannog had 211 households, with a total population of 708. Of this number, 298 were male inhabitants, and given the average age distributions for Wales at this time, around 30 per cent would be under fourteen years of age, with around 4–5 per cent being aged sixty-five or over. The likely potential labour pool for maritime occupations in Llangrannog around 1914 (given that some boys went to sea at a young age and also that men could still be working into their sixties) would have been in the region of 200.

In 1915 the number of men found on merchant crew agreements giving Llangrannog as their place of birth totalled fifty-seven: this was around 25 per cent of the male working age population of the parish. Although, there were certainly more than this due to the incomplete nature of the surviving crew agreements. In addition, there would have also been mariners who were at sea and whose agreements were not filed in 1915.[16] The Llangrannog men found on the 1915 crew-lists comprised eight masters, seven mates, ten second mates, two third mates, four bosun, eleven able seamen, one able seaman and lamps, two ordinary seamen, seven seamen, one first engineer, one second engineer, one steward, one mess room steward, and one fireman/trimmer. This distribution of occupations aboard ship was weighted firmly towards being on deck. The youngest among these crews were two sixteen-year-olds, an ordinary sailor and a mess room steward; while the oldest, a mate, was sixty-six. In the majority of crew agreements, it is possible to see the port that the men signed on at as well as the initial destination, though subsequent ports are noted only if crew joined or discharged, deserted, died or fell ill and were left behind. While the majority of these men had signed on foreign-going agreements, there were a few who were engaged on vessels in the home and coasting trade. Though it should be borne in mind that men might serve on a number of agreements in the course of a year and that they could be in the home trade one voyage and foreign-going the next.

The following examples show the broad range of experiences of these men. In 1915 John Davies, aged sixty-six, served all year as mate on the Cardigan-owned sloop *Margaret and Ann*, 33 GRT (1877). This was the smallest, oldest and only sail vessel on which any seamen from Llangrannog in this sample is to be found. Other men from Llangrannog who can be found on home trade agreements in 1915 include R. W. Mathias, aged thirty-eight, bosun on the Dublin-owned steamer *Patricia*, 780 GRT (1913), who had signed on at Dublin on 4 January 1915, and D. J. Davies, aged forty-one, an able seaman, who signed on to the London-registered *Streatham*, 1207 GRT (1914), in February 1915, leaving the ship at Sheerness in June. D. J. Davies would later serve as bosun on the defensively armed *Greavesash*, 1263 GRT (1917), which was torpedoed by SM UB-74 on 26 February 1918 off Cape Barfluer. Davies was one the eight men who lost their lives.

Some Llangrannog men found themselves on vessels that were under Admiralty charter. At Newport in October 1914 G. S. Davies, aged thirty-one, signed on as second engineer on the Evan Thomas, Radcliffe steamer *Picton*, 5082 GRT (1906), then under Admiralty charter with the entire crew to receive the 'war bonus' of £1 per month. There were a number of other Welshmen aboard. Although the *Picton* was sailing under sealed orders it is possible to trace some movements from entries on the agreement. In the middle of October, a fireman joined at Port Said and at end of November a fireman/trimmer from Cardiff was left sick at Hong Kong. In December 1914 three hands deserted at Moji in Japan, two of them Cardiff men (an apprentice and an able seaman). In January 1915 at San Francisco the master (R. Roberts of Edern) went off sick and the mate was promoted (W. Williams of Dinas Cross). The *Picton* was at Norfolk (Va.) at the beginning of March and back at Hull at the end of the month where a fireman joined. Most of the crew on this agreement, including Davies, signed off at North Shields in May 1915. Leaving Barry on an Admiralty chartered vessel in November 1914, J. E. Davies, aged twenty-five, was signed on as second mate on the *British Transport*, 4143 GRT (1910), again all the crew received the 'bonus' and he discharged at Poplar, London in August 1915. On 17 March 1918, J. E. Davies was second officer on the London and South West Railway's steamer

Southwestern, 674 GRT (1874), sailing Southampton to St Malo, when the ship was attacked and sunk by SM UB-59, only six of the crew survived. Davies was drowned and his body later found washed ashore in France.

The majority of men from Llangrannog found in the 1915 crew lists were on foreign-going agreements and could be found sailing on all the major oceans of the world, the standard form of words on agreements often specified any ports between 75° North (above the Arctic circle) and 60° degrees South (where the Southern Ocean begins). Old sailors had a saying 'below 40 S there is no law; below 50 S there is no God'. A number of Llangrannog mariners found themselves at sea when war was declared, men such as E. Evans, aged thirty, the mate on the *Braziliana*, 3827 GRT (1907), which left Cardiff for Bombay in December 1913, and who did not discharge until April 1915 at Avonmouth. Similarly, in April 1914, W. Davies, aged forty-eight, the master of the London-registered *King Howel*, 4343 GRT (1906), had departed Newport for Bahia Blanca. Three other Llangrannog men were among the crew of the *King Howel*; R. Evans, aged twenty, an able seaman, G. Jones, aged sixteen, an ordinary seaman and David Owens, aged fifty-six, who was the bosun. They would all discharge at Liverpool in March 1915. Davies, Owens and Jones remained aboard for the next voyage from Liverpool for ports in the United States starting in April 1915, and two other Llangrannog men joined for this trip D. J. Thomas, aged sixteen, a mess room steward and Evan Owen, aged twenty-two, a sailor.

Following the outbreak of the war, seamen (excepting those who were reservists and those who volunteered for King and Country), continued to work as usual. In August 1914, D. Owen Jones, aged thirty-two, signed on as third mate on the brand-new Anglo Saxon Petroleum Company tanker, *Cassis*, 4792 GRT (1914). Aboard the Field Line's *Westfield*, 3453 GRT (1901), which sailed Cardiff for Port Said in September 1914, there were three Llangrannog men: D. Rees, aged nineteen, sailor; D. Rowlands, aged thirty-two, bosun and lamps; and S. J. Owen, aged twenty-three, second mate. In October 1914, W. M. Lewis, aged twenty-four, joined the crew of the Evan Thomas, Radcliffe steamer *Swindon* (123162), 5084 GRT (1912), at Cardiff as second mate. In February 1915 the *Swindon* was at Tacoma, Washington State, by mid-April at Barcelona, and then called at Genoa before arriving at Gibraltar at the end of April. In June 1915 the *Swindon* was at Messina, by mid-July Norfolk (Va.), then back at Messina in mid-August before discharging at Barry at the end of that month. In May 1918 Lewis was first-mate on the *Snowdon* (106801), 3188 GRT (1904), which was sunk 84 miles off Malta by SM U-63, while sailing Cardiff to the Greek Island of Milos with a cargo of coal. Lewis was one of two men killed; he was twenty-eight years old. The other casualty was the master, J. L. Owen, aged twenty-nine, also from Llangrannog who three years earlier in January 1915 had signed on as second mate on the *Penistone*, 4139 GRT (1913), sailing Newport to Naples. Among Llangrannog men found joining ships in November 1914, were T. O. Jones, aged forty-six, mate on the Newport-registered *Lord Tredegar*, 3856 GRT (1914), Barry to Rio, and D. J. Jenkins, aged twenty-nine, third mate on the *Civilian*, 7871 GRT (1902), Liverpool to Galveston. Jones returned to Barry on 2 March 1915 and three weeks later at Glasgow he signed on the *South Pacific*, 3660 GRT (1913), proceeding to Australia via New York.

Early in 1915, three Llangrannog men can be found signing on for African ports. In January 1915, E. Davies, aged twenty-seven, was master of the Cardiff-registered and owned *Nora* (123193), 3933 GRT (1907), sailing Barry to Bizerte in Tunisia. In February, Evan D. Jones, aged forty-seven, master, and second mate B. Watkins, aged forty-three, both left Penarth bound for Dakar on the West Hartlepool registered *Claremont*, 3883GRT (1904). In March 1915, there were three Llangrannog men were aboard the Golden Cross Line's Cardiff-registered *Arvonian*, 2794 GRT (1905). The master J. R. Jones, aged thirty, had previously been employed on another Golden Cross Line steamer the *Cymrian*, 1014 GRT (1905), Evan O. Thomas, aged thirty-two, an able seaman (promoted on his next ship to second mate) and D. J. Jones, aged twenty-one, an able seaman who had previously been third mate on the *Standish Hall*, 3995 GRT (1912), in April 1914. On 15 June 1915, J. R. Jones received a gold watch from the Admiralty at a presentation held in Avonmouth in recognition of his gallant conduct when the *Arvonian* was attacked by a U-boat 20 miles off Le Havre on 22 April 1915 while transporting troops to France. His vessel had first avoided a torpedo and then with troops aboard firing at the conning tower and periscope of the surfacing submarine, Jones had attempted to ram the attacker, narrowly missing the U-boat that then steered off. Speaking at the presentation Jones acknowledged the part played by his crew in the evasion, and noted that had his ship been defensively armed, he felt that would have been the end of the matter.[17]

In July 1915 two Llangrannog men were aboard the W. & C. T. Jones owned *Onwen*, 4250 GRT (1914), which left Newport for Alexandria: W. J. Evans, aged nineteen, a sailor, and J. Owen, aged thirty-five, the mate. Owen had previously shipped as mate on the *Onwen* in September 1914 and later served as mate on another W. & C. T. Jones vessel, the *Llongwen*, 4683 GRT (1907). Owen was among the fourteen men who died when the *Llongwen* was sunk 90 miles off Algiers by SM U-39 in July 1916. Signing on in July 1915 was T. Jones, aged twenty-four, second mate, on the brand new Ellerman Lines steamer *Lesbian*, 2554 GRT (1915), which was brought down after fitting-out from Middlesbrough to London. Jones then remained aboard for the steamer's first voyage to Cape ports. On 24 August 1915, ordinary seaman Evan O. Evans, aged fifteen, signed on to the *Winnfield*, 3422 GRT (1901), then under the management of J. C. Gould of Cardiff, sailing Barry to Archangel. Evan O. Evans later served in the Mercantile Marine Reserve based at HMS *Victory* in Portsmouth, he died in the Royal Naval Hospital Haslar aged eighteen in 1918.[18]

Other men from Llangrannog aboard the *Winnfield* with Evans in 1915 were the bosun, David Owens, and able seaman R. Evans (both had previously shipped together on the *King Howel* in 1914), as well as J. H. Owen, an able seaman, aged twenty, who had previously shipped on the Plymouth-registered *Ruahpehu*, 7885 GRT (1901), Cardiff for Sydney. A number of the other crew on the *Winnfield* were Welsh: the master E. L. Taylor was from New Quay but lived in Llangrannog, the mate was from Swansea, the second mate from Llantrisant, and one of the firemen was from Cardiff. The foregoing is not an exhaustive list of Llangrannog men in the mercantile marine during the First World War and there are doubtless men missing from the above record. Llangrannog War Memorial records the names of ten men of the mercantile marine who died during the First World War, though one, D. Hughes Jones, master of the *Dalewood*, 2420 GRT (1911), which was torpedoed in 1918, was originally from Aberystwyth. W. M. Lewis and J. L. Owen who died on the *Snowdon* are recorded as being of Rhydlewis, but both men had given Llangrannog as their place of birth when signing on ship. Three other Llangrannog mariners are commemorated on the memorial but not found in the 1915 crew-lists: John Thomas Davies, aged twenty, an able seaman on the *Commonwealth*, 3353 GRT (1896), sailing from Béni Saf, Algeria to Middlesbrough with iron ore, which was torpedoed by SM UC-71 off Flamborough Head in February 1918 with the loss of fourteen men; Daniel Thomas, aged twenty-six who was second mate on the *Don Arturo*, 3680 GRT (1906), belonging to Buenos Ayres and Pacific Railway Company, which was torpedoed and sunk in June 1917, 90 miles west-south-west of the Scillies by SM U-62 while sailing from Algiers to the Tees (twelve other Welsh crew were lost); and David Jones, aged fifty-four, master, who lost his life when the defensively armed *Greldon*, 3322 GRT (1903), was torpedoed without warning by SM U-96 in October 1917 off the coast of Ireland with the loss of twenty-eight lives.

Of some sixty or so men from Llangrannog in the mercantile marine during the war, nine lost their lives as a result of enemy action. A number of other features are discernible in the foregoing examination of the merchant seamen of Llangrannog. With just one exception they all served on steamers, with the majority of these steamers in the 3–4,000 GRT range. The majority of these men worked aboard ships that were less than a decade old and by far the largest proportion of these men signed on board at one of the south Wales coal ports, often on to ships that were Welsh-owned or managed.

International Crewing

Another feature of the merchant service at this time, particularly on foreign-going ships was the fluid nature of manning and the multi-national nature of crews. A perusal of the agreements for such vessels during the period reveals that men were frequently drawn from all corners of the world. The rapid growth of the British merchant service since 1870 and the ongoing manning requirements for the Royal Navy had seen the supply of British seamen unable to keep up with demand. Anxieties about the increasing numbers of 'foreign' seamen on British merchant ships and falling British recruitment to the service had been linked in part to the unattractive conditions, particularly relating to food, which had been part of the object of the 1906 amendments to the Merchant Shipping Acts.[19]

An examination of three consecutive agreements for the Evan Thomas, Radcliffe-owned *Jane Radcliffe*, 4074 GRT (originally built as the *Windsor* in 1897 and renamed in 1911), running from November 1914 to November 1915, demonstrates the high turnover of crew, their international make-up, as well as the strong presence of Welsh crew in responsible positions. Nonetheless, even on the ships of a company with a reputation for appointing 'Cardi' mariners, the overall proportion of Welsh crew could be quite low.

The first agreement covers a voyage from Cardiff to New Orleans starting in November 1914, returning via various American east-coast ports and Naples and terminating at South Shields in February 1915.[20] The crew was to be considered complete with twenty men, with a total of thirty crewmen listed over the period, including two Scottish apprentices. The master J. Williams, aged forty-two, from New Quay (Cards.), the mate W. B. Birwick, aged thirty-three, from Cardiff, and third engineer A. E. Davies, aged thirty-two, from Cardigan, had all come over from another Evan Thomas, Radcliffe ship, the *Llanberis*.[21] Some of the other crew had also joined from other Radcliffe ships: D. A. Rees, the first engineer, from Burry Port, had joined from the *Clarissa Radcliffe* (1913), and A. H. Bigham, the second engineer, from Chepstow, had come from the *Llangorse* (1900). The second mate who joined from the *Windsor* (1911) and the steward from the *Llangorse* were both English. The final Welsh member of the crew was W. John Jones, an eighteen-year-old mess room steward from Newcastle Emlyn who had previously shipped on the Jenkins Brothers steamer *Italiana*, 2663 GRT (1883).

Among the other crew were: a Londoner (ship's cook); an Estonian; a Greek; a South American; two Swedes; a Dane; two Germans (one a naturalised British citizen the other from Wiwdau, Brandenburg); two Cephalonians (one a sailor, the other a fireman who had joined at Galveston on 7 December 1914 and deserted ten days later); four Irish; a Scot; and an Italian fireman who had joined in Norfolk (Va.) on 18 December and who deserted at Naples in January 1915. One of the able-bodied seamen who had signed on in Cardiff (an American) deserted at Norfolk (Va.) in December, while another American, a fireman, joined the ship at Naples in January 1915. The fourth engineer, who was from Worcester but living at the time in Tredegar, was on his first ship.

The second agreement covers a voyage from the Tyne to Savona or Spezzia starting on 10 February returning via Baltimore before terminating at Hull on the 26 July 1915.[22] There were a total of twenty-nine men on this agreement. Of the previous Welsh crew, the master, mate, mess room steward, and the first and second engineers had all remained aboard, as did the Scottish apprentices. The fourth engineer from the previous trip was promoted to third engineer. The rest of the crew had turned over. Among the crew joining was the second mate D. Williams from Skewen. One of the seamen failed to join at South Shields and the recently promoted third engineer was hospitalised in Savona in March: his replacement, a Swede who joined in Savona, deserted along with the Swedish fourth engineer (also taken on at Savona) at Baltimore in April.

The third agreement[23] covers a voyage from Hull via the Tyne to Port Said starting August 1915 and terminating at Glasgow in November. With the exception of the master, first engineer, the English steward (who had joined the last voyage) and the apprentices, all the crew turned over. Joining the crew was a second engineer from Neyland, and a fourth engineer from

Port Talbot on his first ship. One of Scottish apprentices having completed his four-year indenture when they arrived at Port Said signed back on as third mate. An able seaman failed to join at Hull, and a Norwegian able seaman discharged at Gibraltar due to illness.

The international nature of crewing can also be seen reflected in the ethnic composition of Cardiff seamen's boarding houses. In 1911, out of 181 such establishments there were for example ten for Arab seamen, four for Chinese, twenty-six for Greeks, thirteen for West Indians, twenty-four for southern Europeans and fourteen for northern Europeans.[24] By 1914 the increasing incidence of whole sections of crew being made up of Asians, 'lascar' or Chinese was proving problematical.[25] The term 'lascar' (an Anglicisation of the Portuguese adaptation of an Arabic word) was used to denote sailors from any area east of the Cape of Good Hope – thus, it incorporated Indian, Malay, Chinese and Japanese crewmen. Often these men were on separate agreements with different wage or overtime rates and provision scales to those of the European crew and were often provided with their own cooks.

On the eve of the First World War, there were 51,616 men classified as lascars in the mercantile marine (16 per cent of total crew) and 31,396 as classified as 'foreign', many of whom would have been Black undocumented British subjects.[26] Elder Dempster frequently employed firemen and trimmers from West Africa on their fleet. Crew members from Wales such as W. Morris, fourth engineer from Porthmadog, W. Jones, carpenter from Pwllheli and T. L Hughes, second mate from Anglesey who were aboard the *Benue*, 3123 GRT (1905), between November 1914 and December 1915 would have found the vast majority of the 'black gang' were from Sierra Leone, though others revealed the track of the company's trade along the coast of West Africa.[27] These were men who had been born in Liberia: from Sherbro Island, the port of Monrovia and county of Sinoe; Béréby (now San-Pédro) on the Ivory Coast; Okubi, Ghana; Ouidah, Benin, as well as Lagos, Burutu, Onitsha (on the river Niger), Okrika (near New Harcourt) and Calabar, in Nigeria. They were engaged on standard agreements, though their rate of pay was below average. Trimmers were receiving £3 10s., though by September 1915 they were also receiving a 10s. war bonus.

Among the lascars were Yemeni and Somali seamen who were to form some of the earliest Muslim communities in Britain, many of whom would settle in the dock area at Cardiff. One estimate suggests that there were some 700 permanently settled there by 1911.[28] On cargo ships lascars often made up the 'black gang' of firemen, trimmers, and greasers. One such example was the Newcastle-registered *Drumfries*, 4121 GRT (1905), leaving Cardiff for Leghorn/Livorno with coal in May 1915. Many of the men signing on at Cardiff as firemen and trimmers were from British Sylhet (north-east Bangladesh), but others were from a variety of places from the Indian subcontinent, including: Lucknow (Uttar Pradesh); Tripura (Eastern Bengal); Chittagong (southern Bangladesh); Midnapore (West Bengal); and the Punjab. On certain liner services, lascars could also form the majority of the stewarding complement.

As the numbers of this very visible non-unionised maritime workforce grew and their presence in the port towns and cities increased, arguments that had started as an employment issue spilled over into wider social and cultural concerns. In the months immediately prior to the outbreak of war a campaign in the Bristol Channel ports against the employment of cheap Chinese and Asiatic labour was started with a demonstration by seamen, transport workers and other trade unionists at Cardiff.[29] Further public protests were then held in Swansea, Barry and also at Milford Haven. Their concerns were set out in the following resolution:

> Sir, I am instructed by the No. 9 Branch of the Dock, Wharf, Riverside, and General Workers' Union, to send the following resolution for insertion in the Barry Dock News, and in doing so may I point out that in the British mercantile marine there are employed something like 58,000 Chinese and Lascar seamen, this is being added to at the rate of 7,000 per year, and are employed for no other reason than that they are cheap and cost less to feed. But from the ethical standpoint they are a great deal inferior, less trustworthy in the hour of peril, and generally insubordinate. The resolution, which was passed unanimously, was as follows: 'This meeting of workers views with alarm the amazing rapidity with which English sailors are being displaced by Chinese and other Asiatics employed in British ships, and offers its strongest protest against the action of those ship owners who threaten the western standard of life and morals; it declares its firm intention to assist any action, political or otherwise, formulated by the National Transport Workers' Federation, to stamp out the competition of cheap labour, and pledges itself to support the campaign now proceeding in order to bring such pressure upon the ship owners, the

Board of Trade, and the Government as shall be necessary to put an end to this menace of underpaid labour, which threatens the standard of life secured by years of Trade Union effort'. H. Archer Secretary.[30]

At the Swansea demonstration, Alderman George Colwill addressing the assembled crowd was less judgemental in his opinions of the Chinese character, stating that he believed that 'a blackman or a Chinaman or other Asiatics were as good as any Englishman' but that when 'Chinese were brought over to this country to lower the standard of Western European life, and bring the British workers into servility ... it was time to draw the line'.[31] At the same protest Havelock Wilson, president of the National Sailors' and Firemen's Union commented on the growth of Chinese enclaves in UK ports, stating that 'less than five years ago there was not a single Chinese boarding-house in the whole of the British Channel ports, but now the sight in Bute Road, Cardiff, was startling'.

Reports such as the following one that appeared in the *Glamorgan Gazette* in March 1914 had doubtless fed the fears of the threat to the 'western standard of life and morals' noted above:

OPIUM DENS.
A SOUTH WALES HOTBED.
A dark, narrow-roofed room, a reeking, sickening atmosphere, a very ordinary bed, on which is stretched full length a yellow-faced, dull-looking man, sucking away at the end of a pipe, the bowl of which is held over a lighted lamp. You are in the presence of a Chinese opium-smoker; if he receives you kindly he will give a half turn, and holding the pipe towards you, will request you to 'Try a shimoke.' There are several such opium dens in Cardiff. A gentleman whose business brings him into intimate touch with the colony of the Celestials informed a Press representative that in practically every Chinese house in one of the city districts opium smoking is indulged in to an increasing extent. The den is not of the same character everywhere. In many cases the smoker retires to the privacy of his own bedroom, where he spreads out the paraphernalia of his enjoyment and proceeds to business. In other houses there is a common room or bench, where several of the victims are herded together, each smoking his own pipe, or, as is often

the case, passing the pipe from one to another. There is a colony of about 200 Chinese in Cardiff, mostly sailors, and although all these cannot be said to be victims of the Giant Drug, it is stated that a very high percentage of the number indulge in the habit.[32]

The problem of opium use was not confined to dens ashore, as can be seen in the following example. In May 1915, Brice Thomas from Cardiff was second mate aboard the *Jersey City*, 4669 GRT (1914). Between January and July 1915, the 'black gang' aboard were largely from Hong Kong and made up seventeen out of a crew of thirty-two. On inspection by US customs at New York in May 1915, the officers found a quantity of smoking opium and paraphernalia appraised at a value of $122.50. Attached to the crew agreement was a US Treasury Department letter noting that a penalty of the same value was to be incurred by the shippers. It would seem that this was neither an uncommon event nor one that was strictly enforced in the case of Asian crews, as the letter further noted that 'it is the practice to entertain applications for relief [from the fine] in such cases, and if such an application is to be filed, I would request that it be presented in a reasonable time, whereupon it will be submitted to the Secretary of the Treasury for his consideration and action'.[33]

Following the outbreak of the war, reports concerning the insubordinate nature of Asiatic crews tended to reinforce existing prejudices. One such news story concerning the U-boat attack on the Liverpool steamer *Delmira*, 3459 GRT (1905), off Barfluer in 1915, on which D. R. Solomon of Porthmadog was the chief engineer, included the claim by members of the crew that the captain's attempt to escape from the submarine SM U-37 would 'have succeeded had it not been for the refusal of the Chinese crew to work in the stoke hole'.[34] At Barry Police Court later that year, seven Chinese members of the crew of the Admiralty-chartered transport *Strathavon*, 4402 GRT (1907), were charged with disobeying and assaulting the officers of the vessel. This incident took place on 16 October 1915 while the vessel was at Havre Roads. The chief officer of the *Strathavon*, who was the prosecution witness, stated in court that:

> About 3.30 p.m. he told the bo'sun to bring the men out to swing the boats out. There was a lot of grumbling, but he took no notice of that. They came upon the boat-deck after keeping him waiting for quarter of an hour. He told them to swing the boats out, and

they all started arguing together that it was Saturday afternoon and not the right time to do it; Witness told Ah Sam to shift a guy, and the latter replied: 'Do it yourself'. Chang Kom used a filthy expression to witness. Witness told them that he was not there to argue with them. They were to swing the boats out or he would speak to the captain. They refused, and witness spoke to the captain, who asked him to bring Ah Sam down. He told the second mate, who was on the boat-deck, to bring Sam down, but the latter refused. The second officer took hold of Ah Sam by the shoulder, and told him: 'The captain wants you down there; you had better go.' When witness turned round again, he saw the second mate surrounded by the crew who were armed with iron stanchions, and logs of wood. Witness ran to the second mate's assistance, but he got clear, and was running towards his room. A piece of wood 'came flying through the air,' and just missed witness' head. This was thrown by Ah Kee. The second officer, returned on board with a revolver, and as soon as they saw him, the men made a rush at him, but he threatened to fire. The men probably thought the revolver was not loaded, for they came on, and the second mate fired into the air to frighten them. The men then 'caved in,' and went to the fo'c'sle ... In making their statements for the defence, the men said they had been with the ship for two years, and the captain had had no trouble with them before. Ah Kee said their new officer did not treat them properly.[35]

They were each sentenced to a month in prison. Two other Welshman had served on the ship over the course of this agreement, but neither was aboard at the time of the incident.

By November 1915, whatever the truth behind the attitudes towards Asiatic crews, the Admiralty responded to concerns in the following manner:

CHINESE CREWS
As an outcome of a recent conference at the Admiralty, re the exclusion of Chinese sailors and firemen from Admiralty transports, the following notice has been issued by the Admiralty: In Admiralty transports crews should, as far as possible, be either British or coloured. No other nationalities should be engaged unless it is found impossible without delay to transport to secure crews of British or

coloured persons. This rule shall not necessarily apply in the case of any ship which at the time of registering had on board a crew of Asiatics signed on at Asiatic ports.[36]

As can be seen in some of the rhetoric concerning Asiatic crews, another facet of the diverse ethnic make-up of crews at this time was the existence of racial intolerance. Lyon has recently noted of the mercantile marine at this time that:

> It was perhaps a consequence of the harsh environment and working conditions of the seamen of that period that they were notoriously brutal in their treatment of local populations as they travelled around the world, often regarding the native populations as lesser breeds of humanity.[37]

This is somewhat disingenuous, as racism (though not perhaps acknowledged as such) was a pervasive feature of the British Empire at its zenith, and was far from confined to the lower echelons of British society. For example, Winston Churchill, First Lord of the Admiralty (1911–15), held views on race that were not incompatible with those of the worst seamen.[38] Further, the Royal Naval Reserve regulations for 1914 clearly stated that 'Coloured men, natives of India and Mulattos are not to be entered in the Reserve'.[39] In one case, where a Black British subject had entered the Royal Naval Reserve, Commander A. D. R. Pound, while serving on HMS *St Vincent* wrote on 27 August 1914 that:

> 3 RFR [Royal Fleet Reserve] AB's [able seamen] and 12 RNR [Royal Naval Reserve] seamen joined the ship yesterday. One of the latter is a black man. It is a great mistake to enter them as it is hardly fair to make a distinction and mess them apart from the ship's company, on the other hand it would not be surprising if the men objected to having him in their mess.[40]

It is therefore not surprising that racist sentiments among seamen were not frequently reported, though the few instances that were, bear witness to this undercurrent in the merchant service. At Barry Dock police court in December 1915, Thomas J. Macdonald, seaman, was charged with failing to join the Admiralty transport *Charleston*, 1866 GRT (1908). The newspaper report (which quoted racial epithets that reflected the attitudes and mores of the time) noted that Dock-Constable Gill and PC Greening had proved the case, and also recorded that the defendant 'said the captain threatened that he must sleep with three coloured men', and that the defendant's response to this was that he 'wasn't going to sleep with three niggers for nine months'. He was sentenced to a month's hard labour.[41]

In another case heard at Llanelli police court an American seaman was charged with deserting the Glasgow-registered *Madura*, 4484 GRT (1901), then at the North Dock, which as a consequence of his absence was delayed in sailing. The defendant, who had been advanced £2 of his wages, stated to the court that he had been '36 years at sea, and I have no hesitation in saying that half these men cannot do their work. I am the only white man on board with the exception of two. The crew is made up of Greeks, Spaniards and niggers. I would not care about this if they were good men but they are not'.[42] The Bench directed that defendant should be taken back to the boat. A final example of what appears to have been a similar prejudice concerns the prosecution of three Somali Arabs, then living in Cardiff, who were charged with wilful neglect of duty while serving as firemen/trimmers aboard the Admiralty chartered steamer *Ramsay*, 4317 GRT (1902), in 1915. Yusef Ahmed, Hassan Ahmed and Mohamed Abdulla were accused by the ship's master of continual neglect of their duty. Mr Arthur Vachell solicitor, of Cardiff, who was prosecuting stated that the offence 'occurred between the 25th and 30th of October, when the vessel was bound from Algiers to Bombay. Owing to defendants failing to keep up the pressure of steam the vessel lost ten days on the trip'. The ship's master stated that:

> the third engineer had to go into the 'stoke-hole' and work. If they experienced rough weather there would have been considerable danger, through lack of steam instead of using 28 tons of coal a day they were only using 23½ tons. He had trouble daily with the men after they left Bombay. The proper head of steam was 165 lbs., but the average head on this voyage was 140 lbs., and sometimes fell to 90.

The defendants' contention was that the coal was bad; however, Arthur Johnson, the second engineer, said the coal used was 'the best he had ever seen'. Mr T. P. Pritchard, solicitor, of Barry, for the defence, contended that 'it was impossible to keep up the same pressure of steam with Indian coal as with Welsh coal. No evidence had been given showing that the men wilfully disobeyed orders ... [the] Defendants declared that they did their utmost to get a good steam pressure'. Nonetheless, the Bench were satisfied that there was neglect and a fine of 40s. or a month's imprisonment was imposed in each case.[43]

One of the most obvious difficulties that may have been expected when dealing with foreign seamen, that of the language barrier, seems not to have caused much mention. However, in one instance, W. H. Ladd of Cardigan, master of the W. & C. T. Jones *Adenwen*, 3798 GRT (1913), sailing under Admiralty orders in December 1914, noted on leaving Avonmouth that he had on board three firemen/trimmers from Aden (but living in Cardiff) whose knowledge of the English language was either doubtful or not sufficient. He also noted that men with sufficient knowledge were not procurable at that time. These men would very soon experience the dangers of being captured by a U-boat.

The British mercantile marine could not have functioned as it did without the contribution of these men, forming as they did around 28 per cent of the maritime workforce in 1914. The war probably helped further polarise the situation due to so many 'British' sailors being reservists, volunteering or being conscripted. It is difficult to resolve the tensions that this participation engendered, the major fear appeared to be the undercutting of wages posed by Asiatic agreements as much as fear of 'otherness' either on board ship or in the port towns where such sentiments manifested. Many multi-ethnic crews seem to have functioned without any perceptible difficulty under arrangements that were long-standing. The exploitation of Asiatic and Chinese crew on separate agreements reflected similarly long-standing imperialist attitudes and the accompanying social, economic, racial and religious discrimination.

Notes

1 The material in this section originally appeared in *Maritime Wales*, 38 (2017), 51–63. For the development of women's maritime historiography, see J. Stanley, 'After the Cross-Dressed Cabin Boys and Whaling Wives: Possible Futures for Women's Maritime Historiography', *Journal of Transport History*, 23/1 (2002), 9–22.

2 J. Stanley, *A History of the Royal Navy: Women and the Royal Navy* (2017).

3 V. Jessop, *Titanic Survivor: The Memoirs of Violet Jessop, Stewardess*, ed. by J. Maxtone-Graham (Gloucester, 2007).

4 White Star Line had been absorbed into International Mercantile Marine Co. in 1902.

5 See *www.whitestarhistory.com/adriatic* (last accessed 3 November 2024).
6 She also worked on the *Tunisian*.
7 Taken over by the Canadian Pacific Line in 1917, *https://www.norwayheritage.com/p_ship.asp?sh=corsi* (last accessed 3 November 2024).
8 The *Missanabie* was torpedoed 50 miles off Queenstown in 1918 by SM UB 87 outward bound Liverpool to New York. Among the forty-five who lost their lives was assistant pantryman, J. Davies of Llanfairfechan.
9 Among other Welsh crew on this agreement were an eighth engineer from Cardiff, three firemen, an assistant steward from Aberdare, and an assistant steward from Barry.
10 The *Connaught* later served as a troopship, and on 3 September 1917 while returning to Southampton from Havre, it was torpedoed by SM U 48. Three of the crew are recorded on the Mercantile Marine Memorial; one of whom was born in Swansea, an able seaman, W. C. Parker.
11 See *www.findagrave.com/cgi-bin/fg.cgi?page=gr&GRid=107830381* (last accessed 3 November 2024).
12 See *www.findagrave.com/cgi-bin/fg.cgi?page=gr&GRid=15368549* (last accessed 3 November 2024).
13 *Cork Free Press*, 10 May 1915, p. 6.
14 Shane Murphy, *Shackleton's Photographer: The Standard Edition* (Scottsdale AZ, 2001), p. 310, footnote 39.
15 See *http://sunderlandships.com/view.php?ref=103247* (last accessed 3 November 2024).
16 This number does not include men born elsewhere but living in Llangrannog.
17 *Cambrian News*, 2 July 1915, p. 2.
18 West Wales War Memorial Project, Llangrannog War Memorial.
19 Eames, *Ships and Seamen of Anglesey*, p. 485.
20 See *http://1915crewlists.rmg.co.uk/document/185861* (last accessed 3 November 2024).
21 Originally built as the *Llandudno* in 1897 and renamed in 1911.
22 See *http://1915crewlists.rmg.co.uk/document/185859* (last accessed 3 November 2024).
23 See *http://1915crewlists.rmg.co.uk/document/185857* (last accessed 3 November 2024).
24 M. J. Daunton, 'Jack Ashore: Seamen in Cardiff before 1914', *Welsh History Review*, 9/2 (1979), 192, table 4.
25 At Cardiff there had been racial outbursts against the Chinese in 1911 with boarding houses and laundries being attacked and there were disturbances involving unemployed 'negro' seamen in 1911/12; Daunton, 'Jack Ashore', 194.
26 Humayan Ansari, *The Infidel Within: Muslims in Britain since 1800* (2004), p. 37.
27 Recent research on West African seamen, Wales and the First World War undertaken by Deanna Groom and Helen Rowe of the Royal Commission on the Ancient and Historical Monuments of Wales was presented at the 'BAME Seafarers in the First World War' workshop at the University of Portsmouth in 2018; *https://porttowns.port.ac.uk/workshop-report-bame-seafarers-first-world-war/* (last accessed 3 November 2024).
28 N. Evans, 'The South Wales Race Riots of 1919', *Llafur*, 3/1 (1980), 6.
29 *CDL*, 11 May 1914, p. 6.

30 *BDN*, 29 May 1914, p. 6.
31 *CDL*, 18 May 1914, p. 3.
32 *Glamorgan Gazette*, 27 March 1914, p. 3.
33 Letter attached to crew agreement January to July 1915, *http://1915crewlists.rmg.co.uk/document/207625* (last accessed 3 November 2024).
34 *Cambrian News*, 2 April 1915, p. 7, the paper incorrectly reported that the attack was by U32; further, though damaged the ship did not sink and drifted ashore and was later re-floated.
35 *BDN*, 29 October 1915, p. 6.
36 *CDL*, 27 November 1915, p. 5.
37 Lyon, *Merchant Seafaring through World War 1*, p. 7.
38 See for example, Priyamvada Gopal, 'Why can't Britain handle the truth about Winston Churchill?', *The Guardian*, 17 March 2021. Churchill continues to be a controversial figure in British history, however, even his most ardent defenders concede that he occasionally made disobliging remarks about Indians, Chinese, Palestinian Arabs and other groups. Andrew Roberts and Zewditu Gebreyohanes, 'The Racial Consequences of Mr Churchill: A Review', *Policy Exchange* (London, 2021), p. 18.
39 Royal Naval Reserve Regulations (Men) 1911 + addenda (1912) Revised to 31 July 1914 Para 20.
40 Lilley, 'Operation of the Tenth Cruiser Squadron', p. 94.
41 *BDN*, 3 December 1915, p. 6.
42 *Llanelly Star*, 22 January 1916, p. 3.
43 *BDN*, 17 December 1915, p. 2.

5 1915
Mines, U-boats and Close Calls

Figure 6: Postcard of German minelayer c.1915

Figure 7: U-boats at Kiel, 1914, courtesy of the George Grantham Bain Collection, Library of Congress

While attacks on merchant shipping by German surface raiders continued into the start of 1915, by April these had ceased and no British merchant shipping was lost in this way for the rest of the year. One of the modern aspects of the war at sea was the widespread use of mines. Such weapons had proved their deadly worth in the Russo-Japanese war 1904–5 and several nations including Britain had tried, unsuccessfully, to have them banned at the second Hague Peace Conference in 1907.[1] As we have already seen, this menace had caused the loss of some fifteen British merchant vessels between August and December 1914. During the course of the war, the Germans laid a total of around 43,000 mines, with some 25,000 of these laid at points around the British Isles. The total allied losses from mines during the war amounted to about a million tons or 586 ships.[2] The vast majority of these mines were the moored hertz-horn types, which were initially deployed by surface craft and latterly by the UC class mine-laying U-boats introduced in 1915. In 1915, a total of forty-two merchant vessels (excluding fishing vessels) were lost to mines – totalling 77,000 tons – compared to just nine lost to surface vessels. The following examples show the range of circumstances and varied outcomes of hitting mines for both Welsh crew and Welsh vessels.

On New Year's Day 1915, the Cardiff-registered *Westgate*, 1742 GRT (1881), sailing Bilbao to Middlesbrough with a cargo of iron ore, hit a mine in the Downs[3] but was safely towed to port with no loss of life. Among the crew of the *Westgate* were: the second engineer, G. Baker, aged thirty-three, and G. Martin, mess room steward, aged eighteen, who were both from Cardiff; the donkeyman, W. Watts, aged forty-five, from Penarth; and two sailors from Cilgerran, brothers Sid Davies, aged seventeen, and J. Davies, aged nineteen. The *Westgate* had been regularly running back and forth between Bristol, Cardiff, Barry, Swansea and Spanish ports. According to a report in the *Cambria Daily Leader*, at the time of the incident the ship had been 'sheltering from the bad weather and while swinging to her anchor her stern struck a mine and her rudder, steering gear, and stern-post were blown away ... the majority of the officers and men, belong to Cardiff and district'.[4] Then, one week later in the very early hours of 7 January 1915, as the crew of the Newcastle-registered *Elfrida*, 2624 GRT (1907), were taking soundings in preparation for anchoring 2 miles from Scarborough, the ship hit a mine and immediately began to sink. The *Elfrida* had been sailing from the Tyne for London with 4,150 tons of coal. Despite the suddenness of this event, the entire crew of twenty-one, including the master W. M. Pepperell from Cardiff, managed to get clear in two boats. Pepperell and twelve of the crew were picked up at 3.40 a.m. by the steamer *Glenesk* and landed at Hartlepool, while the rest were later picked up by a minesweeper and landed at Scarborough.[5]

One month later, on 7 February 1915, the Swansea-registered *Tangistan*, 3738 GRT (1906), left Swansea for Algiers with a cargo of patent fuel and coal. While the deck and engineering crews were largely European, all the firemen in the stokehold were listed as 'Arabs'. After discharging the original cargo at Béni Saf, in Algeria, 6,000 tons of iron ore for Middlesbrough were loaded. At 12.30 a.m. on the 9 March 1915, steaming north past Scarborough, *Tangistan* struck a mine and sank in the North Sea 9 miles north of Flamborough Head. The crew consisted of thirty-eight hands, all of whom were lost except one. The sole survivor was a twenty-six-year-old Irish sailor who lived in Pier Street, Swansea and who was picked up by the steamer *Woodville* and then taken to Hartlepool. In the account he gave to the *South Wales Weekly Post*, he recalled that:

> after the explosion amidships all below immediately rushed on deck and found the steamer quickly settling. He put on a life-belt and made for a boat on the port side. Two other men got in and they immediately lowered away, but the boat had scarcely touched the water when the Tangistan gave a heave and sank. None of the boats could have got away from the ship, and must have been drawn under. He added. 'I was still holding on to a line when the ship sank and was being dragged down. I let go and came to the surface. I heard the voices of a number of Arabs who were calling out. I got hold of a box and saw some clinging to some wood. I shouted to them to get hold of a better piece, but they did not understand. Two ships passed and the Arabs shouted for help, but both vessels were too far away to hear. I had been in the water two hours when the Woodville came up. By this time the Arabs had disappeared'. The Tangistan sank about four minutes after she was struck. The rescuing boat cruised among the wreckage, but could find no more survivors.[6]

The captain of the ship David Edmunds, aged forty-five, from Burry Port, is commemorated with a plaque in St Mary's Church, Kidwelly, as is D. J. Rosser, the chief engineer, who lived in Skewen, and L. Jenkins, the third engineer, a former rugby player, also from Skewen. A number of the other members of the crew were living in Swansea; they included N. C. Olsen (Swansea), H. Podesta (Brynmill), E. Pauleson (Hafod), James Simmonds (The Strand) and John Brustad Neilson, the ship's carpenter who was living in St Thomas.[7] A further report (incorrectly attributing the loss to a torpedo) in the same paper covered the story from the side of the *Woodville*'s crew:

> In conversation with members of the crew ... I learned that those on the Woodville say the Tangistan [was] signalling to Flamborough Head station as she passed the promontory, and observed that she used a large round light above the bridge for the purpose. The light, they said, would be seen all round, and doubtless was picked up by the submarine. The fact that the Tangistan was carrying ore would make her all the more liable to be marked down, and the Woodville's men thought the submarine followed her up the coast. The sound of the explosion was not heard on the Woodville, and it was two hours later when the cry of 'Steamer ahoy' was heard, A boat was lowered and O'Toole, the only survivor ... was seen kneeling on a large, white-painted wooden covering. He was holding a box in front of him to stop the waves from dashing over him. He was shivering with cold. The first thing he asked when pulled in the boat was, 'HAS ANYBODY GOT A FAG?'[8]

A week after this incident, on 13 February 1915 in the Dover Straits, the *Wavelet*, 2992 GRT (1905), belonging to Needham Brothers of Hartlepool and sailing Pensacola, Florida for Leith with pitch-pine, hit a mine 11 miles north-east of Goodwin Sands, and though damaged was beached; however, twelve lives were lost as a result of launching one of the lifeboats. One of those drowned was J. Jones, the mate who was from Aberaeron. The following report was printed in the *Abergavenny Chronicle*:

> BRITISH STEAMER STRIKES MINE.
> TWELVE MISSING.
> The West Hartlepool steamer Wavelet was mined off the Kentish Knock on Monday, and the master, Captain Cole, finding that his ship was in a sinking condition, beached her in Pegwell Bay. Eleven of the crew and a passenger were drowned. As the vessel appeared likely to founder at any moment, the first officer and eleven others

got into one of the ship's boats, but owing to the heavy gale and rough seas it capsized and all were drowned ... Captain Cole, in an interview, stated that the vessel's side was torn out for a length of thirty feet. A huge portion of the steel hull was hurled on to the deck by the force of the explosion, and fell at the feet of Second Engineer ... who only escaped death by inches. The charthouse was completely wrecked, and Captain Cole stated that the deck was strewn with pieces of iron from the mine and bolt-heads and rivets from the damaged hull. A huge column of water was thrown up by the mine. There was a second explosion which damaged the propeller. It was at first thought that the ship's bottom had been blown out, which accounted for the launching of the boat and the unfortunate loss of twelve lives.[9]

Further afield, in the Barents Sea in the summer of 1915, there were a number of Welsh crew members on board three vessels on the Archangel run that fell afoul of mines laid by the German auxiliary cruiser *Meteor*. On 11 June 1915 the Whitby-registered *Arndale*, 3583 GRT (1906), sailing under Admiralty orders from Cardiff with coal, sank approaching the White Sea. Three apprentices' lives were lost, including one from Cardiff, Edward William John who was twenty years old. Among the survivors were the second mate and third engineer, both from Cardiff and the ship's cook who was from Newport. Then on 24 June 1915 the London-registered *Drumloist*, 3118 GRT (1905), sailing Archangel for London with railway sleepers sank at the entrance to the White Sea after striking mines. No lives were lost. The mess room steward aboard at the time, T. J. Williams, aged sixteen, was from Glamorgan. In the third such instance the mined vessel managed to make it to port. On 26 July 1915 Glasgow-registered *Madura*, a cargo steamship of 4484 GRT (1901), sailing for Leith with flax, oilcake, wheat and wood, hit a mine just off Danilov Island but reached Archangel. On board were a carpenter from Newport and an assistant steward from Barry aged fifteen.

Mine-laying by U-boats commenced in mid-1915 and as a result the number of merchant shipping losses began to increase. As the following examples show, some ships were luckier than others and while sustaining damage, either made it to port or were beached. On 31 July in the Dover Straits, a passenger and cargo steamship *Galicia* 5920 GRT (1901), belonging to the Pacific Steam Navigation Company, Liverpool, was sailing London for Liverpool with general cargo. Two miles from the North Goodwin Light

Vessel, *Galicia* hit a mine that had been laid by SM UC-1 (Egon von Werner), but was successfully beached at Deal, and later re-floated. Among those aboard at the time were the bosun who was from Holyhead, an able seaman from Porthmadog, another able seaman from Port Dinorwic, a leading fireman from Holyhead and a sixteen-year-old cadet also from Holyhead.

On the 30 August 1915, two vessels with Welsh crew members aboard ran into a minefield that had been laid by SM UC-5 (Herbert Pustkuchen) near the Longsand Light Vessel, off Clacton. The first was the Tatem's of Cardiff *Honiton*, 4914 GRT (1915), which had only been in service for five months and was sailing Buenos Aires for Hull with linseed and maize. Although successfully beached at Shoeburyness following the explosion, the damage was sufficient that the vessel was later declared a total loss. No crewmen were lost on this occasion; among those aboard was an apprentice from Abergavenny. The second was the Newcastle-registered *Bretwalda*, 4037 GRT (1911), which was sailing Newcastle for Marseille with a cargo of coal. Although damaged the *Bretwalda* was towed in, beached on Mucking Flat, Canvey Island and later re-floated: three of the crew were from Wales, the master who was from Rhydlewis, the mate from Aberarth and the ship's steward from Cardiff.

Earlier in August, a second mate from Anglesey was witness to the following unfortunate incident. The *Princess Caroline*, a small Glasgow-registered passenger-ship, 888 GRT (1910), which was sailing Liverpool for Aberdeen with 900 tons of general cargo, was stopped by a naval patrol boat and instructed to steam 3 miles to the east to avoid a newly laid German minefield. As a direct result of following these orders a mine detonated aft under No. 4 hatch, which blew the covers and deck area into the air. The *Princess Caroline* sank about three minutes later, 14 miles off Kinnaird Head, Fraserburgh. Four men were found to be missing, probably blown overboard by the explosion. The survivors rowed to shore, and landed at village of Pennan, Aberdeenshire, the next day.

The final example here of a ship with Welsh crew aboard that was mined in 1915 is that of the cargo steamship *Ballater*, 2286 GRT (1894), sailing Valencia for London with fruit. The *Ballater* was mined on 21 November in the South Edinburgh Channel, but was successfully towed in. On board at the time were four Welsh crew: the mate Daniel Jones Evans from Llanon; the first engineer N. Bastian, and the mess room steward E. M. Peterson, both from Barry; and H. G. Blowen, the second engineer from Newport (Mon.). Earlier that year in June, the *Ballater* had been involved in the rescue from heavy seas of two trawler crews that had been attacked in the Atlantic fishing grounds off south-west England by SM U-34 (Claus Rücker). Most of the rescued men landed at Milford Haven were from the Cardiff-registered *Hirose*, 274 GRT (1906), which had been sunk on 2 June 1915. However, four were survivors of an attack the previous day on the Milford Haven trawler *Victoria*, 155 GRT (1890), which cost the lives of five of the crew, including A. G. Coles, first engineer, aged thirty-six, from Cardiff, and F. Slate, a trimmer, forty-eight, from Haverfordwest. In addition, the skipper's nephew, a twelve-year-old boy who had gone along for a pleasure trip was also killed. The details of this incident were widely reported in the local press at the time.[10]

U-boats

U-boat attacks on merchant shipping had begun in October 1914 but up to December 1914 there had only been three such losses and one narrow escape, though this situation changed rapidly and during the course of 1915 U-boat attacks accounted for nearly 750,000 tons of British merchant shipping representing 227 vessels. The emergence of the U-boat threat was unexpected: at the outbreak of the war the Admiralty considered them to be useless (though this opinion altered quickly following the sinking of the 'Live Bait Squadron' in September), while the German High Command regarded them as experimental vessels.[11] What is often referred to as a campaign of unrestricted submarine warfare began in February 1915 (though this was suspended in August), and both British and neutral vessels now found that they were liable be destroyed without warning. However, in the event only around a quarter (fifty-seven out of 227) of the vessels lost in 1915 were sunk without warning, the majority of attacks conforming to at least some of the provisions of cruiser or prize rules.

By the end of the war some 375 U-boats had been commissioned, 329 of which saw service. These fell into a number of classes, of which there was a continual development throughout the war. The three main classes were coastal minelayers, coastal attack boats and ocean-going torpedo attack boats. The UC type I class were the world's first operational mine-laying submarines (the type II starting with UC 16 were not introduced until 1916) and were in service from the summer of 1915 onwards. There were fifteen of this type built and each carried a dozen mines and had a deck-mounted machine gun with 150 rounds. They were only capable of just over 6 knots on the surface. Of the UB class of coastal attack boats, seventeen were of the

UB type I and had all been commissioned by May 1915. These craft had two bow tubes, carried two torpedoes and had no deck gun. There were capable of 6.5 knots on the surface and had a crew of fourteen. Two of them (UB 9 and UB 11) were probably used for training and completed no patrols. The UB type II boats were faster, capable of 9.5 knots surfaced; they carried a compliment of twenty-three men, with four torpedoes and a deck-mounted 50 millimetre (mm) or 88 mm gun with 120 rounds, though the first two of this type were not commissioned until late December. Excluding fishing vessels, only sixteen of the 225 merchant vessels sunk by U-boats in 1915 were due to attacks by UB class boats. By far the majority of the British merchant shipping lost to U-boats in 1915 was accounted for by the various types of ocean-going attack boats.

At the outbreak of the war there were eighteen of the earlier Körting kerosene (paraffin) engine versions of the ocean-going U class which were operational, though four of these were used only for training (U 1-4). These boats had two bow and two stern tubes, carried six torpedoes and had a 105 mm gun with 300 rounds and a crew of thirty-five. These types of boat could make between 13.5 and 14.5 knots on the surface. However, five had been lost in 1914 with no success (U-5, U-11, U-13, U-15 and U-18) leaving just nine of these craft available for patrol at the start of 1915. Of the diesel-engine types from U-19 forward that succeeded the kerosene-fuelled boats, a number were already in service at the start of the war.[12] In total there were some twenty-six of this class put into commission by the end of 1915.[13] The majority having two bow and two stern tubes, six torpedoes and a 105 mm deck gun with 330 rounds and a crew of thirty-five (from type U-43 they were equipped with an 88 mm gun, with 276 rounds and a crew of thirty-six), they were capable of between 15.5 and 17 knots surfaced.

There were also five export-class type U66 boats that had been built for the Austro-Hungarian Empire but which were not delivered due to the risks involved in getting them to the Adriatic following the outbreak of the war. These craft had four bow and one stern tube, carried twelve torpedoes and a deck mounted 88 mm gun with 264 rounds, all five had been commissioned in 1915 though only two were in service by the end of the year (U-66 and U-67) and none of this class had any successes before the spring of 1916. Thus, during 1915, the total number of U-boats (excluding minelayers) that either already were or became available for operations comprised: nine of the kerosene-fuelled and twenty-six of the diesel engine equipped U Class ocean-going attack boats; fifteen of the UB I (which had no offensive armament once its two torpedoes had been used); two UB II coastal attack boats; two export-class U66 types and one A class Norwegian submarine that had been seized and was used for coastal protection and later for training as SM UA. There were also a handful of Austro-Hungarian boats in service.

In addition to the threat to shipping posed by torpedoes, the majority of U-boats at sea in 1915 were also equipped with deck-mounted guns. The deck gun was principally intended as a defensive weapon against small surface-vessels, for which the torpedo was not a suitable weapon. However, it was soon discovered that deck guns were quite effective for offensive purposes and helped to conserve scarce torpedoes. Leaving aside the machine-guns that were fitted to the UC class mine-laying boats, there were two main types of deck gun fitted to U-boats at this time, the 88 mm and the 105 mm. The guns were operated by a three-man crew, a gunner, a layer and a loader, usually under the supervision of the second watch officer. A chain of men was used to bring the ammunition from below the control room floor, then up the conning tower and onto the upper deck. The rate of fire with a good crew was fifteen to eighteen rounds per minute. The U-boats, however, were poor gun platforms in most sea conditions as they tended to roll a lot, and ocean waves frequently washed over, making the gun platform slippery and hazardous. To prevent the crews from being washed overboard, they were fastened with lifelines. Depending on sea and weather conditions, it was not possible to man the deck gun at all times. The guns themselves had no range finders and therefore engagements tended to take place at close range. The deck gun also contributed to hydrodynamic resistance, slowing the underwater speed and increasing the crash dive time. Indeed, deck gun engagements made the U-boat very vulnerable; if sighted, the gun and ammunition had to be secured and the crew had to get below deck, all of which meant that it took much longer than usual to submerge.[14]

Merchant ships that found themselves under attack from U-boats were to follow the Admiralty instructions that were issued to all owners and masters on 10 February 1915. Section 2 of these instructions dealt with the procedure to be adopted upon sighting an enemy submarine. In the first instance, no British merchant vessel was to 'tamely' surrender to a submarine, but instead should endeavour to do the utmost to escape. The reasoning behind this being that a vessel that surrenders is certain to be sunk and the crew cast adrift in their boats. Whereas a vessel that made a determined attempt to escape had an excellent chance of so doing. In the event of a vessel failing to escape, even if torpedoed, it was reasoned that the crew would, in most cases, have time enough to man the lifeboats. If a submarine was seen at a distance, or if a periscope is sighted, merchant captains were instructed to turn, keeping the enemy astern and to run at full speed. If followed on the surface, the advice was to make for the nearest land or shallow water. In the event of being fired upon, captains were instructed to continue on their course at all costs as stopping would certainly result in being torpedoed. When under fire the crew should go below and be ready to plug any shot-holes near the water line. In an attempt to reassure those who might find their vessels fired upon, it was stated that gunfire from most submarines was not dangerous and further if the submarine did not fire it could be assumed it had no gun, and thus there was no real danger if you kept the enemy astern and kept a sharp lookout for any torpedo. In the event of a submarine coming up close ahead with hostile intentions, captains were advised to steer straight for the enemy at utmost speed, altering course as necessary to keep the submarine ahead. The aim was to cause the enemy submarine to dive to avoid collision, which it was reasoned would ensure a better chance of escape. Any vessel being pursued by, or escaping from, an enemy submarine was instructed to fly the largest ensign available half-mast at the foremast head or triatic stay. No ocean-going British merchant vessel was permitted to go to the assistance of a ship that had been torpedoed. Though small vessels of light draught such as coasters and trawlers, were to give all the assistance they could. The final point made clear the dangers of falling for enemy subterfuge and advised that any vessel observed to be making signals of distress without obvious cause should be treated with suspicion and approached with caution, as it may be acting as a decoy for a submarine.

Such instructions and the attendant responsibilities must have weighed heavily on the minds of the civilian masters who throughout 1915 were most likely to be employed on unarmed vessels. One example of a Welsh vessel with a largely Welsh crew who rammed a U-boat is provided in the following account given by a member of the crew of the Llanelli-owned *Lizzie*, (93762) 801 GRT (1888):

> Mr. John Charles, chief engineer of the s.s. Lizzie, who resides at Glanmor terrace, Llanelly, said: 'We left Dieppe on Thursday morning, and on reaching St. Catherine's Point, which is about fifty miles from the French coast, three boats containing a number of men were sighted. It was also discovered that they were being towed

by a German submarine which, when it sighted us lost no time in cutting the painter, thus allowing the boats to drift. The submarine made for us, but the strategy of our skipper was more than a match for her. Our captain ... gave the order at once to turn the boat around at the same time ordering full steam ahead. Without a moment's hesitation we obeyed and we passed the submarine which by this time had become submerged. We must have rammed her, because we cruised about in the vicinity for fully half-an-hour afterwards, but no trace of the submarine could be found except that the surface of the water where we passed over her became very oily ... we [then] took the three boats in tow, and ascertained that they were the crew of the Delmira, a steamer of 3,459 tons belonging to the Bristol and Chilean Steamship Liverpool which left Boulogne on Wednesday, and was torpedoed in the Bristol Channel on the following day. The crew of the Delmira, who state that they were most courteously treated by the Germans, comprised eight British officers and 25 Chinese. They state that they were offered whisky by the pirates, who offered to take them in the direction that they wished to go. After we had taken them in tow for some distance, a British destroyer made her appearance and the crew of the Delmira were transferred to her.'[15]

On returning to Llanelli, the *Lizzie* brought in one of the masts of the *Delmira*, and also a coil of rope from the submarine itself. While the crew at the time believed (mistakenly) that they had sunk the U-boat, the submarine in question, SM U-37, was not sunk by the *Lizzie*, but was lost a month later after hitting a mine. The Welsh members of the crew comprised: J. Evans, of Aberarth, master; John Charles, chief engineer, of Llanelli; William Jones of Aberdovey, able seaman; William Hinkin, from Mold, sailor; and three men from Aberystwyth, Evan Jones, assistant engineer, Richard Clayton, mate, and J. H. Thomas, able seaman. As we have seen earlier, the chief engineer on the *Delmira* was a Porthmadog man.

Other than the exhortations of the Admiralty in regard to the best course of action when encountering U-boats, there were also private inducements on offer to merchant vessels that encouraged actions such as that taken by the crew of the *Lizzie*. The respected journal *Syren and Shipping Illustrated* had offered a £500 prize to the crew of the first vessel to sink a German submarine. In the event this prize along with other money was awarded to the crew of the s.s. *Thordis*, which had rammed SM U-6 at the end of February 1915, though in fact while both periscopes had been damaged the U-boat returned to base and was later sunk by the British submarine HMS *E16* in September. Another reward for £500 was offered for the sinking of the second U-boat by the Cardiff-based Tatem shipping company and there had been a flurry reports in the local Welsh papers of a claim made by the crew of the Hartlepool steamer *Alston*, 3995 GRT (1903), whose second mate and bosun were both Welsh – though this claim was later withdrawn.[16] In fact over the entire course of the war, very few successful instances of ramming were recorded.

Close Calls

Over the course of the year Welsh crew were involved in a number of close calls with U-boats. On 4 February 1915 the Dublin Steam Packet Company's *Leinster* eluded attack by following Admiralty instructions and using a superior turn of speed:

> HOLYHEAD MAIL BOAT CHASED.
> WRECKER ELUDED BY SMART SEAMANSHIP.
> (From Our Own Reporter) HOLYHEAD, Monday. Following upon the news of the sinking of three merchantmen in the Irish Sea, came the intelligence that the Kingstown [Dún Laoghaire] mail boat Leinster was chased yesterday by a German submarine, while on her voyage across the Channel … Leaving Holyhead at 2.13 yesterday afternoon, with 31 passengers on board, the steamer had travelled about half way across the Irish Sea and was 25 miles east of the Kish Lightship when the look-out sighted a grey submarine about a mile distant, coming from the north, with two sailors upon her small deck. That moment began an exciting quarter of an hour for Capt. Birch and the crew of the Leinster. Capt. Birch lost no time in deciding what course to adopt. A German submarine can only make 17 knots an hour: the Leinster can cover over 25. Round went the head of the Leinster from the westward to the southward, and the Germans had then a much smaller mark – the stern of the mail boat instead of her side – at which to launch a torpedo, if they were so inclined. But they never got near enough really to endanger the Leinster. Captain Birch's prompt manoeuvre

saved the situation. For fifteen minutes the submarine chased the steamer, but she could not reach her. Capt. Birch then changed his course to the westward, heading boldly for the Irish shore. The submarine did the same. But the chase was futile, and in a few minutes she disappeared from the sight of those upon the mail boat ... Capt. Birch, interviewed, said, 'Owing to the moderate gale all were below but the crew. We saw the submarine and apparently she had been approaching the mail boat course submerged, for she was about a mile away when we sighted her ... She carried no flag but we knew her by her German grey. As soon as we sighted the submarine we showed her our heels; we changed our course, and she held on. We ran about two miles, then changed again, and she followed on the same tack. She chased us for about a quarter of an hour. But as we were going at twenty-four and a half knots, and when we last saw her she was still coming to the westward'. None of the passengers knew of the danger that had threatened them until the chase was over.[17]

It is certain that Welsh crew were aboard at the time, as around half of the crew employed on the Dublin Steam Packet Company's four ships were Welsh, the majority from Holyhead and Anglesey. On 12 March 1915, also in the Irish Sea, the Reardon Smith & Sons *Atlantic City*, 4707 GRT (1912), was chased by a U-boat 6 miles east of South Rock, Belfast Lough, but escaped. The three engineers aboard were all from Cardiff.

The next two examples of close calls where Welsh crew members were present shows the subterfuge that could be employed on both sides. The first occurred when the passenger and cargo steamship *Orduna*, 15499 GRT (1914), of the Pacific Steam Navigation Company, Liverpool was chased by a U-boat off the Pembrokeshire coast. This attack involved the use by the U-boat commander of a decoy sailing vessel. Aboard the *Orduna* at the time were three Welshmen, an assistant officer's mess room steward, and two third-class waiters. The following story appeared in the *Cambria Daily Leader* in July 1915:

BRITISH LINER ATTACKED.
SUBMARINE HIDES BEHIND A SAILING SHIP.
New York, Saturday. The passengers by the Cunard liner Orduna, which arrived here today, state that a submarine attacked the

vessel with a torpedo without warning at 6 o'clock in the morning on July 9, and, on missing, fired six shells, none of which took effect. In the official report of the attack ... Capt. Taylor, the master of the Orduna, says: 'A submarine was sighted three-quarters of a mile distant eight minutes after a torpedo had been fired. The Orduna was then 37 miles south of Queenstown. I account for the torpedo missing the ship to the Germans misjudging the speed, allowing 14 knots instead of 16, which we were going. Not the least warning was given, and nearly all the passengers were asleep. It was almost another case of brutal murder'. The report adds that the captain, two officers and four look-out men were on the watch, but failed to see any submarine before the attack, and that the periscope could only have been a few inches above the water. After the torpedo was fired the stewards woke up the passengers and assembled them on the upper deck, each passenger having a lifebelt ready to take his place in a lifeboat. As the shots passed over the heads of the passengers the captain was sending wireless calls for help.

One of the passengers aboard, the Danish artist Baron Arild Rosenkrantz described how a few minutes before the attack:

> we saw a small sailing ship just ahead. Two American flags painted on the side were turned to us. Captain Taylor was immediately suspicious and changed the Orduna's course so that the ship ahead was given a wide berth. Many of us were certain that the vessel was hiding a submarine behind her. A few minutes after when the vessel had been left far behind, I looked through my glasses over the sea and saw a white streak coming toward us. It was a torpedo. When the torpedo was half a mile off the Orduna seemed to jump ahead and swerve to one side, the torpedo passing 20 yards behind the rudder'. Twenty minutes later the submarine opened fire, and Captain Taylor swerved again, showing the submarine the liner's stern only, making as small a target as possible.[18]

Within half-an-hour, the *Orduna* had drawn sufficiently far ahead of the U-boat that the firing ceased. Among the passengers aboard the *Orduna* were twenty-one American citizens. An item detailing various expressions of indignation found in the American press was printed immediately below this account. These can be largely summed up by an editorial in the *Philadelphia Public Ledger*, which opined: 'This is no unfortunate accident. None of the excuses hitherto given for German acts of piracy will serve in the case ... There is but one conclusion to be drawn. The Germans will not discontinue her submarine warfare and will not make it more humane.'

On 19 August 1915, three Welsh men among the crew of the *Nicosian*, 6369 GRT (1912), found themselves caught up in what would become one of the most notorious Q-ship incidents of the war. The *Nicosian* had been sailing under Admiralty charter from New Orleans for Liverpool and was about 100 miles south of Queenstown when overhauled and stopped by SM U-27. The boarding party, finding a cargo of ammunition and mules for the British Army, ordered the crew and passengers to take to the boats and were in the process of sinking the vessel when the Q-ship *Baralong* (responding to an earlier distress call from the *Nicosian* and disguised as a neutral American vessel), arrived on the scene and signalled to the U-boat commander the intention to rescue the crew of the *Nicosian* from the boats. This ruse allowed the *Baralong* to get up close to the U-boat before dropping the disguise and firing thirty-four shots in the space of five minutes into the U-boat, which sank quickly. What followed was suppressed by the Admiralty until news leaked in the American press. Most of the surviving U-boat crew were shot in the water by the Marines aboard the *Baralong*, while those who managed to re-board the *Nicosian* met a similar fate.[19] The *Nicosian*, though damaged, made it to Avonmouth. To protect the crew from any future German reprisals (along with those of the *Baralong*, they were put on the German naval blacklist, to be shot on sight if encountered again) the *Nicosian*'s name was changed and the crew issued with new discharge books that omitted the voyage. Among them were the mate who was from Anglesey, an assistant-cook from Penarth and a fireman from Holyhead. The last such example of a close call for Welsh shipping and crew noted here, took place in the Western Mediterranean on 6 November 1915. The *Lady Plymouth*, 3521 GRT (1915), belonging to L. Lougher & Company of Cardiff, had been chased by a U-boat the previous day, and then came under gun attack from another U-boat off Algiers but managed to escape. Aboard at the time was Thomas Lougher, a fifteen-year-old from Radyr on his first ship, who had signed on as purser for a one-shilling passage.[20]

Relatively few merchant vessels had been equipped with defensive guns at this stage of the war. In May 1915 there were 149 so armed, rising sharply to 766 by the end of that year.[21] As a result some successes in fending off

U-boat attacks had been made as the following two examples show.[22] The first such action by a merchant vessel was that of the London-registered *Ping Suey*, 6458 GRT (1899), belonging to the China Mutual Steam Navigation Company. On 29 May 1915, in the English Channel, nearing the end of a voyage from Batavia for London, the ship was attacked twice in the space of five hours. The *Ping Suey* sustained some damage from being shelled, but was saved by defensive gunfire with only one member of the crew being hurt.[23] Aboard to witness this event were an able seaman from Swansea, an ordinary seaman from Bangor, a fourth steward from Wrexham (who was on his first ship), and a fitter from Caernarfon who had joined the *Ping Suey* at Port Said. A few days later, the crew of the Morel Brothers, Cardiff-registered *Pontypridd*, 1556 GRT (1883), were similarly fortunate. On 1 June 1915 in the Atlantic off south-west England, the *Pontypridd* was chased by a U-boat 40 miles south of Wolf Rock, but was saved by the actions of the gun-crew. The mess room steward, who was on his first ship, was seventeen-year-old W. Maddicks from Newport.

The foregoing evidence shows the developing nature of the threats to British merchant shipping in 1915. Predation by German commerce raiders had been brought largely under control following Royal Navy actions in the South Atlantic, and mines, which would continue to be a clear and present danger to merchant crews, accounted for only about 20 per cent of losses in 1915. The major threat to shipping to emerge was attack by U-boat. Only the fastest of vessels were capable of out-running an ocean-going U-boat, and under 10 per cent of merchant ships had been fitted with defensive armament by the end of the year. There were no more than a few dozen U-boats on patrol at any time in 1915. The total number that had been put into commission reached around fifty by December (though twenty of these had been lost to various causes). Nonetheless, over the course of 1915 U-boats alone would account for the loss of 227 British merchant ships.

Chapter 5

1. Rotem Kowner, *Historical Dictionary of the Russo-Japanese War* (London, 2006), p. 238.
2. d'Enno, *Fishermen Against the Kaiser*, p. 67.
3. The name given to the anchorage or sea space between the eastern coast of Kent and the Goodwin Sands, a well-known roadstead for ships stretching from the South to the North Foreland.
4. *CDL*, 4 January 1915, p. 1.
5. See *www.wrecksite.eu/wreck.aspx?65688* (last accessed 3 November 2024).

6   *SWWP*, 13 March 1915, p. 5.
7   See *www.myprimitivemethodists.org.uk/page/death_solves_a_mystery* (last accessed 3 November 2024).
8   *SWWP*, 13 March 1915, p. 8.
9   *Abergavenny Chronicle*, 19 February 1915, p. 3.
10 See, for example, *Haverfordwest and Milford Haven Telegraph*, 9 June 1915, p. 3.
11 R. K. Massie, *Castles of Steel: Britain, Germany, and the Winning of the Great War at Sea*, (New York, 2004), pp. 122, 126.
12 According to Hurd, Germany had twenty-eight U-boats at the start of hostilities: eighteen of the kerosene, and ten of the diesels; Hurd, *The Merchant Navy*, vol. 2, p. 278.
13 SM U 19-46, note SM U 42 was never delivered and served in the Italian Navy; SM U 46 was commissioned in December 1915.
14 I am indebted to *www.uboataces.com/weapon-deck-gun.shtml* (last accessed 3 November 2024) for this information, and while it relates to a later period it should be borne in mind that both the 88 mm and 105 mm guns had a long service and that the realities of operating them had not much changed.
15 *CDL*, 29 March 1915, p. 6.
16 *CDL*, 6 March p. 1; and 30 March 1915 p. 1; also see *BDN*, 12 March 1915, p. 7.
17 *NWC*, 5 February 1915, p. 7.
18 *CDL*, 19 July 1915, p. 3.
19 G. O'Neill, 'The Scandal of the Baralong Incident was Hidden in a Veil of Secrecy', *Iris na Mara/Journal of the Sea*, 1/4 (Dún Laoghaire, 2006), 8–10; see also *https://warandsecurity.com/2015/09/23/allegations-of-war-crimes-at-sea-in-1915/* (last accessed 3 November 2024).
20 Almost certainly a nephew of Lewis Lougher, the company's founder.
21 Hurd, *The Merchant Navy*, vol. 2, pp. 237–8.
22 Fourteen vessels were saved by their own gunfire in 1915.
23 *CDL*, 31 May 1915, p. 1.

6

1915
Captured by U-boats and Sunk

Figure 8: 'Sinking of the Linda Blanche' ('Kaperung und Versenkung des englischen Handelsdampfer') by W. Stöwer, in the German magazine *Illustrirte Zeitung*, 1915

The majority of British merchant shipping losses that occurred in 1915 involved being first captured, then subsequently sunk by a variety of methods. Generally, some warning was given that allowed those aboard to take to the boats; however, changes of German policy and the realities of submarine warfare against commerce saw such principles degrade rapidly. The following examples document the experiences of Welsh crew and vessels subject to such attacks throughout the course of 1915.

On 30 January 1915 Lord Penrhyn's newest steamer, the Beaumaris-registered *Linda Blanche*, 530 GRT (1914), with ten Welsh crew, was sailing from Manchester for Belfast with general cargo including glazed roofing/floor tiles when stopped 18 miles north-west of Liverpool Bar Light Vessel by SM U-21. The ship's papers were ordered to be carried across and the crew given ten minutes to get into the boats with the ship then being sunk by bombs placed below decks. The crew, after rowing for an hour and a half through rough seas were picked up by the trawler *Niblick* and landed at Fleetwood. They comprised John Ellis, master from Bangor; Robert D. Morris, mate from Barmouth; four able seamen, William Williams from Anglesey, Peter Dob and Thomas Lillie both from Port Dinorwic, and John D. Hughes from Porthmadog; Thomas J. Hughes the first engineer from Holyhead; William Paxton the second engineer who was from Newport; and two firemen from Bangor, Alfred Thomas and John Hughes. The crew later commented on the gentlemanly conduct of the U-boat commander (Otto Hersing) and according to reports in the local press, they had been treated in a very kindly fashion and were given cigars.[1] The attack was commemorated by the German artist and illustrator Willy Stöwer in his 1915 painting *Kaperung und Versenkung des Englischen Handelsdampfer Linda Blanche*. This, however, is far from a true depiction: the *Linda Blanche* was a small and unimpressive coaster quite different from the steamer shown in the painting, and furthermore the 88 mm SK L/30 deck gun with which SM U-21 was fitted is conspicuously absent. The deck gun was, however, mentioned specifically in the report of events printed in the *North Wales Chronicle*:

> From their stories it appeared that the Linda Blanche was steaming about ten knots on Saturday about half an hour after mid-day, when the boy called out, 'Here's a submarine' All hands rushed joyously to the side, thinking to see a British submarine, but were astounded to perceive about a ship's length off a submarine showing the German flag and with a wicked-looking gun on deck aft mounted on a swivel. Through a megaphone came the command in excellent English to stop, an order at once obeyed.[2]

As has been recently discussed by Peter Lyon, the dilemma faced by a civilian master in a situation where he stood to lose his ship regardless of his actions, was the difficult choice between his primary responsibilities for the safety of his crew, passengers and obligations to the owners on the one hand, and the exhortations of the Admiralty to evade capture on the other.[3] The presence of some Welsh crew members on both of the vessels used as examples by Lyon justifies some repetition of the facts here.

On 12 March 1915 two steamers were attacked in the Atlantic off southwest England by SM U-29. The first to be attacked was the *Indian City*, 4645 GRT (1915), whose master was John Williams of Cardiff. Owned by

Reardon Smith & Company, the *Indian City* was sailing Galveston/Newport News for Le Havre with a cargo of cotton and spelter with thirty-seven crewmen aboard. SM U-29 surfaced close by, fired a warning rocket and instructed the steamer to stop. The U-boat commander, Otto Weddigen, gave the crew twenty minutes to abandon ship and then the *Indian City* was torpedoed, caught fire and then sank the next day. In the statement made by Williams to the Admiralty following the event, it was noted that Weddigen had towed their boats for a short while and had offered charts for the Scilly Isles. Williams had also spent a short time on the deck of the U-boat and had drunk a glass of wine with Weddigen. When vessels were spotted approaching, the Germans cut the *Indian City*'s boats loose.[4] They were later towed into St Mary's by one of the patrol boats that had been seen approaching.[5]

Coming up from the south was another British steamer, the Liverpool-registered *Headlands*, 2988 GRT (1882), and it was towards this vessel that SM U-29 proceeded, still on the surface. Among the crew of twenty-three on the *Headlands* were three Welshmen – a fireman/trimmer from Barry, an ordinary seaman from Caerleon and a sailor from Swansea. The *Headlands* sailing Marseille for Swansea/Bristol, had spotted the burning *Indian City* and obeying the law of the sea (though not Admiralty instructions) steered towards the stricken ship. Twenty minutes later the conning tower and mast of the U-boat were seen and the *Headlands* master, Herbert Lugg, made the decision to run. SM U-29 was, however, too fast for them and was within hailing distance within half an hour. Ignoring orders to stop, the *Headlands* maintained course until hit by a torpedo abaft the engine room; all the crew made it into the boats and were picked up shortly thereafter.[6] The *Headlands* was taken under tow but sank before reaching port. Admiralty reports on these incidents, while commending the action of Captain Lugg, took a dim view the decision of Captain Williams and noted 'it is considered that the more correct conduct of a British Master would have been to use his utmost endeavour to escape and not stop his ship or quit it until there was no hope of saving her'. Another factor at play was that as the government was underwriting merchant ships to 80 per cent of their value, the Admiralty felt that any compensation, including that for personal belongings should be dependent on ships *not* being instantly abandoned.[7]

The loss of a crew's belongings was a sufficiently important issue for it to be mentioned specifically in some reports following U-boat attacks, as demonstrated in the following example. On 11 March 1915, in the English

Channel, the cargo steamship, *Adenwen*, 3798 GRT (1913), owned by W. & C. T. Jones of Cardiff, while sailing Rouen for Barry in ballast, was captured by SM U-29 (Otto Weddigen), 20 miles north-west of the Casquets, off Alderney. The following newspaper report recounts in some detail the experience of the crew:

> On Thursday of last week news reached Cardigan that the German submarine U 29 had sunk the steamer Adenwen captained by a Cardigan man ... She is a comparatively new boat being only two years old and is commanded by Capt. W.H. Ladd ... now residing with his wife and two children at Cwmins, St Dogmaels ... 'Our ship' said Capt. Ladd 'was in the service of the Admiralty. We were lucky that we were not caught on our way to our port of destination, or there would have been great loss of life. We left a French port, in ballast, on the Thursday morning very early, as we were not allowed to sail by day. At about six o'clock in the morning we sighted a submarine following. We immediately turned our stern to her and tried to get away. Unfortunately we failed to get sufficient steam up and after about an hour's run ... the submarine came close to us. We were steaming about ... 10 knots. We had no chance of getting away ... as the German was able to do 18 knots. She was awash when we saw her, the conning tower and the top of the hull being visible. She shot up two rockets and signalled to us to stop. He said he would torpedo us if we did not so, but if we did he would give us a chance for our lives.' ... 'We lost all our belongings' continued Capt Ladd. 'After we got into the boats the Germans boarded our ship and put bombs in the engine room, two of which we saw explode with a dense volume of smoke. The ship listed to starboard, and the last we saw of her was with her stern level with the water. We were flying the American Ensign when we were challenged, and the commander of the submarine asked me by whose authority I did so. On my replying that I did it on my own he replied 'Well it did not work this time.' 'How did they treat you' asked the reporter. 'Our own fellows could not treat us better' replied the Captain. 'One of the Arab firemen fell into the water as he was getting into the boat, and they sent him a suit of dry clothing, and said he would get a cold if he stayed in his wet ones. They gave us a quantity of cigars, and asked if we had any

bread aboard the boats. They also took the two lifeboats in tow for three quarters of an hour, and took us towards the English coast. We eventually fell in with the Norwegian steamer Bothnia, and the submarine commander requested her to take us aboard, which they did, and we were landed safely at Brixham'.[8]

A number of the other crew were also Welsh – the mate was from Blaenavon, the second mate was from Cardigan, while the steward, assistant steward and the first and second engineers were all from Cardiff. It is worth noting that though captain Ladd had followed the Admiralty instructions given to merchant masters for such encounters with submarines, it was the lack of available speed that ultimately determined the outcome. It is of further interest that the *Adenwen*, which at the time of the attack was under Admiralty charter, was flying the American Ensign. Although the *Adenwen* was damaged by the bombs, it nonetheless stayed afloat and was discovered later in the day by the French destroyer *Claymore* and towed into Cherbourg. Following temporary repairs, *Adenwen* arrived back at Cardiff on 1 April 1915.

The next two examples show the increasing lack of humanity shown by U-boat commanders to British merchant crews. On the 27 March 1915, a Welsh engineer, Griffith Davies from Pwllheli, survived the sinking of the British passenger steamer *Aguila*, 2114 GRT (1909), by the German submarine SM U-28 (Georg-Günther Freiherr von Forstner), 47 miles south-west of the Smalls.[9] The *Aguila* had been sailing Liverpool to Lisbon, Madeira and Canary Islands with general cargo and three passengers aboard. At about 5.30 p.m. the *Aguila*, when signalled to stop, instead put on full speed in an attempt to escape but was soon overhauled. The U-boat approached to within about 300 feet and opened fire with shrapnel and solid shot. At 6 p.m. the engines were stopped, and as the way came off the ship, the boats were lowered; but the U-boat continued to fire, killing the bosun, donkeyman, a stewardess[10] and a female passenger, and wounding others. The following newspaper report gave first-hand accounts of the attack:

> On Saturday night, at half-past six o'clock, the submarine fired across the Aguila's bow and summoned her to stop, but Captain Bannerman speeded up the engines to fourteen to clear. The pirate, however, made eighteen knots and quickly overtook them. The effort of the Aguila to escape seemed to arouse the pirates' anger. Four minutes only were given to crew to clear, but before that time

had expired the pirate opened fire, which was kept up while the crew were launching the ship's boats. This murderous action of the Germans resulted in chief Engineer Edwards, Boatswain Anderson, and donkeyman McKirkman all of Liverpool being killed. Thomas Crawley, Handel Road, Liverpool, seaman, said he was assisting the Boatswain to launch No 3 boat when the boatswain was hit by shrapnel in the left side. He had to leave him, on the boat deck. Donkeyman McKirkman fell overboard dead. Crawley added: 'Shots were flying all around me and I don't know how I escaped. I was the last man to leave the Aguila. Seeing my chance I caught a lifeline and swung myself off over the side.' Among the wounded men at Fishguard was Mr King third engineer … who had a nasty wound in his right side and a piece of shrapnel in his cap. He explained that the pirates continued firing for nearly two hours and that he received his wound whilst going down into the boat. Seamen Christianson and Lawson and Cook Nogley were bandaged about the head and arms. They were fired on indiscriminately by the pirates.[11]

One of the boats capsized, which brought the total death-toll up to eight. The submarine offered no assistance and went away after sinking the ship.[12] The following day SM U-28 claimed another victim in the same area, this time with much greater loss of life. On 28 March 1915, the Liverpool-registered *Falaba*, 4806 GRT (1906), was overhauled after a short chase, about 60 miles west of St Ann's Head. The first unarmed passenger ship to be attacked during the war, the *Falaba* carried a crew of ninety-five and 147 passengers, including seven women; a total of 242 persons.[13] About ten minutes after the warning to take to the boats was given, a torpedo was fired from a distance of about 100 yards. The *Falaba* took a list to starboard and sank in eight minutes: it was quite impossible to transfer this number of people to the boats in such a short space of time. As a result, 104 lives were lost, among them the first American citizen to be killed by a German submarine. It has been argued that this heavy loss of life was quite unnecessary and would not have occurred if the German commander had allowed the master reasonable time to abandon ship.[14] William Osbourne Hughes, aged thirty-one, a clerk from Conwy was among the crew who died, and among the survivors was Joshua Thomas, a carpenter/seaman from south Wales.

Following the sinkings of the *Aguila* and *Falaba* there was a marked shift in the rhetoric used in the Welsh press. In the place of reports conceding civil and gallant conduct, or the provision of cigars, wine, brandy, dry clothes or the towing of boats to relative safety, readers were confronted by murderous pirates' intent on a policy of hate, prepared to kill civilians as they manned the lifeboats instead of offering assistance. One sub-headline to a report on the inquest into the sinking of the *Falaba* read: 'HUNS LAUGH AT DROWNING VICTIMS.'[15] This usage of the term 'Hun' was quite recent. It had stemmed from a speech made by the Kaiser Wilhelm II to German troops departing to quell the Boxer Rebellion in 1900, which had extolled the merciless savagery of Attila: no quarter given, no prisoners taken. The ruthless and brutal actions of the German Army against civilians in Belgium in 1914 saw the use of the term revived and then used widely in the press and in propaganda to characterise the barbarous nature of the German people.

The use of the term 'pirate' in the reports in the Welsh newspapers grew as attacks mounted, and while it became trite journalistic shorthand for U-boats and their crews, it was clear that these men were not pirates. The description was first applied in relation to the far-flung activities of German auxiliary cruisers, in the Indian Ocean and South Atlantic but transferred to U-boats as the nature of the war against commerce evolved. Throughout the war, there were no specific provisions in international law regarding the operation of submarines.[16] This was due in part to the novel nature of this technology; in the most recent military conflict, the Russo-Japanese War of 1904–5, neither side had possessed submarines. It is unsurprising then, that the subject formed no real part in discussions at the Second Hague Peace Conference of 1907 or the London Naval Conference in 1909. There was an assumption that the rules then existing for surface vessels would apply – but this was not a shared consensus, even where it was recognised. Customary international law viewed merchant vessels as non-combatants that could only be attacked after warning was given, and in keeping with Article 3 of The Hague Convention 1907 (VI), in the event of the sinking or the destruction of an enemy merchant vessel, provision was to be made for the safety of those on board and of the security of the ship's papers.[17]

However, the issue of the exact definition of what constituted a non-combatant vessel was clouded by the decision taken in 1913 to begin defensively arming British merchant vessels. This had initially been a response to the perceived threat from enemy converted auxiliary cruisers to the normal operation of the mercantile marine, and forty such ships had been defensively equipped by March 1914. It was the British position that so-equipped merchant vessels were not commissioned auxiliaries as construed by the 1907 Hague Convention No. 7; that is, they were not under direct authority of the State, or commanded by a duly commissioned servant of the State and the crew (with the exception of the gunners) were not subject to military discipline, and should therefore be treated as non-combatant shipping and not warships. While all this might be true, the question as to whether the fact that such vessels were armed should remove them from the category of vessels entitled to the customary protections of international law was a different matter. Those who sought to justify the practice contended that arming merchant vessels did not preclude non-combatant status and protections, and referred back to a long history of arming merchant ships. Historically such measures had been for protection against pirates and privateers, but in 1914, outside of a few places, there were no longer pirates operating on any of the sea routes plied by British ships, and privateering had been prohibited by the 1856 Declaration of Paris.[18] The widespread use of the term 'pirate' in the press attached connotations of illegality to attacks against merchant shipping, as well as reinforcing belief in the political rhetoric that justified defensive armaments on merchant ships.

In the following examples a pattern of behaviour emerges; merchant ships were more likely to follow Admiralty instructions and at least attempt to run from U-boat attacks, with the result that they were then fired upon, often with scant regard to the outcome and given little if any time to abandon ship when overhauled. On 5 April 1915, the Cardiff-registered *Northlands*, 2776 GRT (1900), owned by Jones, Hallett & Company, with a crew of twenty-four, was sailing from La Goulette for Middlesbrough with iron ore when captured by SM U-33 (Konrad Gansser) and sunk by torpedo. Two Welsh men were aboard – the second mate who was from Swansea, and the first engineer who was from Cardiff. The following report of events appeared in the *Cambria Daily Leader* a few days later:

> Her crew was landed at Deal early yesterday morning and told the following story: 'We were going along all right, keeping an eye open for hostile submarines when we suddenly saw one rise to the surface about 200 yards away and make for us at the rate of 16 knots. We tried to get away by increasing our speed and by steering a zig-zag course, but the submarine was travelling so fast that, we could see that it was all up with us. Then they fired a gun at us, and some of her crew came up on the deck of the submarine and signalled with hand flags for us to stop ... Her commander was evidently in

a hurry, as he shouted out in bad English, "Clear out and hurry up for I am going to sink you." ... He gave us two minutes to obey his order. As the first boat was being lowered something went wrong with the tackle, for the stern broke away and dropped into the sea, but we managed to hang on by the aid of the seats in the boat, and none of us were lost. The second boat got away alright. There were 12 of us in each boat, and as we were pulling away from the ship we saw the torpedo coming. It hit the vessel amidships with a deafening report, sending a volume of water and quantities of wreckage around us and on us. The Northlands gradually settled down by the head, broke in halves, and sank in about ten minutes.'[19]

Before the men took to the boats, the wireless telegraph codes and Admiralty instructions were burnt in the galley fire, and the ship's papers were saved by the master.

On 6 May 1915 in the St George's Channel, the Liverpool-registered *Candidate*, 5858 GRT (1906), while sailing Liverpool for Kingston (Jamaica) was captured and sunk by SM U-20 (Walther Schwieger) 13 miles off Coningberg Light Vessel, to the south-east of Waterford Harbour. The *Candidate*'s master, A. B. Sandiford, had put on full speed on being fired upon without warning by the U-boat and had attempted to run for a bank of fog. However, the fog lifted and without sufficient speed to outrun the attacker (the *Candidate* being capable of only 10 knots) the only option was to take to the boats. Among the rescued men were three able seamen from Wales; J. W. Williams of Caernarfon, W. W. Parry of Bagillt and Robert Owen of Ffestiniog who, along with the rest of crew, were taken to the John Cory Sailor's Rest and Bethel in Milford Haven. A full report of the experience was carried in the *Haverfordwest and Milford Haven Telegraph*:

> Early on Friday morning the patrol boat Grimsby trawler Lord Allendale arrived in the Haven with the crew of the Liverpool steamer Candidate ... The men were rescued from their boats by the trawler which was in charge of Skipper Bart Foster, Milford Haven ... There were 11 of them all told, all being saved. As they filed up the gangway of the mackerel stage they presented a pitiable sight, some of them with just a trousers and shirt on, no boots or stockings, half a dozen quiet lads in their early teens. On the way up to the John Cory Bethel our representative spoke to several

of them. One of the messroom boys described how whilst in the messroom two shells hurtled through and narrowly missed him. He lost no time in getting on deck, practically all of the men agreed that the Germans deliberately fired at them from two guns, and where ever there was a group on deck, there they directed the fire. As they were getting the boats down they poured an incessant fire on them and it was a miracle that none were hit. Robert Owen, a seaman had a very narrow escape. He was in the first boat lowered as the ship was going top speed and it almost filled with water. The pirates shot at it and it sank. Owen with his right hand damaged held on to a rope until rescued by one of the other boats. Another seaman said he was in his bunk when a shell came through and caused him to move. The companion ladder two yards away from him was smashed by a shot and he had to get away with hardly any clothing. A seaman on the bridge said he and the chief officer had to 'duck' repeatedly to avoid the shells and finally he had to jump from the bridge. The bridge and funnel were shot away but it was only after they left in their boats that the Germans put a torpedo in each side of her. They hung round till she sank in an hour and 20 minutes. They were rowing in the boats 7 hours before being picked up.[20]

The Sailor's Rest and Bethel at Milford Haven, where the crew were taken (built in 1907), was one of a string of charitable edifices set up by John Cory, the philanthropist, coal owner and shipowner, to provide shelter and comfort for the shipwrecked and suffering.

Later that month, on 29 May 1915 at the south-western end of the English Channel, the *Dixiana*, 3329 GRT (1901), was captured by SM U-41 (Claus Hansen) and sunk by torpedo. There are a couple of noteworthy circumstances attending this incident – the U-boat was rigged with sails as a means of subterfuge, and following the sinking, the ship's crew who had been adrift for some hours, turned down assistance from a steamer that was heading in the wrong direction for their purposes:

BOUND FOR SWANSEA
STEAMER SUNK BY SUBMARINE OFF USHANT.
... the Greek steamer Zanos Sifnias arrived in Barry Roads on Monday with 27 members of the crew of the steamship Dixiana,

which was sunk off Ushant by a German submarine. The men have now landed at Barry. The vessel was torpedoed 45 miles off Ushant on Saturday. She was bound for Havre and Swansea with a cargo of cotton and pig iron. The master, according to one report, was deceived by the appearance of a small craft bearing sails, which proved to be an enemy submarine which had adopted this device to mystify shipping. A shell was fired from the submarine, and the occupants of the steamer were ordered to clear out without delay. In half an hour the Dixiana disappeared. After having received eight shells in her hull she was still afloat, but the submarine sent along a torpedo, which finished the task of destruction. Fortunately, the boats had been swung out in readiness ... and the crew succeeded in entering them.

The chief steward W. H. Morgan and the cook, C. Haddock, both from Cardiff, gave the following account of the events that occurred after taking to the boats:

After about four hours in our boats we came across a French steamer which offered to take us aboard but as she was bound for Bordeaux we declined. After spending the night in the open boats, we came across a large four-masted ship, which came within a couple of lengths of us and actually stopped but she went on again and took no notice of us. We were eventually rescued some hours later by the Greek steamer Zanos Sifnias. This boat bore down upon us and took us aboard, and we ascertained then that we were really further from land than when we abandoned the Dixiana. We were treated with great kindness aboard this Greek steamer, and given every possible comfort.[21]

There were two other Welshmen aboard the *Dixiana* at the time – W. M. Harris, the second steward, aged fifteen, from Cardiff and on his first ship; and J. Coyle, an ordinary seaman from Penarth, aged sixteen.

On 16 June 1915, two Welsh engineers were aboard the Manchester-registered *Trafford*, 215 GRT (1896), sailing Cork for Lydney in ballast, which was sunk by gunfire 30 miles west-south-west of Tuskar rock, off Rosslare by SM U-22 (Bruno Hoppe). The rescued crew later arrived at Milford Haven aboard the steamer *Turnwell*, 4264 GRT (1901), which had also been attacked by SM U-22 in the same area earlier. The incident was reported in the *Cambria Daily Leader*:

> The London steamer Turnwell, bound from Liverpool to New York, went into Milford Haven yesterday disabled after a remarkable experience with a German submarine in the Irish Sea. Her crew are all safe. When the Turnwell was 30 miles west-north-west of the Smalls at one o'clock on Wednesday morning a submarine came alongside and ordered the crew to abandon ship. The 30 hands got into their boats, and the Germans went aboard the Turnwell and placed bombs in her hold. When they left they attacked the steamer Trafford, of Manchester, and sank her by shell fire. The crew got safely away. The captain of the Turnwell stood by; and observing that his ship still floated, he, with his men, went back aboard her. They found that the Germans had ransacked the cabins and taken off everything of value. The crew set to work at the pumps, kept the Turnwell afloat, and succeeded in making Milford Haven under her own steam, having on board the crew of the Trafford, who had been picked up by a patrol boat and transferred.[22]

In some cases, the bravery and efforts of crews to save their ships and cargo were recognised by the Admiralty. In the following example, two Welsh firemen received the Distinguished Service Medal, and a second mate who was from Abergele received a 'mention'. On 28 June 1915 the Liverpool-registered *Armenian*, 8824 GRT (1895), was on voyage from Newport News to Avonmouth with 1,422 mules for HM Government when attacked by SM U-24 (Rudolf Schneider) off Trevose Head, Cornwall. The *Armenian* was unarmed, but had a top speed of 14.5 knots, and the captain decided to make a fight of it. The following account of the *Armenian*'s fate reveals that on sighting the U-boat, the captain:

> headed for the submarine with the intention of ramming her. The enemy, however, opened fire and Captain Trickey turned his ship stern on to the submarine so as to decrease the target. Several shots fell ahead and astern of the merchantman until the range was found, when the wireless telegraph house was wrecked. Another shell entered the firehold and started a fire. Captain Trickey with his officers and men set to work to subdue the flames, but other

fires were caused by subsequent shells. One struck the steering gear, putting it out of action, and another fell on the engine-room hatch, sending debris on to the engines, which were, however, kept at full speed. During this phase of the one-sided action twelve of the crew were killed and others injured. Captain Trickey still held on to his course.

When the unequal ordeal had lasted nearly an hour, the funnel was struck, the shell passing down into the body of the ship. The stokehold was put in darkness and the boilers were so damaged that steam could not be maintained. The master then realised that escape was impossible. He hoisted the white flag and blew the ship's whistle in token of surrender, preparations being made simultaneously to abandon ship. Whether the submarine failed to notice the British signals or was determined to punish to the uttermost so persistent an opponent will never be known. At any rate the shells continued to fall on the crippled vessel, damaging the boats' falls and causing some of the boats to hang by one fall only, with the result that many men were thrown into the water. Eventually all the surviving members of the crew were able to get away.

The captain, satisfied that no one was on board, himself left. But shortly afterwards an improvised raft was seen leaving the Armenian with the chief engineer, the veterinary surgeon, and the purser; they also were rescued. When all six boats were clear of the ship, the submarine approached and, getting into position on the port quarter, fired a torpedo into the Armenian. Under Captain Trickey's orders, the hatches of the lower hold had previously been battened down, the ballast tanks pumped out, and the refrigerator boxes secured, thus giving additional buoyancy to the vessel. Consequently the first torpedo left the Armenian still afloat and another was discharged, this time into the stokehold, with the result that the ship forthwith began to sink rapidly. Owing to the action of the captain, the enemy had to expend about fifty shells, as well as two torpedoes. As she sank rapidly the Armenian, with a length of 530 feet, presented a remarkable spectacle; half her length was reared into the air.

The ship having been dispatched, the submarine ... dived and disappeared. The commander showed, however, a measure of humanity; before diving he rescued three or four men from the water. Captain Trickey's boat being the only one with a compass, the other boats were collected and connected astern. A course was then made for land under sail. At 7 o'clock the following morning the Belgian steam trawler President Stein took the men on board and at noon turned them over to the destroyers Mansfield and Milne, which landed them at Avonmouth that afternoon. The unequal action resulted in the loss of twenty-nine lives, including the fourth engineer and twenty American cattle attendants. The Admiralty marked their appreciation of the master's efforts to save his ship and its valuable cargo by conferring upon him the Distinguished Service Cross. The quartermaster, W. A. Goss, and two firemen, J. Davies and E. G. Talbot, received the D.S.M., and the second officer, Mr. H. O. Davies, and the chief engineer, Mr. J. Crighton, obtained 'mentions'.[23]

J. Davies, who was from Ebbw Vale, and E. G. Talbot, who was from Cardiff, were two of only twelve merchant firemen to receive the Distinguished Service Medal throughout the entire war.[24] W. H. Perts, aged twenty-seven, the ship's chief cook from Cardiff, was one of the twenty-nine men lost. Among the other survivors, second mate H. O. Davies was from Abergele, third engineer C. W. Sharp engineer was from Flint, and ordinary seaman E. R. Talbot was from Cardiff and on his first ship.

U-boat attacks continued throughout the summer. On 21 August 1915, two days after the first of the notorious *Baralong* Q-ship incidents (where the surviving crew from SM U-27 were shot in cold blood as revenge for the sinking of the *Arabic* and *Lusitania*), the crew of the Cardiff-registered *Ruel*, 4029 GRT (1913), belonging to Turnbull Brothers Shipping Company, were – in the words of one commentator – 'singled out for a demonstration by the enemy of the brutal methods he was prepared to adopt in the hope of breaking the spirit of the British merchant seaman'.[25] The *Ruel* was sailing Malta for Barry Roads in ballast and, after being chased and shelled, was captured by SM U-38 (Max Valentiner) and sunk by gunfire 45 miles south-west of Bishop Rock, Scillies. The men having taken to the boats were then subjected to small-arms fire. Among the crew who endured this appalling treatment were the mate E. Roberts from Ffestiniog; the bosun J. Jones from Porthmadog; and the fourth engineer A. Hardy, the mess room steward W. Griffiths, and an apprentice L. Smith, all from Cardiff. One man was killed, and eight others were wounded. In a subsequent statement made under oath by the master, the second mate and Lieutenant D. Blair, R.N.R. (who was at time in charge of the Royal Naval Reserve base at Penzance), it was stated that:

> when in the act of abandoning the steamer Ruel in a sinking condition due to attack by a German submarine, we were fired on while alongside and pulling away from the above vessel, the wounds of those injured showing that both shrapnel and rifle bullets were used ... the submarine was distant about 150 yards, and close enough for the crew to observe that we and the remainder of the crew of the steamer Ruel were abandoning the ship and had given up any further attempts to escape.[26]

The case of the *Ruel* later formed part of Sir Edward Grey's response to a German memorandum concerning the *Baralong* incident, which demanded 'that the commanding officer and other responsible parties on board HMS *Baralong* shall be brought to trial for murder and duly punished'.[27] The survivors from the *Ruel* were picked up soon after the sinking by the armed trawler *Dewsland* and the drifter *Campania* and landed at St Mary's in the Scillies. On the same day as the ordeal of the crew of the *Ruel*, SM U-38 attacked another steamer on which Welsh crew were present. The Evan Thomas, Radcliffe's *Windsor*, 6055 GRT (1911), with a crew of forty, was sailing Barry for Leghorn/Livorno with coal when captured and sunk by gunfire 70 miles south-west of Wolf Rock, near Land's End. There were no casualties. Among the *Windsor*'s crew were the mate from Newborough, Anglesey; the second mate, third mate, the second engineer, an ordinary seaman and an apprentice, all from Cardiff; the first engineer from Llanelli; and a sixteen-year-old apprentice from Newport (Pembs).

The final example of a steamer captured and sunk by U-boat in 1915 where Welsh crew were present involved the small coaster *Cottingham*, 513 GRT (1907). This ship had very likely accidently run down and damaged SM UC-2 off Lowestoft in July. At the time, a claim was made by the crew for the reward offered by W. J. Tatem, which was noted earlier. Although this claim was dismissed,[28] the crew were granted £200 by the Admiralty for the part that they played.[29] On Sunday 26 December while sailing Rouen for Swansea in ballast, the *Cottingham* was captured by SM U-24 (Rudolf Schneider) and sunk by gunfire about 16 miles off Lundy. Among the seven men who lost their lives were three from Wales

– L. H. Benoke, seaman, aged sixty-three, of Pembroke; J. Lewis, fireman, aged sixty, born in Carmarthen; and R. Roberts, aged sixty-three, fireman, from Swansea.

While the vast majority of attacks were against merchant steamers, sailing vessels that had no chance of outrunning an attacker were not immune from the attentions of U-boats as the following examples show. On 5 May 1915 in the Atlantic off the south of Ireland the three-masted wooden schooner *Earl of Lathom*, 132 GRT (1885), was captured by SM U-20 (Walther Schwieger) and sunk by gunfire 8 miles south-west of Old Head of Kinsale. The crew of five included T. O. Jones, the master, who was from Moelfre. The schooner had been sailing Connah's Quay/Mostyn for Limerick with fire clay goods and general cargo; there were no casualties. Then, on 21 May, the fully rigged steel ship *Glenholm*, 1968 GRT (1896), was captured by SM U-27 (Bernd Wegener) and sunk 16 miles off Fastnet Rock, County Cork. There were two Welshmen aboard; the mate who was from Cardigan and a sailor from Cardiff. This loss was reported briefly in the *Cambria Daily Leader*:

> The crew of 29 hands from the sailing ship Glenholm, owned by Mr. Novice, of Liverpool, were landed at Berehaven this morning, their ship having been sunk 15 miles S.W. of Berehaven last evening by an enemy submarine. The crew were signalled to leave the ship, and she was immediately sunk, 39 rounds being fired. The Glenholm left Chile on January 3rd with a cargo of 3,000 tons of nitrate.[30]

The third example involving Welsh crew for which we have a more detailed account occurred on 12 June 1915 in St George's Channel. The four-masted iron barque *Crown of India* was not long out from Barry for Pernambuco, Brazil with 3,000 tons of coal when it was attacked by SM U-35 (Waldemar Kophamel), which opened fire on the unarmed ship from half a mile away. Among the crew of the barque were two Swansea men – a sail maker and a sailor – and one of the apprentices aboard was from Porth. The following account appeared in the *Haverfordwest and Milford Haven Telegraph* four days later:

> At about 6.30 on Sunday morning two more crews, victims of the German submarine campaign on the west coast were brought

into Milford Haven by the steam liner 'Queen Alexandra', 23 men from the 'Crown of India' and 10 from the Norwegian barque 'Bellglade' ... These were the first crews from sailing ships to land here in such circumstances.

A representative for the paper who spoke to two of the men who had been aboard the *Crown of India* reported that:

> one of them, a Swansea man ... said they were 36 hours out from Barry when attacked. He was at the time up in the main royal yard, and another man was on the mizzen when the first warning shot passed through the main upper topsail and the other a point off the port quarter ... Capt. Branch [the master] told our representative that they left Barry Dock on Friday ... and when 70 miles west-south-west of St. Anne's Head two shots were sent across his ship. He had previously observed the submarine so he knew what this meant, and put up his flag, and they then got the two boats out the men getting into them in good order. They pulled hard to get clear of the vessel and were nearly half-a-mile off when the Germans sunk the ship after ramming nine shells into her ... Seeing a Norwegian barque in the distance he headed his boats in that direction, but soon found that the submarine was on the same track, and therefore altered his course. He witnessed the attack on the Norwegian and afterwards the two crews were picked up.[31]

About half of the incidents examined above took place in the St George's Channel/Irish Sea area. U-boat activity clustered in the major shipping lanes of strategic ports, and the incoming and outgoing trades from Liverpool, Avonmouth, Cardiff and Barry made the western approaches to the Irish Sea and Bristol Channel a magnet for attacks. Though this was a dangerous area, there is some bias in the sample as much of the evidence is drawn from the Welsh newspapers, which were more likely to report incidents off the coast of Wales and especially when survivors were brought safe to Welsh ports. Over the course of the war most U-boat attacks would take place in the English Channel and on the coast of Northern France, while in the North Sea, the shipping lanes serving the Tyne and Tees ports were also particularly hard hit.

Marooned Men and Hostages

Another of the possible dangers faced by merchant seamen during the war was that of being marooned in a remote location. One such case reported in the *Cambria Daily Leader* in March 1915 concerned the French barque *Jean*, 2207 GRT (1902), that had recently left Port Talbot bound for Antofagasta with 3,500 tons of coal, which informed readers that:

> Lloyd's agent at Conception Chile, cables: The steamer Skerries reports that the barques Jean and Kildalton were sunk by the SMS Prinz Eitel Friedrich in December last. The crews are at Easter Island, but refused to be taken off. The English captain is reported mad.[32]

The *Kildalton*, 1784 GRT (1903), was a three-masted barque that had been sailing Liverpool to Callao when captured. The captain, W. Sharp, aged sixty-four, was from Shetland and his crew had been imprisoned on the SMS *Prinz Eitel Friedrich* before being landed on Easter Island. They did not leave until March 1915 when a Norwegian trading ship called there.[33] Some of the French crew remained longer, as they had been in touch with their consul and were waiting for instructions. Some of the detail of the crews' sojourn and the conditions on Easter Island are contained in the account of the first archaeological expedition there.[34] From this account, the mad captain appears to have been that of an unidentified vessel flying the Chilean flag, which had called at the beginning of December (before the crews of the barques had been landed), and the cause of his trouble appears to have been the consumption of three bottles of whisky a day.

While the foregoing did not, as far as can be ascertained, involve any Welsh men (though it is possible some may have joined the *Jean* at Port Talbot), the risk of being marooned was real enough. A number of Welsh crew were aboard the Bear Creek Oil Shipping Company's tanker *Elsinore*, 6542 GRT (1913), when they were marooned on San Cristóbal Island, the most easterly of the Galapagos archipelago, in September 1914. The following report appeared in the *Cambria Daily Leader* when some of the crew returned to Britain later that year:

> Men of the crew of the Liverpool steamer Elsinore, whose whereabouts has been a complete mystery to their friends, made their

appearance today, telling a tale suffering at the hands of the Germans. Two months ago the Elsinore was found by the German cruiser Leipzig in the Gulf of California, and since then it has been uncertain where the crew had been landed. The men have had an adventure which they will never forget. Two lieutenants with an armed force from the Leipzig boarded the Elsinore taking the master (Captain Roberts) with them to the German cruiser, and upon returning to the Elsinore Captain Roberts informed his crew that the vessel was going to be sunk. They must get the lifeboats provisioned. The commander of the Leipzig then sent the Elsinore to the bottom ... the crew were ... put on board a German depot the Marie, and they do not say they were at all well treated there. They were made to work hard, filling bags of coal for transhipment to the Leipzig. Captain Roberts advised them to do as they were told, and for three days they carried on this laborious work. They were on the Marie for eight days and nights receiving very scanty food and shocking accommodation, sleeping on the bare iron decks, with a sentry standing over them ... They were at last put ashore at Chatham Island – one of the Equatorial group of Galapagos or Tortoise Islands off the coast of Ecuador ... There the crew of 29 hands were left by the German commander telling them that they must not leave for 14 days. Two days later, however, a small sailing ship arrived to load sugar and took Captain Roberts and part of the crew to Guayaquil, in Ecuador. The remainder of the crew were imprisoned on the island for 20 days. They were badly housed in a building which one of the South American Governments had formally used for a convict settlement ... The castaways were on friendly terms with the natives, who are engaged on a sugar plantation; but they suffered very much from want of proper food, only getting rice and jam and what fish they were able to catch. At the end of three weeks another vessel came and rescued the remainder of the marooned men, taking them also to Guayaquil.[35]

R. G. Evans of Porthmadog was the mate on the *Elsinore* and both he and Roberts (who was from Widnes) later sailed together on another tanker, the *Camillo*, 5315 GRT (1908), in April 1915. Evans was not the only Welsh crew member on the *Elsinore*, however, as three other men – the chief engineer J. Nicholas from St Dogmaels, the second engineer Asa J. Evans from

Cardigan, and J. E. Patton, a fireman from Cardiff – were also aboard. The following account, written by Asa Evans provides considerably more detail of the events that befell these men:

> It was whilst on voyage from Corinto (Nicaragua) to San Luis (California) that the unexpected happened. We left Corinto on the sixth of September and everything went on smoothly until we got to the Gulf of California (Mexico). We were aroused on the morning of September 11 at 2.15 by a shell fired across our bows, and a powerful search-light playing on our ship. This was a warning to stop our engines, which we did immediately. At this time none of us knew whether we were stopped by a friend or by the enemy, but we had not long to wait before we realised that it was indeed the enemy. About half an hour after the first shot was fired we were boarded by a crew of two officers and ten men with loaded rifles. They proceeded to the saloon to examine the ship's papers. After ascertaining that we sailed under the British Ensign, and having made a search through our engine room and bunkers for oil and coals, they left us. Before leaving we were told to get our boats ready, with as little clothing as each of us could carry in our handbags, as they were going to set us adrift in our own boats when they got to a convenient place to sink our ship ... They also gave us instructions to turn our ship round and head back the same way as we had come, and to take all orders by signal from the Leipzig. About 11 a.m. we sighted another steamer on the horizon making towards us. We all met at noon, and then got orders to stop. This steamer turned out to be another German – the transport Marie, carrying coal for the Leipzig. We were again boarded, this time by seven officers and ten men, all armed to the eyes. They then gave us orders to take to our boats and pull for and go aboard the Marie. When we got on board we found that we were going to be closely watched and guarded. They had already posted a guard there, consisting of one officer, a signalman, and nine marines, fully armed, and a good watch was kept over us day and night. It was from here that we witnessed the sinking of the good ship Elsinore. In all it took twelve explosive shells to do the dastardly work, and the last we saw of our good old ship was about 4 p.m.; she was then a mass of flames and stately as ever,

slowly sinking on an even keel. We then proceeded for Galapagos Islands aboard the Marie and accompanied by the Leipzig. On September 18 we arrived at Albemarle (the chief of the Islands) and bunkered the Leipzig. On September 19 we left Albemarle for Hood Island, where we arrived on Twentieth, leaving at 2.30 a.m. on the 22 for St. Cristobel Island, where we were put ashore ... on the same day and abandoned to our fate – to find our way back to the mainland (a distance of about 600 miles) as best we could ... On September 24, two days after landing, our captain and half the crew (we were 40 all told) sailed for the mainland in a sloop owned by the Governor of the Islands. As this boat was not capable of carrying any more men, the remainder of us had to stay behind and take our chance when another boat called. As it turned out we had three weeks to wait before the happy day for our departure dawned. When the day did come we shed no tears. On October 25 we left the Island on a 20 ton sloop, and it was a picnic with a vengeance. The cargo consisted of 14 tons of sugar; she carried provisions and water for 13 days. There were 23 hands including crew, and hardly room to swing a cat round. The Elsinore's crew slept in the hold on top of the sugar bags, whilst the remaining officers and engineers slept in what they called the cabin, fitted out with two shelves or bunks 8ft by 2ft. The two officers shared one bunk and the fourth engineer and I the other. We are both built on rather fine lines, otherwise we should have fared badly. It took us 13 days to get across to Guayaquil (Ecuador). Hard boards again for 13 days, and our diet consisted of one ounce of bread, coffee, rice and beans at 11 a.m. for breakfast, and beans and rice for dinner and tea (combined) at 5 o'clock ... Neither of us had a wash or a shave from the time we left the Island till we got to the mainland as we could not afford the water. You should see the sight we presented. Robinson Crusoe was not in it! On October 25 we arrived at Guayaquil and saw the British Consul. We were put on board the R. M. S. Ecuador, whose commander is an old acquaintance whom I had not seen for over 16 years – Captain W. H. Morgan, St. Dogmaels – bound for Panama. Mr. Nicholas, two apprentices and I proceeded to San Francisco to join the S. S. Cordelia, another of the company's boats; the rest of the crew got back to England.[36]

Neither Nicholas nor Evans appears on the crew list for the *Ecuador*, 1768 GRT (1881), at this time, but they may have travelled as passengers. However, Nicholas and Evans both joined another of the Bear Creek Oil Company's ships, the *Oberon*, 5142 GRT (1907), at Panama on 6 November 1914, as stewards on nominal wages, leaving the vessel at Port San Luis, California. They then both joined the *Cordelia*, 6533 GRT (1912), at San Francisco on 29 November 1914, signing on as chief and second engineer with both men signing off at Vancouver in May 1915. J. E. Patton, who had also been on the *Elsinore* when it was captured, signed on as a fireman on the *Oberon* at San Francisco in December 1914 and arrived back in South Shields in April 1915.

Prior to the war it was not unusual to find Welsh seamen on vessels running down to load cargoes of grain off the Atlantic coast of Morocco. By 1914, following the two Moroccan crises and the formation of the French Protectorate, this situation had altered markedly, and on the north African coast, crews ran the risk, if sunk or stranded, of being held to ransom. On 3 November 1915 in the western Mediterranean, the defensively armed steamer *Woodfield*, 3584 GRT (1905), while sailing for Salonica was captured by SM U-38 (Max Valentiner) and sunk 40 miles east-south-east of Ceuta, Morocco. Two Welsh men were among the crew, the master Robert Hughes, aged thirty-six, from Criccieth (born in Porthmadog), and first mate Thomas Jenkins, aged fifty-five, from Cardigan. The carpenter, Daniel Adolfsen, aged thirty-five (born in Norway) was married and living in Barry. On the morning of 3 November 1915, while sailing from Avonmouth for the Dardanelles with a cargo of petrol, the *Woodfield* was attacked by SM U-38 about 50 miles east of Gibraltar. After a fight that lasted more than three hours the *Woodfield* was sunk. The crew got away into the boats, two of which reached the Spanish enclave of Melilla. The third drifted ashore on the coast of Morocco where the occupants were taken prisoners by hostile Moors and held to ransom. Their eventual release was secured by the Spanish government and the survivors were taken to Melilla. The following report, which subsequently appeared in the *North Wales Chronicle and Advertiser*, contains a letter written by Robert Hughes while at Melilla in December 1915 to his brother:

> I do not know what they are going to do with us. They are very slow coming to some settlement. I do not see how they can intern us as we are ship-wrecked mariners. The ship was sank thirty miles

from land. The submarine left us at that distance. I am wounded through the shoulder and right thigh, but am out of all danger now and in a few days will be hopping about as well as ever. The doctor comes for me every day and takes me up to the hospital in a motor-car to see the other members of the crew. We have all been under the X-ray. The twelve men that were in the hands of the Moors are now here. I should like to tell you about our experience. I can assure you it was no fault of ours that the Woodfield was lost. We struggled hard for three hours. The shells were bursting on deck and spreading like hailstones. Eight crew were killed and fourteen injured. The carpenter was struck. He had life in him when the last boat left the ship. I stayed behind with him and did all I could to try and get him round, but it was no use; he died in my arms. The old ship took a lot to sink, and to finish her they had to send a torpedo. After the torpedo had hit us I made a jump from the steamer and got on a little raft. How I managed to swim I don't know. My arm and leg were injured. The pains were terrible, but I clung for all I was worth to the raft. The sea was rather rough. At last I was picked up by the 1st mate's boat and we were called alongside the submarine. They gave us a bottle of brandy and some bandages. At 2 o'clock the following morning we landed at Melilla. The third mate's boat had landed there two hours before us, so that they were waiting for us and had ambulances on the quayside, and the wounded were taken right to the hospital and we were well treated.[37]

The men were later transferred to Malaga. At the time of the report SM U-38 was believed to be an Austrian submarine (which it was not); however, it was operating from an Austrian base at Cattaro, Montenegro at the time of the attack.

The LNWR steamer *Hibernia* had been requisitioned by the Admiralty for use as an armed boarding steamer and renamed HMS *Tara* retaining most of the original Welsh crew. In November 1915, while heading for the Port of Sollum in Egypt, the *Tara* was torpedoed off Tripoli by SM U-35. Out of a crew of 104, a dozen men, mostly from the engine room, were lost in the explosion and subsequent sinking. The remaining ninety-two men were taken prisoner and held captive for four months in the Libyan Desert before being rescued.[38] Their captors were the Senussi, a Muslim politico-religious

Sufi school and clan who had fought French colonial expansion in the Sahara from 1902 to 1913, and then the Kingdom of Italy's colonisation of Libya beginning in 1911. During the First World War, they fought the Senussi Campaign against the British in Egypt and Sudan. Five of the men from the *Tara* died at Bir Hakkim while being held prisoner and one died after his rescue in a hospital at Alexandria. Of the eighteen men who lost their lives, fifteen are commemorated on the Holyhead War Memorial.

Early in 1916, and while the men of the HMS *Tara* were still being held captive, another British merchant crew fell into the hands of hostile 'Bedouin'. On 4 January 1916, the unarmed London-registered *Coquet*, 4396 GRT (1904), while sailing Torrevieja for Rangoon with 6,200 tons of salt, was captured by SM U-34 (Claus Rücker) and sunk 200 miles east of Malta. At the time of the attack there was a moderate breeze and heavy swell, a lookout was being kept, and the two lifeboats were slung out ready for lowering. The fate of the men who took to the boats was later reported in some detail in the *North Wales Chronicle*:

> By the sinking of the s.s. Coquet during the early part of this year, the mercantile marine lost a very capable and highly respected officer in the person of the late Mr Arthur Griffiths, chief officer of that ill fated vessel ... [following the attack] ... Two boats were launched, one in charge of the captain and the other under the command of ... Griffiths. After being adrift for about six days and suffering extreme hardship the crew of the captain's boat made for the Tripolitan Coast and subsequently were captured by Bedouin Arabs. In the encounter with the Arabs, three men were killed, and two, including the captain, wounded. The injured men were deserted by the Arabs, and later succeeded in making their escape to a British patrol boat which later appeared on the scene. Since then Captain Groom has reached England, and presented an exhaustive report to the Admiralty on the whole occurrence. Of the boat in charge of Chief Officer Griffiths, nothing more has been heard or seen, since it parted company with the captain's boat on January 6th, and the presumption is that it was lost with all on board. Griffiths was the third son of the late Mr and Mrs Griffiths, of Nazareth, Penrhyndeudraeth. He was a native of Festiniog. Mr Griffiths was 39 years of age, and had been for many years a member of the Merchant Service Guild.[39]

It also transpired that the men in both boats had all their navigational instruments taken from them by the U-boat commander before leaving them adrift. Fifteen men, including Griffiths, are listed on the Mercantile Marine Memorial, but it is not known if there were other Welshmen in the boat that made land. The ten men who later escaped had been held for some eight months.[40]

The nature of the war against commerce changed over this period. Prize or cruiser rules worked better for commerce raiders than for the U-boats that had no spare men to form a prize crew and little spare room aboard for captured crews, though they would and did take masters, engineers and gun-crew as prisoners. The operation of Q-ships and the defensive arming of merchant ships muddied matters. Submarines were at their most vulnerable when surfaced (depth charges did not come into effective use before 1916), and towing boats to safety meant that the submarine could not dive. All these developments had been foreseen. In 1912, the then retired Admiral Sir John Fisher, who been First Sea Lord between 1904 and 1910, delivered a report to the British cabinet clearly predicting that submarines would become one of the chief weapons of naval warfare. Outlining the unsuitability of cruiser rules for submarines, he concluded that compliance with such rules would quickly be dropped in favour of survival. In early 1914, while acting as an unofficial adviser to the Admiralty, Fisher prepared a memorandum warning that the advent of the long-range ocean-going submarine would fundamentally alter traditional British naval strategy, and that the threat posed would be not one of invasion, but of starvation.[41] The then First Lord of the Admiralty, Winston Churchill, would later recall that, 'There was a general belief even in the Admiralty where I presided, that no nation would ever be so wicked as to use these underwater vessels to sink merchantmen at sea'.[42]

Notes

1   Eames, *Ships and Seamen of Anglesey*, pp. 508–9.
2   *NWC*, 5 February 1915, p. 7.
3   Lyon, *Merchant Seafaring through World War 1*, pp. 71–3.
4   Lyon, *Merchant Seafaring through World War 1*, p. 72.
5   See *http://forgottenwrecks.maritimearchaeologytrust.org/indian-city* (last accessed 3 November 2024).
6   L. Cope Cornford, *The Merchant Seaman in War* (New York, 1918), pp. 49–52.
7   Lyon, *Merchant Seafaring through World War 1*, p. 73.

8 See *ww1ceredigion.wordpress.com/tag/s-s-adenwen/* (last accessed 3 November 2024).
9 His survival is reported in the *North Wales Chronicle*, 1 April 1915, p. 6.
10 Martha Emily Jenkins, born in Liverpool but of Welsh extraction.
11 *Cambrian News*, 2 April 1915, p. 3.
12 On the same day, SM U 28 also sank the West Hartlepool-registered, *South Point*, 3837 GRT (1912), which was sailing Fowey/Cardiff for Philadelphia with China clay in bulk and casks. Aboard at the time was a second cook from Cardiff and a sailor from Newport (Mon.); no lives were lost.
13 The cargo included 13 tons of ammunition.
14 A fuller account of this incident can be found in Hurd, *The Merchant Navy*, vol. 1, pp. 308–12.
15 *Haverfordwest and Milford Haven Telegraph*, 31 March 1915, p. 2.
16 L. E. Davis and Stanley L. Engerman, *Naval Blockades in Peace and War: An Economic History Since 1750* (Cambridge, 2006), p. 19.
17 H. S. Levie, 'Submarine Warfare: With Emphasis on the 1936 London Protocol', in M. N. Schmitt and L.C. Green (eds), *Levie on the Law of War: International Law Studies Volume 70* (Newport, 1998), pp. 296–7.
18 Levie, 'Submarine Warfare', pp. 302–4.
19 *CDL*, 7 April 1915, p. 6.
20 *Haverfordwest and Milford Haven Telegraph*, 12 May 1915, p. 3.
21 *CDL*, 1 June 1915, p. 8.
22 *CDL*, 18 June 1915, p. 8.
23 Hurd, *The Merchant Navy*, vol. 2, pp. 8–10.
24 The other ten recipients were all merchant ratings on auxiliary craft.
25 Hurd, *The Merchant Navy*, vol. 2, p. 33.
26 Hurd, *The Merchant Navy*, vol. 2, p. 33.
27 *CDL*, 5 January 1916, p. 6.
28 *Abergavenny Chronicle*, 8 October 1915, p. 6.
29 P. Akermann, *Encyclopedia of British Submarines 1910–1955* (Cornwall, 2002), p. 256.
30 *CDL*, 22 May 1915, p. 5.
31 *Haverfordwest and Milford Haven Telegraph*, 16 June 1915, p. 3.
32 *CDL*, 1 March 1915, p. 3.
33 W. L. Putnam, *The Kaiser's Merchant Ships in World War 1* (Jefferson NC, 2001), p. 85.
34 K. Routledge, *The Mystery of Rapa Nui* (London, 1919).
35 *CDL*, 27 November 1914, p. 4.
36 *Cardigan & Tivy-Side Advertiser*, 21 May 1915, p. 5.
37 *NWC*, 31 December 1915, p. 3.
38 R. S. Gwatkin-Williams, *Prisoners of the Red Desert* (London, 1919); see also W. Davies, *The Sea and the Sand: The Story of HMS Tara and the Western Desert Force* (Caernarfon, 1988); and G. S. Griffiths, *Holyhead to Bir Hakkim (and Back): The Full Story of H.M.S. Tara* (Wrexham, 2015).
39 *NWC*, 8 December 1916, p. 7.

40 A full account of Groom's ordeal following their arrival Ras Amana on the north African coast after six days can be found in Hurd, *The Merchant Navy*, vol. 2, pp. 216 ff.
41 Eames, *Ships and Seamen of Anglesey*, p. 507.
42 J. D. Lyons, 'Churchill on Science and Civilization', *The New Atlantis*, 28 (Summer 2010), 75–84.

7 Changing the Rules
Unrestricted Submarine Warfare 1915; Convoys 1917–18

Figure 9: Port Talbot Docks 1915, courtesy Llyfrgell Genedlaethol Cymru/National Library of Wales

The Devil to Pay: Unrestricted Submarine Warfare 1915

Perhaps the most abiding image of the war against commerce in the First World War is that of the British merchant crews who were torpedoed without warning. Early in 1915, the Germans made a statement of intent regarding the new rules of engagement to be applied to British and neutral merchant shipping: from 18 February these could be subject to sinking without warning. In fact, prior to this, on the 30 January, three British merchant vessels had already been sunk in such a manner by SM U-20 (Walther Schwieger); one of which made it to Le Havre with the help of a tow but later sank, the crew of another were picked up by a French minesweeper and the third crew were completely lost.[1]

The first such incident involving Welsh crew occurred on the 20 February 1915 in the Irish Sea. The Merevale Shipping Company's Cardiff-registered, *Cambank*, 3112 GRT (1899), with twenty-four crew aboard was torpedoed without warning by SM U-30, 10 miles east of Point Lynas, near Amlwch, Anglesey. Three lives were lost in the explosion, and one man drowned while abandoning ship. The crew of the Bull Bay lifeboat *James Cullen* were alerted by the torpedo explosion, launched and met up with the survivors who were in two boats, and towed them in until the arrival of armed yacht *Oriana*, which in turn towed these boats into Amlwch. Among the survivors were four Welshmen: the master, the second engineer, the mate and the mess room steward, all of whom were from Cardiff. The following detailed report of this incident was printed in the *North Wales Chronicle*:

STEAMER TORPEDOED OFF ANGLESEY
SUNK WITHOUT WARNING.
GERMAN SUBMARINE'S RAID NEAR AMLWCH.
A German submarine ... has appeared again in the Irish Sea. There she has sunk two British steamers, the Cambank, of Cardiff, a vessel of 3000 tons, and the small Irish collier Downshire. The Cambank ... was torpedoed without warning at eleven o'clock on Saturday morning, about five miles off Amlwch, Anglesey. The third engineer and two men were killed and the donkey man was drowned. The remainder of the crew saved themselves in their own boat, and eventually were towed to Amlwch Port, where they were taken charge of by the local agent of the Shipwrecked Mariners' Society. The vessel had just taken the Liverpool pilot on board and resumed her journey when she was torpedoed ... The crew of a vessel which docked at Liverpool during Saturday stated that about a quarter to ten o'clock they spoke to the Cambank, who warned them that there was a submarine about. Both vessels were bound for Liverpool, but the Cambank was much the slower of the two, and while the faster boat reached port without incident, the Cambank met with disaster. Lloyd's agent at Holyhead stated that the captain of the Liverpool pilot steamer reported having, at 11.15 on Saturday morning, put a pilot aboard the Cambank. Fifteen minutes later she was torpedoed by a submarine, and sank in twelve minutes.

CHANGING THE RULES

ENEMY CRAFT APPEARS OFF POINT LYNAS.
HOW THE 'CAMBANK' WAS SUNK.
The Cambank loaded at Huelva, Spain, a cargo of about 4800 tons of pyrites and copper ingots, the latter consisting of about 800 tons. She left Huelva a week ago for Garston. Experiencing very heavy weather in the Channel, she put into Falmouth, and later continued her voyage to Garston, and arrived off Amlwch between nine and ten o'clock on Saturday morning, and, as usual with Liverpool-bound boats; took on a pilot, in this instance Pilot Pass, of the Mersey Dock and Harbour pilots, and then continued her voyage to Garston. When about ten miles east of Point Lynas, a submarine suddenly appeared about 300 yards distant, and instantly, without any challenge or warning, sent a torpedo at the Cambank. Both Captain Prescott, in command of the vessel, and Mr Pass, the pilot, saw the periscope of the submarine, and almost simultaneously they saw the trail of a torpedo approaching them at a terrific speed. The Cambank's helm was put hard over at once, but answered but slowly, and practically did not change her course to any extent, and the torpedo struck her plump amidships. A shattering explosion followed, and tons of water were flung on the deck of the Cambank, which immediately began to sink, and Captain Prescott promptly ordered the boats to be lowered. There were 25 men to be saved, but only 21 answered the last call, for three who were down below at the moment of the explosion were killed outright. All the others got safely into the boat with one exception, who, being excited in jumping from the ship to the boat, missed the boat and sank immediately.

EXPLOSION SEEN FROM THE SHORE.
The tremendous force of the explosion may be estimated from the fact that, though the tragedy occurred thirteen and a half miles away, people on the hills ashore distinctly heard it. There are persons who actually saw the explosion and the sinking of the ship and gave the alarm; and in this way the Bull Bay lifeboat was notified and hurried to the scene of the disaster, where the crew of the Cambank was found rowing about, several of them half naked, and all of them hungry, cold and wet. The Bull Bay lifeboat took them in tow, and later on a patrol boat came on the scene and took both

in tow and landed them at Amlwch Port about three o'clock. Here a great crowd was waiting to see the rescued men, who, however, were taken in charge by the local agent of the Shipwrecked Mariners' Society and clothed and fed and warmed. This, it may be noted, was done by the society, although only one of the rescued men was a member of the society. The society, furthermore, gave each of the men a railway pass to his own town, for which they all left by the mail train. The crew was a mixed one, but it is to their credit that nothing in the shape of a panic developed in their calamity. They all, of course, lost everything except what they had on at the time the ship was torpedoed. During the hours from 3 till 7.40 the men rambled about the town surrounded by hundreds of the inhabitants, who evinced the greatest hospitality to them, and followed them to the station and gave them a cheering send-off. Despite their nerve shaking experience the men are in excellent heart … The crew of the Cambank expressed the opinion that the loading of the vessel at Huelva was watched by many German spies, and that her destination and course were accurately ascertained before she left Huelva.[2]

While the comments made by the crew regarding spies may seem implausible, or indicative perhaps of a more general paranoia, in neutral Spain a vast intelligence campaign was undertaken by the Germans. Their spy networks enrolled the services of all kinds of characters (including prostitutes, waiters, dancers, police agents and anarchists), especially in the main urban centres, along the coasts, at the borders and on the islands, in order to sabotage the production of goods destined for the Allies. They also informed on the sea routes and departures of merchant vessels so that these could be intercepted by submarines.[3]

On the 24 February 1915, three steamships were torpedoed by SM U-8 (Alfred Stoss) off Beachy Head. Among them was the London-registered *Rio Parana*, 4015 GRT (1902), sailing Tyne for Portoferraio, Italy, with a cargo of coal. The torpedo hit the *Rio Parana* on the starboard side. With the ports and doors stove in and the saloon flooding, the ship was abandoned and then sank. The *Rio Parana*'s master was J. Williams of Pembrey, who was sixty years of age. This was the same captain Williams who had been earlier captured by the German surface raider SMS *Karlsruhe* in October 1914.[4] Williams later commented on these events in a newspaper interview:

[His] second adventure occurred last week, off Beachy Head, in the English Channel. The boat was the Rio Parana, 6,700 tons, belonging to the London and American Maritime Trading Company and bound from the Tyne to Elba. On February 24th, between 3 and 4 P.M., they were either mined or torpedoed. 'You don't know which, Captain?' 'How do you know,' He replied, 'how can you know, unless you see a submarine? There was nothing visible. You can see the trail of a torpedo coming along the water, but nothing was seen that day. It all happened in one second, and the boat began to sink in about 40 minutes. As the boat began to sink very quickly, we got away in our boats. We were in the boats for an hour or two in bitterly cold weather, and were eventually picked up by a British torpedo boat and landed in Newhaven the same evening. None of us were drowned, and there was no accident.' The crew, numbering 31, were taken to London, and provided for by the Ship-wrecked Mariners and Fishermen's Society. They were paid off in London on the following day. But for a cold, I am none the worse. Asked what his future plans were, Captain Williams said: 'Going to sea again; as soon as I get well. Not going to let the Germans frighten me. Someone has got to go to take command of ships. If all stopped at home now there would be no grub'.[5]

On 18 March 1915 there were a number of Welsh crew aboard the Cardiff-registered *Blue Jacket*, 3515 GRT (1904), sailing La Plata for London with maize when torpedoed by SM U-34, off Selsey Bill. Though damaged, the steamer later put into Southampton Water. The Welsh crew aboard comprised second mate G. Owen from Criccieth; third engineer A. Richards from Milford Haven; second engineer George Richmond from Newport (Mon.); and the mess room steward Allen Rees, from Rhydyfelin, who was on his first ship:

TORPEDOES FAIL TO TAKE FULL EFFECT.
The Cardiff steamer Blue Jacket ... which put into St. Helens (Isle of Wight), yesterday, reported that she was torpedoed about 5.30 p.m. on Thursday without any previous warning when 15 miles from the Owers Lightship. The chief officer ... who with a portion of the crew, were landed by a trawler at Newhaven, stated that they left La Plata with about 5000 tons of grain for London on February 9.

When they entered the Channel they put their lifeboats in readiness for any emergency, and when the explosion took place the boats went in the water. The torpedo struck the ship in No. 1 hold, and the force of the explosion was so great that it blew off the hatches, and sent the whole lot including a quantity of the cargo, into the air. The ship's two boats stood by the vessel for about an hour and a half. The first boat's crew, with the chief officer, were picked up by the Ramsgate trawler Concord and this trawler brought them to Newhaven Harbour. The captain, with his party in the second boat, stood by the vessel, the forehold of which was full of water. The Blue Jacket ... is owned by Mr. George Hallett, Bute Street, Cardiff.[6]

On 4 April 1915 there were a number of Welsh crew present when the *City of Bremen*, 1258 GRT (1899), sailing Port Talbot for Nantes/Bordeaux with coal, was torpedoed by SM U-24 (Rudolph Schneider). The ship capsized and sank in five minutes, 20 miles off Wolf Rock, four of the crew were lost; the survivors were landed at Penzance. Among those who survived were four firemen/trimmers who were from Swansea, Cardiff, Kenfig Hill and Neath, and a steward/cook from Llandenny. Among the four men who lost their lives was William John Watters, the second engineer, aged fifty-one, who was from Swansea. The following appreciation appeared in the *Cambria Daily Leader* a few days later:

> The many friends of Mr. Will Watters, late of 14 Stanley Terrace, Mount Pleasant, Swansea, who was on the City of Bremen which was torpedoed by a German submarine without any warning last Sunday morning, will always treasure the memory of his heroic death. They feel proud to have known and loved him. Down below in the engine-room gladly doing his duty with no chance to escape when the deadly torpedo shattered his ship, he was as great a hero as our brave soldiers in the trenches or our jolly Jack Tars on the North Sea. Inscribed on the nation's roll of honour art no braver names than those of our sailors who, in this our hour of need, face the terrors of mine and Submarine to bring us food from the ends of the earth.[7]

A fuller account of the events and of the impact on his family was given in the *Herald of Wales and Monmouthshire Recorder*:

SWANSEA MAN DROWNED.

The torpedoing of the Port Talbot trader, City of Bremen, by a German submarine on Sunday brought great sorrow to a Swansea home. The Second Engineer ... whose, wife and two children live at 14, Stanley Terrace, Swansea ... was one of four members of the crew, and the only Britisher, drowned when the vessel was sunk by pirates. Mrs. Waters [sic] and her son and daughter, aged 15 and 11 respectively, spent the holiday out of town and on their return at about 8 p.m. on Monday discovered a telegram awaiting them. It had arrived earlier in the day, and was from ... the owners of the City of Bremen, and announced the death of Mr. Waters. Mrs Waters fainted when she realised what the telegram conveyed, and kindly neighbours came in and sought to soothe her grief ... One of the crew stated in an interview yesterday that it was his belief that the submarine followed the vessel during the night and waited until daybreak to make sure of her nationality. No warning was given to the crew of the City of Bremen, and the vessel sank five minutes after being struck by the torpedo. The submarine disappeared immediately. Half the crew were on deck at the time and the vessel turned turtle, engulfing four men. The captain and twelve members of the crew were picked up after being in their boats four hours.[8]

On 7 May 1915 the most well-known example of a British vessel being torpedoed without warning and with attendant serious loss of life occurred. The story of the *Lusitania*, 30396 GRT (1907), is significantly well known so as not to warrant a detailed repetition here. Having sailed from New York on 1 May for Liverpool with 702 crew members and 1,287 passengers aboard, on approaching waters in which U-boats had been reported the lifeboats were swung out and the bulkhead-doors closed. Torpedoed on the starboard side between the third and fourth funnels by SM U-20 (Lt-Cdr Walther Schwieger) the liner took a list to starboard, sinking fifteen minutes later some 15 miles south of Old Head of Kinsale. In all, 1,198 lives were lost; 413 crew and 785 passengers (128 of whom were American civilians), including 291 women, ninety-four children, one matron, thirteen stewardesses and one typist. Some 761 survivors were rescued by trawlers and other craft that headed out from the Irish coast. It should be noted that there is still some remaining controversy over whether the ship could be considered a legitimate military target based on the fact that a considerable portion of the cargo was munitions, though this was denied by the British government at the time and for a long while afterwards.[9]

A number of Welsh crew were aboard, some of those who lost their lives and whose bodies were not recovered are commemorated on the Mercantile Marine Memorial.[10] Among these was Owen Owens, an able seaman who was born in Holyhead in 1850, whose father had also been a stoker in the mercantile marine. Three other Welshmen whose bodies were never recovered were J. Davies, aged sixty-two, a trimmer from Denbighshire; T. O. Hughes, aged forty-one, an assistant storekeeper from Flint; and F. Davies, aged thirty-seven, a printer from Newport (Mon.). The death of stewardess Mary Jones, aged forty-three, of Llanfairfechan, whose body was recovered and is buried in common grave C in Queenstown churchyard, has been discussed earlier. There were also a number of Welsh crewmen among the survivors. The bosun, John Davies, was born in Cardigan, Cardiganshire in 1853. His father was a coachman and his uncle was in HM Coastguard Service. The family home was at St Dogmaels, but when quite young he ran away to sea, and while still a boy joined the Cunard Steam Ship Company. Fellow survivor second cabin passenger Ernest S. Cowper wrote about the disaster a year later in *The New York Times*. In his account he especially praised Davies and his efforts:

> But the bravest of all that brave assembly was rugged old John Davies, the boatswain. Many there are on both sides of the Atlantic today who owe their lives to him. He stuck to his job until the ocean took him off his feet. He worked the forward falls on the lifeboats which got away from the starboard side, and smoked as he did it. He was assisted by two boyish-looking well groomed wireless operators, who, catching John Davies' spirit perhaps, pulled out their cigarettes and smoked as they worked the after falls with him. They were drowned.[11]

Davies never received any recognition from his company or his country. Having been landed at Queenstown, he made his way back to Liverpool, and without any footwear he walked from the Pierhead to Bootle, a distance of some 5 miles, without complaint.[12] John Idwal Lewis, aged twenty-nine, was the senior third officer aboard. He was born on 29 August 1885 and was a native of Porthmadog. His first ship was a three-masted barque. In

1912, he left sail and entered the world of steamships, working on the Moss Line and Blue Funnel Line. In 1913, he earned his master's certificate. He had served aboard *Lusitania* since October 1914. Lewis was in charge of lifeboats 1–11 on the starboard side. During the sinking, he assisted the first officer Arthur Rowland Jones[13] in filling and lowering the lifeboats, although very few lifeboats from his section of the ship got away. Lewis went down with the ship but resurfaced and then clung onto an overturned collapsible boat to stay afloat. He was rescued by a trawler.[14] William Williams, the *Lusitania*'s master at arms, responsible for security aboard, had been born at Tremadog in 1869, but by 1915, his family home was in Everton. He had joined the *Lusitania* at Liverpool on 12 April 1915 at a monthly rate of pay of £5 10s. After the ship had gone down, Williams was in the sea for some time and eventually came across the *Lusitania*'s captain clinging to some wreckage. He was able to help the captain to stay afloat until they were both rescued by one of the ship's boats, after which they were picked up by a small steamer and eventually landed at Queenstown.[15]

Following the loss of the *Lusitania*, some pertinent questions relating to naval protection of merchant shipping were put to the First Lord of the Admiralty Winston Churchill, in the House of Commons. The MP for Liverpool, R. P. Houston asked whether Churchill was aware, prior to the sinking, that U-boats were active off the south coast of Ireland, in St George's Channel, and the Irish Sea; did he know that the *Lusitania* had been expected at Queenstown; did he know that on the previous day two Liverpool liners, the *Candidate* and the *Centurion*, had been torpedoed and sunk in those waters; and given that the Admiralty had provided escort vessels to convoy government-contracted steamers from the south coast of Ireland to Liverpool, had any such arrangements been made to protect or convoy the *Lusitania*? Churchill's response was that the Board of Trade had ordered an inquiry into the tragic circumstances but also spelt out that:

> in no circumstances will it be possible to make public the naval dispositions for patrolling the approaches to our coastline ... and, secondly, that the resources at our disposal do not enable us to supply destroyer escort for merchant or passenger ships, more than 200 of whom on the average arrive or depart safely every day.[16]

The Liverpool-registered *Centurion*, 5495 GRT (1908), which left Liverpool for Durban, flying no flag and with the ship's name covered as a precaution, had been torpedoed on the 6 May 1915 without warning by SM U-20 in St George's Channel. The weather was foggy at the time of the attack and Schwieger, not wanting to miss his chance, had been too impatient to wait for the vessel to be identified before firing the torpedo.[17] Among the forty-four crew who successfully made it off in the boats was W. O. Jones from Porthmadog, the second officer. Two other Welshmen were also signed on for the last agreement running from April – an able seaman from Mostyn and a seaman from Criccieth – but it is unclear whether these men were aboard at the time.

On 15 June 1915, the sinking of the *Strathnairn*, 4336 GRT (1906), caused heavier casualties than had occurred on any ordinary trading-vessel since the *Tangistan* had been lost on 9 March.[18] The Glasgow-registered *Strathnairn* was sailing Cardiff/Penarth for Archangel with 7,000 tons coal, in fine and clear conditions, when torpedoed and sunk by SM U-22 (Bruno Hoppe), 2 miles west of Ramsey.[19] In all, twenty-one crew were lost (many of them Chinese), mostly drowned. Survivors included the second mate and a number of Chinese crew who got away in a gig, rowed east and were picked up early the following morning by the schooner *Amanda*, 97 GRT (1867), of Padstow and landed later that day at Milford Haven. The first engineer and a Chinese carpenter had to jump overboard and clung to a capsized boat for nine hours before being picked up by the *Abbotsford* of Glasgow and landed at Swansea. Among those lost was the third mate, Benjamin Bruce Evans, aged nineteen, from Whitchurch, Cardiff. The following account was reported in the *Cambria Daily Leader*:

> Eleven survivors were brought into Milford Haven by the steam barge Thomond, the Chinese walking over the docks into the town barefoot, with the few belongings that they could save, and were escorted to the John Cory Sailors' Rest for the night. One of them in broken English was able to give an outline of the tragic occurrence, and tried to describe how the boats capsized and his shipmates were lost. He also showed how the submarine crept round the ill-fated ship to the stern, apparently to ascertain her name ... The only British survivor is the second officer, Mr. James Wood, of Belfast, who gave his version very clearly when met after reporting the affair, he said: We left Cardiff at 8 o'clock on Tuesday night. The ship was struck by a torpedo without the slightest warning ... The force of it burst the boiler, and soon the ship

listed heavily to port. We never saw the submarine till after she had done the foul work ... As soon as possible after the ship was struck the four boats were got out. Mine, however, was the only one to get clear away, for one was smashed, and the other two capsized on being cut clear of the davits. The captain and other officers were in these. The submarine, never offered to assist the solitary boat.' In fact, Mr. Wood, observing the Strathnairn was not sinking quickly, pluckily attempted twice to get back to the ship but each time he was foiled by the submarine driving him off. He could not see the number of the submarine, as little more than the periscope was visible. At 12.45 midnight they were picked up by the schooner Amanda, of Padstow, transferred to the steamer Rosabella, Chester, and at the entrance of Milford Haven were again transhipped to the Thomond.[20]

In Hurd's account of the incident, it was noted that:

the second mate (Mr. J. H. Wood), who was asleep in his cabin, after being relieved by the chief officer, was thrown out of his bunk by an explosion. When he reached the deck he noticed that, although way was still on the ship, a lifeboat and a gig had been lowered and had been smashed against the vessel's side. Captain Browne came to the conclusion that the vessel was sinking and slipped down a lifeline into a lifeboat which had been lowered with a number of Chinese seamen in it. Owing to the boat's painter being cut before the boat had been released from the dropping gear, it also collided with the vessel's side and all the occupants were washed out of it. Realising the error which had been made in lowering the boats too soon, Mr. Wood waited until the ship was stopped before launching the remaining gig. Fortunately the Strathnairn, though a little deeper in the water, had taken only a slight list to port, and the gig was successfully launched with the assistance of the remaining ten Chinamen on board.[21]

Later in the year, on 14 November 1915, the *Treneglos*, 3886 GRT (1906), owned by the Hain Steamship Company was returning from Port Louis, Mauritius with a cargo of sugar. While steaming at full speed the ship was torpedoed without warning by SM U-34 (Claus Rücker) and sunk 70 miles west-south-west of Gavdos Island off the Isle of Crete. A terrific explosion in the engine room killed the third engineer and two firemen outright.[22] Among those who survived the attack were the mate who was from Penarth, the second mate from Newport (Pembs.), a fifteen-year-old mess room steward from Barry, the second engineer from Newport (Mon.), and an apprentice from Penarth. The presence of two gunners on the crew list suggests that the ship was defensively armed. The penultimate example considered here of a vessel attacked without warning, involved the Cardiff-owned Evan Thomas, Radcliffe *Patagonia*, 6011 GRT (1913), whose master, David Davies, aged forty-five, was from Neath. On the agreement covering the final voyage there were another nine Welsh crew listed, including four other members of the master's family: his wife, H. M. Davies, stewardess, aged thirty-seven; his daughter, Iris Beryl Davies, stewardess, aged seventeen; and both his sons, W. J. Davies, cadet, aged fourteen, and Howard Davies, cabin boy, aged twelve – all of them were from Cardiff and all on their first ship. The other Welsh crew members were: D. J. Evans, mate, from St Dogmaels; D. T. D. Jones, second mate, from Wern Mill Cardiganshire; G. Phillips, third mate from Cardigan; H. Edmunds, second engineer from Machen; W. B. Thomas, third engineer from Swansea; Ivor B. Harries, fourth engineer also from Swansea; R. J. Watkins, assistant purser from Cardiff; and Gwilym George, an apprentice who was from Abercastle, Pembrokeshire. On 15 September 1915, while in service as Russian naval transport and sailing Odessa for Nicolaieff in ballast, the *Patagonia* was torpedoed aft by SM UB-7 (Wilhelm Werner) and sank 10.5 miles north-east of Odessa – luckily, the entire crew survived.

The final account of a ship torpedoed without warning in 1915 considered here concerns that of the sinking on 30 December of the P&O steamer *Persia*, 7974 GRT (1900). The *Persia* was sailing London/Marseille for Bombay, with 317 crew (eighty-one European and 236 Asian) and 184 passengers on board when it was torpedoed by SM U-38 (Max Valentiner) off Cape Martello, Crete. The torpedo struck the port side forward, the boiler exploded, and the *Persia* foundered very quickly. Only four of the lifeboats were successfully launched. In total 334 lives were lost, among them the master and two stewardesses. Some of the victims drowned, as the ship's boats were sucked down by the sinking ship. The majority of the 167 survivors who made it into the boats were picked up on the second night after the sinking by a minesweeper, and the remainder (eleven who had clung to a broken lifeboat), were rescued by the SS *Ningchow* and then landed at Alexandria. One of the survivors was the ship's joiner, J. D. Thomas who was from South Wales. Valentiner would be put on the list of war criminals for this attack.

By 1915 the risks faced by the mercantile marine had increased dramatically. In 1913 some 110 British vessels had been lost through wreck and accident: in 1915, twice this number was lost to U-boats alone. There was a lull in attacks without warning in the waters around Britain from October 1915 when, in response to American protests over the sinking of passenger liners, the U-boat fleet instead concentrated its attention in the Mediterranean (where there were no American ships). In March 1916 such attacks resumed, though with some restrictions applied to the rules of engagement with regard to passenger ships and unarmed merchant vessels. In 1915 only 21 per cent of merchant ships attacked by U-boats were sunk without warning, increasing to 29 per cent for 1916.[23] The dangers faced by merchant seamen became much worse with the resumption of unrestricted submarine warfare in 1917, a year that saw the loss of 25 per cent of all inbound shipping (there were only six days where no British merchant ships were lost), and vessels that were sunk without warning reached 64 per cent of total losses.

Ultimately it was the introduction of convoys that would have the greatest impact on reducing merchant losses. The Royal Navy had started the use of convoys on the Harwich to Hook of Holland route in July 1916 to protect the vital neutral trade in foodstuffs with the Netherlands. It proved a resounding success with only seven vessels lost by the end of the war out of 1,861 sailings. In February 1917, at the request of the French Navy, convoys were introduced for colliers (at that time experiencing a high rate of losses) sailing for France. This was similarly successful with only fifty-three ships lost out of 39,352 sailings. Following the alarming rise in merchant losses after the re-introduction of unrestricted submarine warfare in February 1917, the first experimental convoy for merchant ships left Gibraltar on 10 May 1917. Two days later the first transatlantic convoy sailed, and from their inception until the end of hostilities, only around 150 ships were lost out of 16,539 sailings.[24]

The Bitter End: Convoys 1917–18

With the widespread use of convoys from mid-1917, the normal conduct and business practice for the majority of British mercantile shipping was altered fundamentally. By the end of 1917, 90 per cent of steamers in the main overseas trades sailed in convoys. Regardless of whether crew were signed on under normal commercial, T.124 or Mercantile Marine Reserve arrangements, they now proceeded largely in convoys of ships with similar speeds and destinations that were shepherded through the most dangerous waters of the major steam routes. The impact of convoys on shipping losses was dramatic. This very welcome news garnered widespread coverage in the press. In a syndicated 'War Supplement' carried in a number of Welsh newspapers in August 1918, an article about the valuable work performed by the Royal Navy in relation to convoy duties gave the following figures:

> Taking for the purposes of comparison British steam vessels of over 500 tons gross sailing to and from the United Kingdom in the main overseas trades, in the period from April to June, 1917 before the convoy system was established, 5.41% were sunk by enemy action. In August of the same year, when the system was beginning, the losses were nearly 4% but during September to November ... this figure had dropped to 2.11% of the total sailings. For the period March to June 1918 losses on the main overseas routes had fallen to 1.23% of sailings.[25]

Following the introduction of the convoy system, Milford Haven became one of the three ports of concentration for outward bound vessels from western ports and was used for the slower 7.5 knot convoys.[26] The level of activity at Milford Haven can be seen from the following summary of traffic there during the last week of July 1918: as well as an incoming convoy from Gibraltar, two outward convoys were escorted, one containing thirty-one ships, the other twenty-seven, in addition, smaller convoys of between four and seventeen colliers sailed daily for Rosslare, and there were also twenty-one individual escorts for vessels to destinations such as Holyhead or Barry.[27] Between August 1917 and the end of the war, 113 north Atlantic convoys sailed outward from Milford, comprising 2,646 ships; of these, only a dozen were lost to U-boats.[28]

In March 1918 selected journalists spent a week seeing first-hand the work of the convoy system and sailing on escort vessels. In the resulting three-part article, which appeared in the *Cambria Daily Leader*, some idea of the realities of being in convoy for merchant masters can be gleaned. Attending a captain's conference held before the sailing of a convoy of thirty vessels, it was reported that:

At this meeting, a naval captain set out the plan for the convoy on a blackboard with red and blue models of ships pinned to its surface, the colours signifying merchantmen or escorting craft. Speed, armament, destination, and other factors, were all taken into consideration in determining where this or that ship should take up station; speed, calculated on the capacity of the slowest ship in the convoy, was decided; distance between ships in line or column made known; the action to be taken under this or that circumstance laid down; and a host of other points.[29]

This article also repeated a number of points for the general enlightenment of captains who had not had the benefit of such a lecture. There were warnings against using wireless and other apparatus that would reveal the presence of a ship to a near-by U-boat; warnings against risking a ship, cargo and lives through the neglect of simple precautions such as keeping all possible bulkheads and doors closed, so that should the ship be struck by a torpedo the creation of virtual watertight compartments would improve the chances of making port. Another important caution was against making glaring lights at sea; noting that some cooks made 'a flare' in the dim early morning light while getting galley fires going and how careless seamen failing to close a porthole, could show a tell-tale light.

The official ships' logs for commissioned vessels engaged in convoy escort duty are terse, brief and to-the-point records of the day-to-day realities of convoy work and its vagaries. These records also show some of the common experiences of the merchant ships making up the convoy and their crews: the zigzagging, the regular drills and exercises, the gunnery practice, the deployment of paravanes to sweep for mines, the shepherding of laggards and dealing with vessels that for a variety of reasons might signal that they were 'not under control' and therefore unable to comply with convoy signals, the recording of ships leaving or joining the convoy and of ships sighted and signalled to. In port, they recorded the coaling and provisioning, cleaning, scrubbing, chipping and painting, and the comings and goings of officers and crew.

The memoir of Tom Coppack of the family firm of Coppack Brothers, Connah's Quay, who were engaged in the coastal trades, provides some rare and detailed insights into the experience of merchant seamen once the convoy system had been introduced. In 1916 Coppack had joined the Royal Naval Volunteer Reserve and trained as a signalman at Crystal Palace.

Following a short stint aboard a steam yacht with the Queenstown Patrol, in August 1917 he was attached to the armed merchant cruiser HMS *Moldavia*, 9500 GRT (1903), a P&O liner that had been requisitioned in 1915 by the Admiralty. When Coppack joined the ship's company, the *Moldavia* had just moved to new escort duties for convoys sailing on the central Atlantic West African routes. Coppack missed the *Moldavia*'s first convoy for reasons that are discussed below, but he was present for the second convoy that left Sierra Leone in mid-September 1917. This convoy consisted of around thirty ships, each capable of averaging about 10 knots, formed into seven columns of four ships each, the two with the heaviest armament covering the rear. The *Moldavia*'s third convoy out of Dakar consisted of thirty-nine ships. According to Coppack none of these had been in convoy before and their captains had no previous experience of station keeping, signalling or zigzagging. On this return leg, Coppack was assigned as signalman aboard a 5,000-ton steamer that, having first discharged a cargo of south Wales coal at Sierra Leone, had been moved up-river to load groundnuts for Lever Brothers at Liverpool.[30]

Of a later convoy from Gibraltar aboard a Greek steamer carrying iron ore from Huelva to Rouen, Coppack recalled that the voyage from Gibraltar to Cherbourg took thirteen days, during which time the ship was in and out of four convoys.[31] On joining the Queenstown patrol, Coppack had been instructed that other than the official log book, no crew member was allowed to keep any record of daily events, to do so would run the risk of heavy punishment at Naval Detention Quarters ashore. Despite knowing this, after joining the *Moldavia* in the summer of 1917 he attempted to inform his mother (in a coded letter) of the date of his return from Dakar. The letter did not pass the censor and Coppack was confined to barracks for one month without pay and with leave stopped.[32]

The protection afforded by convoys was not the sole preserve of steamers on the main arterial trade routes. Early in 1918 Hugh Shaw, the master of the schooner *Kate*, (70473) 68 tons net (1875), had loaded coal at Newport for Fecamp on the Normandy coast, but was instructed to proceed to Falmouth where he joined a convoy across the English Channel that was escorted as far as Cape Barfluer. The *Kate* then loaded flint at Fecamp for Cardiff and although ordered to proceed to Cayeux, Somme, to join a return convoy, Shaw instead took advantage of a good wind and risked crossing unescorted. He would later recall that a friend of his, the master of the schooner *Kindly Light* who was just a few miles ahead of the *Kate* on 2 February 1918, was attacked by a U-boat and sunk by gunfire.

The next freight was Cardiff for St Briuec in Brittany, and the *Kate* sailed first for Falmouth before joining a convoy of about twenty sailing coasters. The *Kate* later had a six-pound gun mounted at Swansea for defensive purposes. Continuing in the trades to France, Hugh Shaw and the crew of the *Kate* were at Paimpol in Brittany when the Armistice was signed.[33] The convoying of sailing vessels had a similar impact on losses through enemy action. In August 1918, *The Glamorgan Gazette* reported that between January to August 8,981 sailing vessels had been under escort around the western coast of France and of these only twenty-seven were torpedoed.[34]

It was not only cargo and crew that were conveyed on the fleet of the mercantile marine, as has been previously noted crews working West African routes were susceptible to tropical diseases. At the end of August 1918, on his first convoy aboard another of the escort vessels on the West Africa route, Tom Coppack contracted malaria. He recuperated on board ship and once recovered was assigned to duties on the *War Prince*, 4286 GRT (1917), out from Sierra Leone.[35] Of this convoy he recalled that about a dozen crew died aboard the armed merchant cruiser HMS *Hildebrand*, 6991 GRT (1911), from spotted fever (a tick-borne disease similar to typhus) and blackwater fever (a complication of malarial infection), and that there were also cases aboard the *War Prince* among the lascar firemen resulting in the ship being quarantined on arrival at London. While both these fevers were to be found at sea on the West Africa routes, the official logs for the *Hildebrand* record only three deaths in 1918. On 14 September a member of crew on one of the ships being convoyed, the Elder Dempster steamer *Prah*, 2520 GRT (1899), was recorded as having died from remittent fever and pneumonia and was buried at sea the following day. In October, two men died aboard the *Hildebrand*, one from diphtheria, the other from lobar pneumonia.

Tom Coppack was in his late seventies when he recounted his experiences as a convoy signalman, and more than fifty years had elapsed since the events he described. It is perhaps unsurprising then that some of his narrative does not exactly match with the accounts given in the official ships' logs. The episode of ship-board mortality that Coppack was recalling was not due to any tropical illnesses but a different infectious disease altogether, the 'Spanish flu', and the ship involved was the HMS *Mantua*, which was in service on the central Atlantic Convoys (principally Plymouth/Devonport to Sierra Leone/Dakar) from March 1917.

The origins of this global influenza pandemic cannot be ascertained with any certainty, though outbreaks assumed to be associated with the first wave were first recognised in US military camps in March 1918.[36] Other research suggests that the origins may lie in earlier outbreaks at the densely occupied infantry base depots at Étaples in northern France, where, by late December 1916, dozens of soldiers were reporting sick with aches, pains, coughs and shortage of breath. The mortality rate among the sick was as high as 40 per cent. At Aldershot Barracks in March 1917 similar symptoms and mortality rates were experienced.[37] Others have pointed to another probable vector; the recruitment and transportation of the men who formed the Chinese Labour Corps who were urgently needed to alleviate man-power shortages caused by casualties. The first men started arriving in France in mid-1917 and by the end of the year there were 57,000 Chinese working with the British Armed Forces in France and Belgium. This number would double by the time the Armistice was signed. Whatever the origin, it is clear that the global spread of the virus was greatly facilitated by mass movement of men by sea. An outbreak on the Grand Fleet at Scapa Flow, Orkney and Rosyth in the middle of April 1918 saw 10,000 men taken ill. The impact of this outbreak was made clear when in July 1918 First Sealord Admiral Sir Rosslyn Wemyss told Cabinet Secretary Sir Maurice Hankey 'the influenza is rife in the Navy ... many Destroyers have been unable to go to sea, so that the loss of several merchant ships is directly attributed to this issue'.[38]

Wartime censorship and reporting restrictions had largely kept the story in the background. Arriving in neutral Spain in May 1918, the absence of reporting restrictions in the press there gained the virus the sobriquet 'the Spanish flu'. The first reports of cases in Welsh newspapers started in June 1918. An article informing readers of the arrival in Swansea of the 'Spanish flu', noted its highly contagious nature and rapid onset, though it was not at that point considered widespread.[39] Two weeks later, *The Times* reported that there were hundreds of cases in the Monmouthshire collieries.[40] In the first wave between the end of June and the middle of August, there were thirty-one deaths at Cardiff and twenty at Swansea. The second wave between mid-October 1918 and mid-January 1919 claimed the lives of another 440 in Cardiff and a further 270 at Swansea.[41] By the time the pandemic was over, the official death toll for Wales was at least 8,750, but may have been as high as 11,400.

In late August 1918, 'epidemics of unprecedented violence' had erupted in three port cities thousands of miles apart: Freetown in Sierra Leone; Brest; and

Boston (Mass.).[42] In the case of the outbreak at Freetown, the most likely initial source was the arrival of the Armed Merchant Cruiser *Mantua*, 10885 GRT (1908), with the central Atlantic convoy in mid-August 1918. The flu had been raging at Plymouth as the convoy was preparing to sail, despite this on the day before departure there were no men on the sick list of the *Mantua*. On the day of departure, 1 August 1918, four men reported sick. By the time the convoy reached Freetown two weeks later, there were 124 men on the sick list out of a total complement of 364. The following day a Mercantile Marine Reserve rating died. By 19 August there were 170 men on the sick list; this was approaching half the crew.[43] Another nine men died before the ship left on the return leg of the convoy on 26 August; all ten men are buried in the King Tom Cemetery at Freetown. By this time the numbers in the sick bay had reduced to thirty men. Despite the ship being ordered into strict quarantine on its arrival at Freetown, the *Mantua* was coaled using local labour, and this was the most likely vector for the outbreak there. Two men died on the return voyage to Plymouth, one of them a Mercantile Marine Reserve steward; both were committed to the deep. In all twelve fatalities the cause of death was recorded as pneumonia. By the time the ship docked at Devonport on 10 September 1918 there were only five men on the sick list. Within three weeks of the outbreak 790 had died in Freetown, by October it was 1,000. There was a heavy mortality on ships in the harbour. On board the pre-Dreadnought battleship HMS *Africa* then attached to the Ninth Cruiser Squadron on Atlantic convoy duties but based mainly at Sierra Leone, on 9 September 1918 out of a complement of 777 officers and men, 476 were reported sick. Over the following three weeks fifty-two men died of influenza.[44]

Evidence for the impact of the pandemic on merchant crews is sparse, though it undoubtedly claimed the lives of many. Hugh C. Morris from Barmouth, whose death at Sierra Leone was reported in September 1918, was an officer aboard an Elder Dempster ship and was most likely a victim of the outbreak there.[45] In October 1918 the *Cambria Daily Leader* carried a brief notice concerning the death of a French sailor from the 'Spanish flu' at Swansea. In what amounts to a tacit acknowledgement of the links between the war, maritime transport and the flu pandemic, in December 1918 a report on the large and impressive funeral at Llanelli of a mercantile marine officer, aged twenty-four, W. J. Morgan, noted:

> Whilst acting as officer on a British liner on Atlantic voyages, rendered extremely strenuous by the ruthless German submarine

campaign, then at its height, he contracted an illness, to which he eventually succumbed, septic pneumonia intervening. Thus he may truly be regarded as another victim of the great European war.[46]

For most of the war, the majority of British merchant crews were largely defenceless against the threat of U-boat attacks. Admiralty instructions for dealing with the submarine threat looked fine on paper, but the individual circumstances of each attack made for difficult decisions on the part of ship's masters and crew. In May 1915 there were only around 150 defensively armed merchant ships, though this number increased over the course of the war, rising to 2,899 by February 1917. As has been seen, such vessels were much more likely to be torpedoed without warning, and throughout 1915 only 42 per cent of merchant vessels attacked in this way escaped.[47]

The eventual successful response to the threat of unrestricted submarine warfare in form of the convoy system, despite its late introduction, saved the lives of many merchant seamen. Although the convoy system would radically alter normative working patterns for many crews, it ultimately helped to ensure the failure of the U-boat campaign. Conversely, at the same time, convoys – both civilian and military – created a perfect vector for the deadly flu pandemic that swept the world in 1918. Modern estimates suggest that some 50 million people died worldwide as a result of the pandemic, a death toll higher than that of the war itself. The First World War accounted for 20 million dead on all sides, of which 10 million were civilians, most of whom died from war-related famine and disease.

Notes

1. They were the *Ikaria*, *Tokumaru* and *Oriole*, respectively.
2. *NWC*, 26 February 1915, p. 7.
3. F. J. Romero Salvadó, 'Spain and the First World War: The Logic of Neutrality', *War in History*, 26/1 (2019), 52.
4. Lyon, *Merchant Seafaring through World War 1*, p. 64.
5. *CDL*, 4 March 1915, p. 1.
6. *CDL*, 20 March 1915, p. 1.
7. *CDL*, 7 April 1915, p. 6.
8. *Herald of Wales and Monmouthshire Recorder*, 10 April 1915, p. 10.
9. See *www.theguardian.com/world/2014/may/01/lusitania-salvage-warning-munitions-1982* (last accessed 3 November 2024).
10. A full list of survivors and victims of this attack can be found at *http://www.rmslusitania.info/people/* (last accessed 3 November 2024).

11 *The New York Times*, 7 May 1916, p. 10.
12 See *www.rmslusitania.info/people/deck/john-davies/* (last accessed 3 November 2024).
13 A. R Jones was born in Liverpool but was living in Prestatyn and married to a local woman.
14 See *www.rmslusitania.info/people/deck/john-idwal-lewis/* (last accessed 3 November 2024).
15 See *www.rmslusitania.info/people/deck/william-williams/* (last accessed 3 November 2024).
16 *SWWP*, 15 May 1915, p. 6.
17 See *www.rmslusitania.info/related-ships/centurion/* (last accessed 3 November 2024).
18 Hurd, *The Merchant Navy*, vol. 2, p. 7.
19 Various positions for the loss were reported by Hurd and the newspapers, the position given here is provided by Wrecksite.
20 *CDL*, 17 June 1915, p. 3.
21 Hurd, *The Merchant Navy*, vol. 2, p. 7.
22 Hurd, *The Merchant Navy*, vol. 2, p. 187.
23 E. A. Gray, *The U-Boat War 1914–1918* (London, 1994), p. 176.
24 P. E. Fontenoy, 'Convoy System', in Spencer C. Tucker (ed.), *The Encyclopedia of World War I: A Political, Social and Military History*, vol. 1 (Santa Barbara CA, 2005), pp. 312–14.
25 *Brecon County Times Neath Gazette and General Advertiser*, war supplement, 24 August 1918, p. 2.
26 Fayle, *Seaborne Trade*, vol. 3, p. 141.
27 J. D. Davies, *Britannia's Dragon: A Naval History of Wales* (Stroud, 2013), pp. 204–5.
28 H. Newbolt, *Official History of the War: Naval Operations*, vol. 5, part 3, appendices (i) (Uckfield, 2001).
29 *CDL*, 26 March 1918, p. 2.
30 Coppack, *A Lifetime with Ships*, pp. 108–9.
31 Coppack, *A Lifetime with Ships*, p. 128.
32 Coppack, *A Lifetime with Ships*, p. 107.
33 Ayland (ed.), *Schooner Captain*, pp. 85–6.
34 *The Glamorgan Gazette*, 23 August 1918, p. 2.
35 Coppack, *A Lifetime with Ships*, p. 135.
36 Matthew Smallman-Raynor, Niall Johnson and Andrew D. Cliff, 'The Spatial Anatomy of an Epidemic: Influenza in London and the County Boroughs of England and Wales, 1918–1919', *Transactions of the Institute of British Geographers*, 27/4 (2002), 452–70, esp. p. 454.
37 J.S. Oxford et al., 'A Hypothesis: the conjunction of soldiers, gas, pigs, ducks, geese and horses in Northern France during the Great War provided the conditions for the emergence of the "Spanish" influenza pandemic of 1918–1919', *Vaccine* 23.7 (2005), pp. 940–5.
38 Arnold, C., *Pandemic 1918: The Story of the Deadliest Influenza in History* (2018), p. 59
39 *CDL*, 22 June 1918, p. 3.
40 Arnold, *Pandemic 1918*, p. 65.

41 Smallman-Raynor, Johnson and Cliff, 'The Spatial Anatomy of an Epidemic', 456, table 1.
42 D. Killingray, 'A New "Imperial Disease": The Influenza Pandemic of 1918–9 and its Impact on the British Empire', *Caribbean Quarterly*, 49/4 (December 2003), 30–49, esp. p. 33.
43 See *www.naval-history.net/OWShips-WW1-08-HMS_Mantua.htm* (last accessed 3 November 2024).
44 Festus Cole, 'Sierra Leone and World War One' (unpublished PhD thesis, SOAS, 1994), p. 235.
45 *Cambrian News*, 27 September 1918, p. 1.
46 *SWWP*, 7 December 1918, p. 2.
47 V. E. Tarrant, *The U-Boat Offensive 1914–1945* (New York, 1989), p. 22.

8 Courage, Compensation and Commemoration 1916–18

Figure 10: *Llandovery Castle* Victory Bond poster, Library of Congress

While this study has largely considered the first seventeen months of the war, throughout the remainder of the conflict many of those working at sea would endure comparable experiences under similar circumstances to those that have already been discussed. At the end of 1915, developments that would change the way the mercantile marine operated, such as the creation of the Ministry of Shipping, the Mercantile Marine Reserve, the National Maritime Board, and the introduction of convoys, were still in the future. Much more work could be done on the experiences of those merchant mariners who served in the Royal Naval Reserve, the Royal Naval Volunteer Reserve and the Mercantile Marine Reserve, but this falls outside the purview of this examination. What follows considers some of the more germane aspects of the experiences of merchant mariners from Wales for the remainder of the war.

Manning issues began immediately at the outbreak of war. Within forty-eight hours some 8,000 officers and men from the mercantile marine volunteered, with most serving in the Royal Naval Reserve.[1] By the end of the war, according to the Ministry of Reconstruction's pamphlet 'Naval Demobilisation' published in December 1918, the Navy employed 80,000 officers and men from the merchant service, including 20,000 Royal Naval Reserve ratings, 36,000 trawler reserve, and 20,000 merchant seamen and firemen on transport agreements.[2] Manning problems, which arose as a consequence of the war, were overcome through the largely harmonious co-operation between the unions and the Shipping Federation both prior to and following the creation of the Ministry of Shipping, the Mercantile Marine Reserve and the National Maritime Board.[3] The need to keep men going to sea greatly strengthened the collective bargaining power of seafarers, and in 1917 when Welsh seamen called for pay to be continued until surviving crew members were back in the United Kingdom, there was an almost immediate response with the government announcing in August that crew would receive a month's pay or full wages until their return to a British port, whichever was the greater.[4] One example of the extent of the search for additional manpower during the war can be seen in the recruitment of scouts for service at sea. In February 1917, a piece in the *Cambria Daily Leader* reported that:

> the managers of the White Star, Dominion and American Lines, have now decided to start a scheme in their larger passenger vessels by which the supply of boys from training ships and training homes will be supplemented by members of the Scouts' Associations in Liverpool, London and Southampton, enrolled as Sea Scouts. These Associations will be invited to recommend boys from 13 to 15 years of age, of certified fitness good character, and smart appearance, who are desirous of going to sea, and from these the marine superintendent will select two bridge boys per steamer, whose duties will consist of assistance in signalling, attending telephones, running messages, and generally helping the quartermaster.[5]

In fact, some sea scouts from Swansea were already serving in this capacity at the beginning of 1915. Joining the Charente Shipping Company's *Patrician*, 7470 GRT (1901), at Belfast on 31 January 1915 were A. Prosser, A. S. J. Green and B. O'Connell, all in their late teens, on their first ship and all from the Mount Pleasant area of Swansea. The *Patrician* (also known as HMS *No. 13*) was one of fourteen vessels that had been hired for use as dummy battleships (sometimes referred to as the special service squadron) with the necessary conversion work carried out at the Harland and Wolff yard. Disguised as HMS *Invincible*, the *Patrician* was stationed in the Aegean until June 1915. When the Dummy Battleship Squadron was disbanded later that year, the Admiralty purchased and converted the *Patrician* into a tanker. Renamed *Tarakol* (then *Vineleaf* in 1917), the ship served as a Royal Fleet Auxiliary oiler for the rest of the war. In September 1915, Prosser, Green and O'Donnell were back at Belfast where they transferred to the *Princess* (also known as HMS *No. 9*), formerly the *Kronprinzessin Cecilie* 8688 GRT (1905), a German liner requisitioned at the outbreak of the war and also used as a dummy battleship. The *Princess* patrolled from the naval station at Aultbea, Loch Ewe, until October when the decision was taken to convert the ship into an armed merchant cruiser. Among the crew of the *Patrician* were two Welshmen, a mate from Cardiff and a quartermaster from Holyhead.

Another two sea scouts from Swansea, also in Belfast in February 1915, B. Reynish and A. Lloyd, were signing on their first ship, the Canadian Pacific's *Montezuma*, 8360 GRT (1899), also known as HMS *No. 3* and disguised to look like HMS *Iron Duke*. In June both scouts were transferred to the *Princess* at Loch Ewe. From July to September 1915, they were on the *Manipur*, 7654 GRT (1906), also known as HMS *No. 11*, which was then converted into a repair ship, the *Sandhurst*. The crews of these various vessels (though not the scouts) were all signed onto T.124 agreements for commissioned ships.

T.124s changed the world of work for merchant seamen, as under such terms they were signed on for the duration of the war and, like those who worked in the ferry companies, were subject to transfer to other vessels as required. An upside of being subject to naval discipline for some crew was the provision from 1914 of pensions, grants and allowances for officers, ratings and dependants of those injured or disabled while serving aboard auxiliaries.[6] These provisions did not apply to those entitled to Workman's Compensation Act (1906), which provided for manual labourers earning under £250 per annum. Not all men who found themselves on T.124

agreements took well to serving under naval discipline. To a certain extent this can be seen in the rate of desertion from Royal Fleet Auxiliary vessels. Over the course of the war, the Royal Fleet Auxiliary had greatly expanded the size of its fleet: in 1914 there were only thirteen vessels in service, by 1918 there were more than 160, mostly tankers of one sort or another.[7] Between 1916 and 1919, some 130 men deserted. Two oil tankers – the *Fortol*, 2629 GRT (1917), and the *Petroleum*, 4686 GRT (1903) – had the worst record, with twenty men deserting from each.[8] When launched the *Petroleum* was largest oil tanker in the world but lacked a buyer until purchased in 1905 by the Admiralty. This was their first oil-fired vessel, but it was found too dangerous to operate as such and was converted to coal-fired boilers. In July 1915 the crew list for the *Petroleum* shows the majority of men, including the second engineer who was from Cardiff, being signed onto T.124 agreements at Scapa Flow. Only two men deserted from this tanker between 1915 and the end of the war, with most of the desertions occurring in 1919, which was possibly indicative of impatience while awaiting demobilisation, whereas the *Fortol* saw fifteen men desert between late August 1917 and the end of hostilities.

Press censorship, brought in with the Defence of the Realm Act 1914, was mainly directed towards avoiding news that might have military or naval value for the enemy, and for keeping in check the opinions of the pacifist and socialist presses. The effectiveness of the activities of the Press Bureau lessened away from the capital with one 'D Notice' (a government notice sent to newspapers or other publications requesting them to withhold information for reasons of state security) from September 1915, complaining that 'some papers ... especially those published in places remote from London, seldom submit matter to the Bureau'.[9] Merchant shipping information, however, continued to be published as normal and it was not until 1917 that the movements and casualties section was dropped from *Lloyd's List*. For the remainder of the war this information was printed separately for restricted circulation only. The German propaganda film *Der Magische Gürtel* ('The Enchanted Circle') (1917) shows the commander of SM U-35 crossing off his latest victim in a copy of *Lloyd's Register* (also shown is the sinking of the Porthmadog schooner *Miss Morris*, 156 GRT, sunk in full sail in April while sailing Genoa for Malaga in ballast). Later in the war newspaper reporting of merchant losses became somewhat more circumspect, ships' names and other details might be omitted from reports. For example, when third engineer Idris Percy Thomas of Porthmadog died as a result of the torpedoing of the defensively armed *Wirral*, 4207 GRT (1911), off Norway in May 1917 bound for Archangel with munitions, the *Cambrian News* reported only that he had been 'on board a steamer which was mined or torpedoed'.[10] Sometimes reporting was reduced to aggregate losses only, which served to depersonalise the news. It was probably for the best: little of such news was uplifting and the regularity and increasing frequency of such losses could be seen as demoralising and worked counter to the patriotism engendered by reports of plucky merchant sailors beset by the unspeakable foe.

As the war progressed there were increasing numbers of defensively armed merchant ships. With this came the need for gunnery training courses for merchant officers and seamen, some of which were undertaken at Cardiff. The outcomes of encounters between defensively armed vessels and U-boats from 1 January 1916 to the 31 January 1917 show that roughly two out of three escaped, whereas for unarmed vessels it was around one in five. However, defensively armed vessels were twice as likely to be torpedoed without warning.[11]

Throughout the war merchant crews continued to be captured by both surface raiders and U-boats. The German propaganda film *Graf Dohna und seine Möwe* released in 1917, contains footage of the capture and sinking of a number of British merchant ships by the SMS *Möwe* in December 1916. Among the captured ships' crews were: Emlyn Jones, a seaman from Trecastle who was aboard the *Voltaire*, 8618 GRT (1907); from the crew of the *King George*, 3852 GRT (1906), were Hugh Davies, a bosun from Aberdovey, and Dominico Gatt, a ship's cook, John Magio, an assistant cook, and James Richardson, a fireman/trimmer, all from Cardiff, Gwilym Heke, a fourth engineer from Pontyclun, James Patterson, a first engineer, George Sawle, a donkeyman, and J. Zasologny, a sailor, all from Barry; from the *Cambrian Range*, 4234 GRT (1906), were Archibald Davies, a fourteen-year-old apprentice from Swansea, and T. G. Jones, a third engineer from Caernarfon; on the *Georgic*, 10077 GRT (1895), whose cargo when scuttled included 1,200 horses, were E. E. Hughes, a refrigeration greaser from Bagillt, and J. J. Peters, a mate from New Quay (Cards.); and from the *Yarrowdale*, 4652 GRT (1912), were George Haines, a seaman from Fishguard, and L. Laverick, a second cook from Cardiff.

Following the capture of the *Yarrowdale* (which it was decided was too valuable to sink) on the 12 December 1916, all the captured crews, some 400 men, were put aboard and sent into the Baltic seaport of Swinemünde, present day Świnoujście, Poland. The majority of these men were then interned at Brandenburg, though others were detained in camps at Schweidnitz, Furtenberg and Wahmbeck Post Bodenfelde. Also among the crew of the *King George* were two Norwegian sailors, resident in Barry, who gave an account of their experiences following their capture. Having been kept in the holds while on the *Yarrowdale*, from Swinemünde they had been taken to a camp at Neustrelitz, where after twenty-five days they were released (they were neutrals) and having been sent across the Danish border returned to Hull via Norway three weeks later.[12]

In January 1919, the *South Wales Weekly Post* ran a story about the experiences of Swansea sailor O. Evans of Cwmbwrla, who was held prisoner on a U-boat for twenty-five days. Repatriated and back in Swansea, Evans had called in at the paper's office to thank the *Post* and its subscribers for his six months' supply of parcels. The paper had been running a parcel scheme for prisoners of war since 1915. Evans had been captured from the defensively armed *Medora*, 5135 GRT (1912), which was torpedoed without warning and sunk by SM U-86 in the Irish Sea, 10 miles south-west of Mull of Galloway on 2 May 1918. Evans, who was the ship's gunner, was taken prisoner along with his skipper and the radio operator. As recounted by Evans:

> The submarine had many narrow escapes, and once a British destroyer almost sank her and she had to dive head first. Off Milford Haven they opened fire on a sailing ship which returned the fire at close range, and one shot struck the submarine but glanced off, and the submarine dived. He and the skipper were on board the submarine for 25 days and returned through the Kiel Canal to Emden. He was treated better on the submarine than after getting to Germany.[13]

How Evans can have been sure about such events or indeed of the position of the U-boat prior its arrival at Emden is unclear. What is certain, while Evans was aboard, the SM U-86 sank another six vessels; four British and two from Norway. Among these were: the *Tommi*, a steel schooner of 138 net tons (1900), which was shelled and sunk on 5 May 1918 in the Irish Sea between Calf of Man and Chicken Rock, all hands were lost, with three of the four-man crew from Wales (the master and the cook were from Amlwch, Anglesey, and the mate was from Criccieth); the defensively armed *Leeds City*, (1908) 4298 GRT, Reardon Smith-owned and registered at Cardiff, which was torpedoed on 6 May off Skulmartin light vessel,

Ballywater County Down, the crew were saved; and the *Inniscarra*, 1412 GRT (1903), of the Cork Steam Packet Company, torpedoed without warning on 12 May 1918 off the coast of County Cork with loss of twenty-eight of the thirty-three crew. Among those lost were the second mate from New Quay (Cards.), the second engineer from Neyland, and a Royal Naval Volunteer Reserve seaman from Llanrhidian. The U-boat commander was Helmut Patzig who would later sink the *Llandovery Castle* hospital ship.

One in four inbound ships were being lost in 1917 and readers of the Welsh papers were confronted with a succession of harrowing survivor accounts. With only a small fraction of crew being taken prisoner following U-boat attacks, survival depended largely on making it into one of the lifeboats, though this did not always result in successful outcomes. On 27 January 1917, the defensively armed Admiralty chartered collier *Artist*, 3570 GRT (1909), was torpedoed without warning and sunk 58 miles west of the Smalls with the loss of thirty-six, lives including the two-man Royal Naval Volunteer Reserve gun crew. Of three lifeboats launched, one was damaged against the side of the ship and later seen in trouble, mountainous seas preventing any assistance being rendered. The other two boats got clear, but ultimately only one made it to safety. One of the survivors, eighteen-year-old cadet Robert D. Owen of Morfa Nefyn, gave the following account to the *Cambrian News*:

> Sixteen got into this lifeboat, and of these nine were firemen, and of the rest there was only one A.B., he being Christmas Edwards of Pwllheli. After rowing for about an hour in that terrible sea and our strength giving way, we saw that the only option we had was to drop our sea anchor and to drift about on this until assistance came, as we were all anxiously waiting to see if anyone had received our S.O.S. signal which we had sent out immediately we were torpedoed. Still keeping in sight of the master's boat, we drifted along and at the same time suffering most terribly from the cold and severe wind, and also wet through, all the firemen having on nothing more than thin dungaree suits, and the only cover possible for us was the sail which we had in the boat. By night time three of our crew had died from the terrible exposure, and as our rations were not very high our 'whack' was rather meagre, it being three biscuits and a little water a day. Sunday morning dawned with no better prospects as regards weather. Tremendous seas were still

running and it was blowing a gale, and our little boat was continually filled up, with the waves breaking on top of us, and everyone that was able had to take a turn in bailing out the water. Sunday passed, the most terrible Sunday we had, as yet ever experienced. Our friends dying around us, one by one, no one knowing whose turn it would be next, by now six had died, and we were obliged to bury them at sea. Night then came, and this again passed with no sign of refuge from anywhere. Monday morning dawned with no better results with the weather, the wind still blowing too hard to put the sail up. Monday, again passed with nothing coming into sight, and each one of us by now was hardly able to move, being numbed with the cold and suffering terribly for want of warm food. Monday night came and during the night, to our great joy, a light was sighted which we made out to be a shore light. I took a bearing with a compass which we had, and after consulting with Edwards we both decided to put the sail up at the dawn of day, weather permitting. Dawn came and adding to our great joy the wind and sea had abated a good deal, so we started our fourth day in an open boat. After a great struggle, our strength nearly exhausted, we managed to put the mast and sail up and, running before the wind and sea, we started our voyage, destination unknown but for the fact that we were making for land somewhere ... An hour later another of our friends died. He was Mr Spencer Jehu of Pwllheli. Early in our trouble he had been humane and kind enough to take off one of his jerseys and hand it over to one of the firemen who was suffering terribly at the time, and that fireman lives today to tell of his kindness. About 9-30 a.m. on Tuesday we sighted smoke on the horizon ... This was a Glasgow steamer. At 2-30 p.m. we were transferred and landed safely ... On landing five had to be taken into hospital and four into lodgings. We were all suffering terribly from frost bites and the effects of the exposure but being well looked after we gradually came on.[14]

Of a crew of forty-five only nine had survived. Spencer Ellis Jehu, who died in the lifeboat was a sixteen-year-old seaman. Among those who were missing were J. O. Jones, a fifteen-year-old deck-boy (on his second voyage) who was also from Pwllheli, and G. Jones, aged thirty-four, leading seaman, Royal Naval Volunteer Reserve from Pontardawe.

In April 1917 there was an account in the *Barry Dock News* of the 'terrible privation and hardship' that overtook Gilbert Williams, aged eighteen, a steward from Barry. Williams had been aboard the collier *Newstead*, 2836 GRT (1894), sailing Barry for Naples when torpedoed by SM U-49 off the northern coast of Ireland early in March. Having taken to the boats with the rest of the crew, along with fourteen others:

> he was tossed about in the open seas for more than a week before being picked up. The only food they had was a few biscuits, and five men died from exposure and starvation. The remainder are all suffering from frost-bite. Williams is now in hospital in Liverpool, where both feet have been amputated, and the donkeyman, who is a Norwegian and lodged at Barry has had both legs off.[15]

Fifteen of the crew lost their lives, Williams was released from hospital in July. In May 1917 the same paper carried an account of the death of Arthur Hughes, aged eighteen, an engineer's steward from Cadoxton. He had been aboard the *Kariba*, 3697 GRT (1904), inbound from Java and Dakar to Falmouth with a cargo of sugar, which was sunk by SM UC-27 (Gerhard Schulz), 260 miles west-north-west from Ushant on 13 April 1917. Hughes had made it into one of the two lifeboats following the torpedoing of the ship, though these became separated in the night. While one boat was picked up the next day, the boat containing Hughes and twenty others was adrift for ten days, during which time ten men, including Hughes, succumbed to exhaustion and exposure. The survivors were picked up by a French trawler.[16] In all, thirteen men were lost, among them were two other Welsh crew members – T. A. Powell, aged twenty-eight, a fourth engineer from Penarth; and able seaman T. E. Varney, aged twenty-four, from Newport (Pembs).

One of the most harrowing tales from the latter part of the war concerned the fate of the steamer *Mariston*, 2908 GRT (1915), in July 1917. Defensively armed and sailing Almeria to Glasgow with a cargo of copper ore, the *Mariston* was torpedoed without warning 82 miles west of Fastnet by SM U-45. Torpedoed twice, the *Mariston* sank quickly, ten men went down with the ship and the remaining nineteen men made it into the water. The U-boat commander, Erich Sittenfeld, who surfaced to survey his work, witnessed the beginning of a shark attack on the survivors, but offered no assistance and left the scene of carnage that was unfolding. The ship's cook, who would be the sole survivor, later recounted that while clinging to a makeshift raft he saw a school of sharks among them and then heard man after man screaming as they were dragged under. He was picked up by a British merchant ship fifteen hours later.[17] Among those lost were two men from Wales – William Eakon, aged fifty-two, the ship's carpenter, who was the husband of Ellen Eakon (née Saunders), of Cadoxton, Barry (he had been born in Stettin); and George Owens, aged thirty, deck hand, Royal Naval Reserve (who was one of the two-man gun crew), the son of Elizabeth Owens and Evan Owens of Cardigan.[18]

Overall, the majority of men who made it into the lifeboats were ultimately picked up and landed ashore. For some, being at sea in an open boat following the sinking of their ship was a recurring experience. One such case was that of Alfred White from Cadoxton. On his first voyage as assistant steward, aged fifteen, he had been on the steamer *Crown of Castile*, 4505 GRT (1905), sailing St John's, New Brunswick for Le Havre with hay and oats when it was captured and scuttled by SM U-28 off the Scilly Isles in March 1915. The ship's company, having been allowed time to take to the boats, were picked up a few hours later by a French steamer and landed at Barry. In 1917, White was torpedoed twice in the space of ten weeks. In June, White had been aboard the defensively armed steamer *Birdoswald*, 4013 GRT (1892), sailing Livorno to Cartagena with hemp when torpedoed without warning by SM U-63. The entire crew made it into the boats, though the master and the chief engineer were taken prisoner. The remaining crew were later picked up by a Spanish brig and landed at Tarragona. On 1 October, White was torpedoed again. On this occasion he was an assistant cook on the defensively armed *Normanton*, 3862 GRT (1912), which was torpedoed by SM U-39 without warning 180 miles north-west of Gibraltar while sailing Barry for Savona in ballast. All the crew made it safely into the boats and were picked up thirty-six hours later by a British steamer and landed in Gibraltar. In all three cases no lives were lost.[19]

In August 1917 a decision was taken that compensation would be granted by the Board of Trade to masters, officers and seamen losing their effects through war risks on British merchant and fishing vessels. This compensation was also extended to the widows of merchant seamen whose ships were sunk by mine or torpedo.[20] However the amount paid was a matter of dispute, and a year later at a mass meeting of Barry seamen, presided over by Mr James Marston, the local secretary of the National Sailors and Firemen's Union, a resolution was unanimously passed calling on the Board of Trade to:

substantially increase the amount paid to torpedoed seamen for clothes lost, the sum of £7. 10s being totally inadequate to provide a seaman with an outfit, due to the present high cost of material, and in the opinion of the meeting £30 would not be too much for the purpose of renewing a seaman's bag.[21]

For those who survived attacks, aid could be forthcoming from a number of sources in addition to the work that was done by the seamen's missions. One such source was the Shipwrecked Mariners' Society, founded in 1839 with the primary objects of caring for shipwrecked persons and assisting the dependants of men lost at sea. According to their president, the first Baron Leith of Fyvie, during 1917, the Society had afforded help 'to no less than 23,720 shipwrecked persons landed on our coasts, and assisted 920 widows, 1,947 orphans and 458 other dependent relatives of men drowned or killed at sea, to date'.[22] The final tally for assistance provided by the Society 1914–18 amounted to £126,836 expended on helping 50,917 sailors and fishermen, 2,656 widows, 4,724 orphans, and 1,121 aged parents.[23] Another source of support was the British and Foreign Sailors' Society, an international Christian charity started in 1818 as the Port of London Society. In 1917 the *Aberdare Leader* reported that during the past year the British and Foreign Sailors' Society had given assistance to 22,997 men from torpedoed vessels, provided 90,741 meals, 62,331 articles of clothing, 3,046 railway warrants, and had expended £20,892 for prisoners of war.[24] A few months later at a meeting of the Ladies Committee of the Swansea branch of the British and Foreign Sailors' Society, it was stated that during the course of 1917 the society had fed, clothed and succoured more than 800 torpedoed and shipwrecked crews, and had sent parcels of food and other necessaries every fortnight to more than 1,000 friendless prisoners of war in Germany. It was also noted that the Swansea Branch had done excellent service, particularly in the work that they did in January 1918 feeding, clothing and succouring 400 survivors of the torpedoed hospital ship HMHS *Rewa*.[25]

The HMHS *Rewa*, 7308 GRT (1906), which had been carrying wounded men from Malta, was torpedoed without warning by SM U-55 on 4 January 1918 off Hartland Point on the Devon coast. Four men died: two firemen, a trimmer and a panniwallah (water carrier), all lascars of the Indian Merchant Service. The remainder of the crew, patients and passengers, having made it into the lifeboats were picked up a few hours later by a steamer and three trawlers out of Swansea. The steamer, the *Paul Paix*, 4196 GRT (1908), having taken on board 121 of the survivors, including twenty wounded, subsequently struck a mine. Despite being damaged, skilful handling brought the steamer safely into Swansea. The *Western Daily Press* described the 'piteous' sight as survivors came ashore, 'a procession of maimed and limping men, some on the backs of others and all without boots, wended its way under willing hands of helpers to the Coal Exchange ... all business being suspended, while others were taken to leading hotels'.[26] At a presentation held at the Swansea Chamber of Commerce in May 1918, the master of the *Paul Paix*, Captain G. Legge of Harbour View, St Thomas, received a gold watch from the ship's owners in recognition of his services. In addition, there was the sum of £25 to be distributed by him at his discretion to the crew.[27]

Milford Haven, by dint of its location, played a prominent part in the reception of the victims of attacks on shipping emanating from or bound to ports such as Liverpool, Cardiff, Barry and Avonmouth. A map published in Germany in 1918 by the cartography firm Carl Flemming AG shows the locations of all successful U-boats attacks on shipping for the period 1 February 1917 to 1 February 1918.[28] This period covers the height of the campaign, and clear concentrations of attacks can be seen. These patterns, though amplified by the resumption of unrestricted submarine warfare in 1917, had remained largely unaltered throughout the course of the war. The majority of losses occurred in the English Channel and its approaches, and also along the northern coast of France. Other concentrations can be seen focusing on the North Sea coal ports and to a lesser extent in the Bristol Channel. There was a large concentration of attacks that occurred in the Western Approaches extending all along the southern coast of Ireland and reaching into St George's Channel and the Irish Sea.

Among the crews who found themselves brought safe into Milford Haven were fishermen, deep-sea sailors, Scandinavians, Chinese and lascar crew, and West African firemen and trimmers. Between 1914 and 1918, a total of 33,864 men stayed at the John Cory Bethel and Sailor's Rest, and 164,700 had visited there. Among this number were 3,895 men from the 148 ships that had been attacked or sunk and whose crews were brought to Milford Haven. The Bethel's sick bay treated 537 men, and the value of meals, beds and clothing that had been provided free amounted to £3,183 13s. 4d. In addition, 32,436 letters were received and posted, thousands of bibles, books and magazines distributed, and 7,560 visits made to vessels in Milford docks.[29]

Other than the charitable aid provided by the Shipwrecked Mariners' Society and British and Foreign Sailors' Society, the compensation due to the families and dependents was mediated through the courts. At Pwllheli County Court in December 1917, a number of claims were dealt with. The *Cambrian News* carried a full report on the proceedings:

> Mr. Hugh Pritchard, who appeared for several dependants of deceased sailors whose vessels have been torpedoed, mentioned, that those cases were now unfortunately frequent and intimated that it might be well to obtain a general indication of the Judge's view in regard to the disposal of money paid into court in the case of widows and sole dependants. His Honour said he considered the money should be made to last as long as possible and thought he could not do better than direct its investment in war loan, the interest on which is far in excess of bank interest.
>
> Mr. Hugh Pritchard: That is so, but unfortunately the moment you suggest war loan to these unfortunate people they seem to think it an indirect way of commandeering their money for the Government. There is undoubtedly, an impression in their minds that the court and lawyers are out to draw in as much money as possible for the Government and that they might never see their money again.
>
> The Judge: That arises from their ignorance and they must be taught differently. They should realise that if the war loan fails everything fails. For my own part every penny I can spare goes into the war loan.[30]

The 1917 War Loan offered a rate of 5 per cent and raised around £2 billion (though only 41 per cent of this was new money), as an incentive to invest there was a 5 per cent discount on face value.[31] It was later converted to 3.5 per cent stock in 1932 but not finally redeemed until 2015.

The awards made in the other cases demonstrate a range of judicial responses to individual circumstances. In one case, a young widow who persisted in having the whole sum (which amounted to £300) paid out to her, was asked by the judge what she would do with the money, to which she replied, 'I will invest it, but I would rather do so myself rather than through the court'. In response the judge countered, 'What difference does it make? In any case you will not see the actual money as it is all paper in these days. The time when people gloated over their money by pouring it out of a bag and back again has gone by'. The judge was here referring to the fact that full convertibility (into gold) had been suspended at the start of the war. In another case, Laura Mary Jones applied for payment of the £300 due in respect of her grandson, Robert W. Jones of Nefyn, who fell victim to an enemy submarine. Robert, whose wife had predeceased him, left one daughter in the care of his grandmother. The judge ordered the investment of the money with the interest to be paid for the maintenance of the girl. In most cases a portion of the money was paid, with the investment of the balance in war loan. In the claim of Mrs Pritchard, of New Street, Pwllheli, whose husband was drowned after twelve months of married life, £150 was paid out and £150 invested. In the case of Mrs Griffiths, of Minydon, Nefyn, whose husband was drowned, the sum of £50 was paid out and the remaining £250 was invested in war loan. The same amount was paid in respect of the late Griffith Jones of Ty Canol, Aberdaron, to his mother, who was his sole dependant. In the foregoing cases, the award was at the upper limit set by the Workmen's Compensation Act 1906 for those *wholly* dependent on the earnings of the deceased. For claimants who were not wholly dependent on the earnings of the deceased, lesser amounts were awarded.

At Barry County Court in June 1918, a number of compensation cases were heard, dealing variously with a claim for an injury sustained on an Admiralty collier, and three cases where the claimants were not wholly dependent on the earnings of the deceased. The claim for injury shows how even a relatively minor accident could prevent a man from returning to sea. The applicant, D. Ross, had lost the third finger on his right hand in an accident aboard the *Polgowan* while in a French port. Ross told the court that he had tried to go to back to sea, but ships refused to take him on account of his hand, and he had not found much alternative employment subsequently. Following the opinion of a medical board, the judge made an award of 15s. per week.[32] The *Polgowan*, formerly the German-owned *Macedonia*, 4347 GRT (1900), had been seized off Las Palmas by HMS *Gloucester* in 1915 and used thereafter by the Admiralty in various roles.

Three other claims were heard. In the case of the death of seaman Ivor Curtis, aged seventeen and from Barry Docks, an order for £100 was made to his parents. It was noted that the respondents (the owners of the steamship *Heatherside*) had paid £75 into the court, but this was deemed insufficient. Curtis had been a scout when the war broke out; he had volunteered immediately and became a signaller on a HM transport.[33] On

24 August 1917 the Admiralty chartered *Heatherside*, 2767 GRT (1909), had been sailing Newport for Malta with coal when torpedoed and sunk by SM U-93 north-west of Cape Ortegal; in all, twenty-seven lives were lost, including two Newport men, the second mate and the carpenter. In the case of Percy John, a twenty-year-old sailor, an order for £125 was made to his parents, the court noting that the deceased man held a gunnery certificate and consequently got higher wages. John had been aboard the defensively armed *Romford*, 3035 GRT (1898), carrying a cargo of phosphates, which hit a mine laid by SM UC-67 2 miles east of Cape Carthage on 10 February 1918; twenty-eight lives were lost, with nine members of the crew commemorated on the Barry Merchant Navy Memorial. In the third case of the day, Florence Kate Smith was awarded £75 for the loss of her son, though neither his name nor the name of his ship was reported.[34]

It has been argued that although long-standing problems remained with regard to manning, security of employment and the unlimited hours of work, by 1918 the lot of British merchant seamen had improved considerably with higher fixed wages, improved living and working conditions, proper representation in disputes with employers and a much-improved safety record. Just thirteen years earlier there had been no standard wages, no statutory scale for provisions, no proper system of compensation for disability or for loss of effects by war action, and no pension or sick-care payments.[35] While this was undoubtedly the case, working conditions, nonetheless, could still be far from optimal. In September 1919 at a meeting of the Swansea Port Sanitary Authority, a number of the issues raised give some insight into conditions for seamen in the immediate post-war period. It was reported that during the past quarter 2,070 vessels had been inspected, and 1,003 defects and nuisances dealt with. Captain W. M. Davies, the chief port sanitary inspector, described the condition of some ships' forecastles as 'dirty and leaky' and said that in some cases of defective quarters, the conditions were as bad as they had been thirty years ago.[36] Though legislation in 1906 had increased the space allowed for crew, it was still behind that of other European merchant fleets, and could not in any case be applied retrospectively to the shipping then in use. The standard ships that were built to conform to the new rules for crew space that were ordered by the government in 1916 did not start to come into commission until mid-1917, with by far the greater number not putting to sea before the end of the war. It was not only conditions on board that were poor and at Swansea the immediate dock environment was also a cause for concern. At the same meeting attention was drawn to the prevalence of organic refuse about the docks thrown overboard from ships, which was a nuisance to people working at the dockside. Comments were also made about the unsatisfactory manner in which ships' provisions were delivered by the retailers, with the condition of the food sometimes disgraceful, meat being received almost black with coal dust.[37] Earlier that year, at Barry, the port sanitary inspector reported that of 309 ships inspected, forty-three were found to be dirty, with fifty-three beds having been destroyed.[38]

With the cessation of hostilities, merchant seamen were not materially much better off than at the outset, despite the recognition of their vital service. In 1917, Labour delegates Ramsay MacDonald and F. W. Jowett were prevented from sailing to the Petrograd peace negotiations from Aberdeen by the National Sailors' and Firemen's Union who threatened to call the crew out on strike. The issue was their refusal to give an undertaking to insist on restitution for the relatives of merchant seamen who had lost their lives as a result of U-boat attacks.[39] Ultimately, there would be no justice, not even for the victims of the worst atrocities committed at sea. Of the eighteen U-boat commanders listed as war criminals, not one was punished or convicted.[40] Any gains made with regard to wages were largely swallowed up ashore by the increase in prices for basic foodstuffs. By late 1917 the impact of the U-boat campaign could be seen in the queues for sugar and shortages of butter and bacon on high streets across the land. Voluntary recommendations from the Food Controller for curtailing consumption quickly turned into compulsory cards and coupons, starting with sugar in January 1918. Food prices had roughly doubled since the outbreak of the war and the immediate post-war period saw rationing and shortages, industrial unrest and ugly race riots in Welsh ports, and trawler-men on strike against new contracts.

Over the course of the war, 2,479 merchant ships had been lost to the enemy. Many of these ships' crews showed conspicuous bravery in defending their ships and were highly proficient in the difficult and often perilous task of getting away the boats. As we have seen, making it into the boats was sometimes the beginning of a much longer ordeal. One author has reasoned of the wartime experience of merchant mariners that 'if the slaughter at sea was less than that on the Western Front, it was a sacrifice better made for the nation's survival'. It is hard to better an assessment of the merchant seaman's character at this time that claims that 'what emerges is the indomitable spirit of the majority', among the officers and men who, doing their duty almost without exception and despite the quality of ratings varying greatly, continued to sign on and man ships.[41]

In September 1917, the *Abergavenny Chronicle* reported that the award of Silver War Badges was to be extended to the officers and seamen of merchant ships who, by reason of wounds received through enemy action, or by reason of illness attributable to war service, were compelled to give up their employment.[42] The Mercantile Marine Service Association had long been campaigning for such recognition. The Silver War Badge, first issued in September 1916, was initially awarded to service personnel who had been honourably discharged due to wounds or sickness, it was also known as the Discharge Badge, the Wound Badge or Services Rendered Badge. The main impetus for its creation was to prevent veterans from being publicly challenged for not wearing uniform by proponents of the Order of the White Feather. Further official recognition of the brave service rendered by civilian seafarers and fishermen came with the creation by the Board of Trade of the Torpedo Badge, which was authorised on 6 June 1918. It was to be awarded to merchant mariners including stewardesses, who having been aboard a ship sunk or damaged by torpedo or mine went on to complete a further voyage (of at least one month's duration) on the articles of a British merchant ship. Bars worn under the badge were added for subsequent similar service, up to five, whereupon the holder could swap the bars for a five-pointed star. Following the cessation of hostilities, recipients of the red woven 'active service' badge were able to exchange it for a gold wire one. In cases where mariners did not survive the further voyage that would qualify them, the award of a torpedo badge was conferred on a living relative. This was the case for second mate Thomas McFadden, born at Mostyn, who, aged twenty-three was one of six men killed when the *Framfield*, 2510 GRT (1894), was mined in October 1916. The gold torpedo badge to which he would have been entitled was presented to his mother, then living in Burry Port.[43]

In 1919 the Board of Trade established the Mercantile Marine Medal, to be awarded to all those who served for at least six months during the war or on at least one voyage through a danger zone. Men who served in coastal trades and fishermen could also qualify.[44] In total, 133,135 Mercantile Marine Medals were issued, with around 10 per cent of these being awarded posthumously. By comparison, according to records held at The National Archives,[45] out of 1,150,000 Silver War Badges awarded, only 155 were awarded to merchant mariners. The inescapable conclusion is that the chances of being invalided out of the merchant service were considerably less likely than ending up in Davy Jones' Locker.

In December 1928, Queen Mary officially unveiled the Tower Hill Memorial commemorating the sacrifice made by the merchant and fishing fleets. The 12,210 names of those with no other grave than the sea inscribed thereon represented the majority of the civilian mariners who were lost during the conflict. The memorial represents a larger loss of life than that at the Commonwealth War Graves Commission cemetery at Tyne Cot in Belgium, where there are 11,965 burials, and which is the largest cemetery for Commonwealth soldiers in the world, for any war. In the end, the war waged on the mercantile marine conducted by commerce raiders and U-boats was not just against the enemy, but also against civilian mariners of all nations, and while many were British subjects, there were many who were not. A little over a decade later, when the economic consequences of the peace led to war again, many of the ships and men that survived these perilous years would again find themselves called upon.

Truth

> Man with his burning soul
> Has but an hour of breath
> To build a ship of truth
> In which his soul may sail –
> Sail on the sea of death,
> For death takes toll
> Of beauty, courage, youth,
> Of all but truth.[46]

Seamen from Wales had witnessed the first loss of the war when the *San Wilfrido* was mined at the mouth of the Elbe, and it would be a merchant seaman from Wales who was the final victim of a torpedo attack against British merchant shipping. In 1918, Peter Madsen, aged fifty-seven, was the ship's carpenter aboard the steamer *Murcia*, 4871 GRT (1915). Madsen had been born in Denmark but was married to a Welsh woman and was living in Newport. On 2 November 1918, while sailing from the Indian port of Bassein (Vasai) to Marseille with a cargo of rice and gunnies (jute sack cloths), the *Murcia* became the last British merchant vessel to be sunk by a torpedo during the war.[47] Attacked without warning and sunk

12 miles off Port Said by SM UC 74, the only fatality among the crew was Peter Madsen.

There were some families that had salt in their blood, with intergenerational participation in a broad variety of maritime occupations. Some would experience almost the entire range of vicissitudes of fortune that could befall a seafaring family in time of war. In the spring of 1915, Mrs Laura Jones Morris of Glyndwr Terrace, Barmouth was probably slightly relieved when her husband, master of the schooner *William Prichard*, 170 GRT (1903), moved to sailing in the coasting trades. Immediately prior to the outbreak of war, the sixty-nine-year-old Hugh Morris was in the salt cod trade, sailing down to Cadiz and then out across the Atlantic for Newfoundland and Labrador. With a first mate from Nefyn as old as he, and half a dozen crew, they were participating in a pattern of trade that stretched back three centuries. Hugh was from a seafaring family, his father Richard Morris (d. 1886) had been owner and master of the schooner *Mary Jones* (255562), 48 net tons, which had been built at Barmouth in 1842.[48] Hugh Morris appears to have continued to sail in the coasting trades and both he and the *William Prichard* survived the war. He was an active member of the community, a Master Mason at the local lodge, and a member of the harbour trust. In 1917 he was a member of the War Savings committee and also served on the jury at an inquest into the bodies of merchant seamen that had washed ashore locally.

Hugh Morris had been a month at sea when war was declared and was not back in Wales before April 1915. During his absence, Mrs Capt. Morris had the company of her son Richard, who was on furlough between August and November 1914 from his post as a lighthouse keeper in the Red Sea (Egypt at this time being a British 'protectorate'). A month later in December, two of their sons, John and William Edward joined the Army. At the same time, a fourth son, Hugh Cynhaiarn Morris, was an able seaman aboard the steamer *Kintuck*, 4616 GRT (1895), sailing Birkenhead for Hong Kong and Shanghai. In stark contrast to the schooner that his father captained, the China Mutual Steam Navigation Company's *Kintuck* was certified for a crew of sixty but sailed with just sixteen British crew members, with the remainder of the ship's complement being made up of Chinese seamen and firemen listed on a separate Asiatic agreement.

William Edward Morris arrived at Gallipoli on the troop transport *Caledonia*, 5066 GRT (1905), in July 1915 with the 1/6th Battalion Royal Welsh Fusiliers and landed at Suvla Bay in August. He somehow survived the ensuing disaster which saw the 53rd (Welsh) Division's numbers reduced by 85 per cent through combat, harsh weather and disease, before they were evacuated to Egypt in December. John Morris, who had married a local woman while on leave in April 1915, would die at Mametz Wood in the summer of 1916 during the First Battle of the Somme, aged twenty-four. In 1917, Hugh Cynhaiarn Morris would spend four days in a lifeboat following the torpedoing of his ship, most likely the Elder Dempster *Ikbal*, 5404 GRT (1894), which was sunk 200 miles off Land's End.[49] As has been seen earlier, he would die at Sierra Leone in September 1918 on another Elder Dempster ship, the *Benue*, most probably from the 'Spanish flu'.

While this book has been concerned primarily with the experiences of merchant mariners in Wales during the First World War, there is a sense in which this work contains a much wider maritime history. In 1914 there were Welsh mariners at sea who had been born in a time before the Lutine Bell was salvaged. This bell, which would subsequently sound for the loss of so many merchant ships in Lloyd's underwriting rooms, was first rung at the Royal Exchange in 1859. These were men who, until they were in their teens or early twenties, had lived in an age where convicts were transported and hanging was still a public spectacle. Men such as able seaman Owen Owens of Holyhead, born in 1850, bosun John Davies of Cardigan born in 1853 (who were both crew on the ill-fated *Lusitania*), Humphrey Shaw of Connah's Quay born 1846, who came out of retirement to help crew the schooner *Kate* in 1915, and Hugh Morris of Barmouth born in 1845, master of the schooner *William Prichard*. Some of the ships at sea in 1914 were of a venerable age, the schooner *George Casson* (1863) and the small steamer *City of Cadiz* (1862) both seized in Germany at the outbreak of war had been half a century at sea. Some of the ships were brand new, some of the crew remarkably young by modern standards, though this was not unusual at the time – the Royal Navy allowed fifteen-year-olds to be on active service.

What is captured here is a view of the multifaceted maritime world inhabited by these Welsh men and women at the peak of the British Empire. A maritime trade largely powered and protected by steam ships, in turn driven by the coal raised, for example, at Elder's Navigation collieries at Oakwood and Maesteg, or David Davies's Ocean collieries in the Rhondda and the Garw, mines whose very names reflected the purpose for which this bituminous coal was raised. The South Wales coalfield was at its peak in 1913 and the money it generated had transformed Cardiff and its docks, and created those at Penarth and Barry from whence many mariners from Wales at this time sailed 'coal out'. A broad array of other types of maritime trades and services took mariners from Wales to all parts of the world, and brought mariners from all over the world to Wales. At the apogee of the British Empire, the uneven relationships in this international legacy of maritime labour can be seen clearly both on board ship and in the port towns and cities where some would lay more permanent roots; these relationships were already of a long-standing nature and continue to play out to this day. In 1914 the United Kingdom imported 60 per cent of its food: 80 per cent of the wheat, nearly all the sugar and two-thirds of the bacon. The contribution and sacrifice made by this diverse but distinct section of the civilian labour force ensured the sugar for the jam, tea for the 'Tommies' and rum for the ration, palm oil for the soap, flour for the bread and 'biscuit', the 'bully beef'. Over the course of the First World War many also engaged in what was an unprecedented global distribution of materiel and men. The Wales in which these mariners lived was in a state of flux, the burgeoning industrial and urban population was turning the political consensus away from Liberalism and despite the Welsh appetite for Christianity, particularly in its non-conformist guises, the secularisation of society continued apace. By 1914 it was becoming clear that the burning issues of the day were material, not spiritual.[50] And it was this material welfare of the nation that the mercantile marine was particularly concerned with over the course of the war.

Notes

1 Lyon, *Merchant Seafaring through World War 1*, p. 234.
2 *CDL*, 31 December 1918, p. 3.
3 A. Kennerley, 'The Seamen's Union, the National Maritime Board and Firemen: Labour Management in the British Mercantile Marine', *The Northern Mariner/Le marin du nord*, 7/4 (October 1997), 15–28.
4 Dixon, 'Seamen and the Law', pp. 290–1.
5 *CDL*, 15 February 1917, p. 2.
6 G. Puddefoot, *Ready for Anything: The Royal Fleet Auxiliary 1905–1950* (Barnsley, 2010), p. 46.
7 Puddefoot, *Ready for Anything*, p. 32.
8 Puddefoot, *Ready for Anything*, p. 45.
9 D. Hopkin, 'Domestic Censorship in the First World War', *Journal of Contemporary History*, 5/4 (1970), 156.
10 *Cambrian News*, 25 May 1917, p. 5.
11 Lyon, *Merchant Seafaring through World War 1*, p. 189.
12 *BDN*, 2 March 1917, p. 7.
13 *SWWP*, 11 January 1919, p. 4.

14 *Cambrian News*, 23 February 1917, p. 5.
15 *BDN*, 20 April 1917, p. 7. The paper erroneously identified the U-boat as U-39.
16 *BDN*, 11 May 1917, p. 5.
17 Cornford, *The Merchant Seaman in War*, pp. 262–4; *Western Australian*, 16 October 1917, p. 6; *Western Mail* (Perth), 9 November 1917, p. 43.
18 See *www.wrecksite.eu/wreck.aspx?13444*; and *www.wwwmp.co.uk/ceredigion-memorials/cardigan-ww1-war-memorial/* (last accessed 3 November 2024).
19 *BDN*, 9 November 1917, p. 2.
20 *CDL*, 14 August 1917, p. 1.
21 *BDN*, 20 September 1918, p. 3.
22 *Haverfordwest and Milford Haven Telegraph*, 28 November 1917, p. 1, letter to editor.
23 See *https://shipwreckedmariners.org.uk/who-we-are/our-history/* (last accessed 3 November 2024).
24 *Aberdare Leader*, 9 February 1918, p. 2.
25 *CDL*, 18 April 1918, p. 2.
26 *Western Daily Press*, 10 January 1918, p. 6.
27 *SWWP*, 25 May 1918, p. 4.
28 *Flemmings Karte beit Schiffsversenkungen unserer U-Boote*, Library of Congress Geography and Map Division G5701.S65 1918 .C2; see *https://lccn.loc.gov/2016432165* (last accessed 3 November 2024).
29 *Haverfordwest and Milford Haven Telegraph*, 26 February 1919, p. 1.
30 *Cambrian News*, 7 December 1917, p. 7.
31 See *www.natwestgroupremembers.com/content/dam/natwestgroupremembers_com/pdfs/war-loans.pdf* (last accessed 3 November 2024).
32 *BDN*, 28 June 1918, p. 3.
33 *BDN*, 15 February 1918, p. 7.
34 *BDN*, 28 June 1918, p. 3.
35 Dixon, 'Seamen and the Law', pp. 293–4.
36 *CDL*, 17 September 1919, p. 2.
37 *CDL*, 17 September 1919, p. 2.
38 *BDN*, 7 February 1919, p. 5.
39 *Llangollen Advertiser*, 15 June 1917, p. 3.
40 Lyon, *Merchant Seafaring through World War 1*, p. 247.
41 Woodman, *More Days, More Dollars*, pp. 322–3, 328, 333.
42 *Abergavenny Chronicle*, 14 September 1917, p. 6.
43 *SWWP*, 12 July 1919, p. 1.
44 All recipients of the Mercantile Marine Medal were also eligible for the British War Medal.
45 TNA MT9/1404.
46 John Masefield, 'Truth', in *The Story of a Round-house and Other Poems* (New York, 1912).
47 Lyon, *Merchant Seafaring through World War 1*, p. 235.

48 *The Barmouth and County Advertiser and District Weekly News*, 15 January 1914, p. 6.
49 *The Barmouth and County Advertiser and District Weekly News*, 10 May 1917, p. 3.
50 D. Densil Morgan, 'Christianity and National Identity in Twentieth-Century Wales', *Religion, State & Society*, 27/3–4 (1999), 330.

Bibliography

Books

1911 Census of England and Wales General Report with Appendices (1917–18).
Akermann, P., *Encyclopedia of British Submarines 1910–1955* (Cornwall, 2002).
Ayland, N. (ed.), *Schooner Captain* (Truro, 1972).
British Vessels Lost at Sea 1914–1918 (London, 1919).
Carter, T., *Merchant Seamen's Health 1860–1960* (Woodbridge, 2014).
Cipriano Venzon, Anne, and Paul L. Miles (eds), *The United States in the First World War: An Encyclopedia* (New York, 1999).
Coppack, T., *A Lifetime with Ships: The Autobiography of a Coasting Shipowner* (Prescot, 1973).
Cornford, L. Cope, *The Merchant Seaman in War* (New York, 1918).
Eames, A., *Ships and Seamen of Anglesey* (Anglesey, 1973).
Eames, A., *The Captain's Wife* (Llanrwst, 2016).
Earl of Dunraven KP, CMG, *Past Times and Pastimes*, vol. 1 (London, 1922).
Davies, J. D., *Britannia's Dragon: A Naval History of Wales* (Stroud, 2013).
Davis, L. E., and Stanley L. Engerman, *Naval Blockades in Peace and War: An Economic History since 1750* (Cambridge, 2006).
Davies, W., *The Sea and the Sand: The Story of HMS Tara and the Western Desert Force* (Caernarfon, 1988).
d'Enno, D., *Fishermen Against the Kaiser: Shockwaves of War, 1914–1915*, vol. 1 (Barnsley, 2010).
de Kerbrech, R. P., *Down Amongst the Black Gang: The World and Workplace of RMS* Titanic's *Stokers* (Stroud, 2014).
Druett, J., *Hen Frigates: Passion and Peril, Nineteenth-Century Women at Sea* (New York, 1998).
Fayle, C. E., *Seaborne Trade*, 3 vols (London, 1922–4).
Fontenoy, P. E., 'Convoy System', in Spencer C. Tucker (ed.), *The Encyclopedia of World War I: A Political, Social and Military History*, vol. 1 (Santa Barbara CA, 2005).
Gittins, S., *The Great Western Railway in the First World War* (Stroud, 2010).
Gray, E. A., *The U-Boat War 1914–1918* (London, 1994).

Griffiths, G. S., *Holyhead to Bir Hakkim (and Back): The Full Story of H.M.S. Tara* (Wrexham, 2015).
Grigg, J., *Lloyd George: War Leader, 1916–1918* (London, 2002).
Gwatkin-Williams, R. S., *Prisoners of the Red Desert* (London, 1919).
Home, W. E., *Merchant Seamen: Their Diseases and their Welfare Needs* (London, 1922).
Hope, B. D., *A Commodious Yard: The Story of William Thomas & Sons, Shipbuilders of Amlwch* (Llanwrst, 2005).
Hope, R., *Poor Jack* (London, 2001).
Hopkins, C. P., *'National Service' of British Merchant Seamen 1914–1919* (London, 1920).
Hughes, D. Lloyd, and D. M. Williams, *Holyhead: The Story of a Port* (Denbigh, 1981).
Hughes, E., and A. Eames, *Porthmadog Ships* (Denbigh, 1975).
Hughes, H., *Immortal Sails* (Prescot, 1969).
Humayan, Ansari, *The Infidel Within: Muslims in Britain since 1800* (London, 2004).
Hurd, A., *The Merchant Navy*, 2 vols (London, 1922).
Jenkins, D., (ed.) *'I Hope to have a Good Passage': The Business Letters of Captain Daniel Jenkins, 1902–11* (Newport, 2016).
Jenkins, D., *Shipowners of Cardiff: A Class by Themselves* (Cardiff, 1997).
Jenkins, J. Geraint, *Evan Thomas Radcliffe: A Cardiff Shipowning Company* (Cardiff, 1982).
Jessop, V., *Titanic Survivor: The Memoirs of Violet Jessop, Stewardess*, ed. by J. Maxtone-Graham (Gloucester, 2007).
Jones, B. C., *Book of Remembrance Seafarers from Wales of the Mercantile Marine & Fishing Fleets who lost their lives during World War One 1914–1918* (2014).
Jones, John Graham, *The History of Wales* (Cardiff, 2014).
Keble Chatterton, E., *Q-Ships and their Story* (London, 1922).
Kemp, P., (ed.) *The Oxford Companion to the Sea* (Oxford, 1976).
Kirkaldy, A. W., *British Shipping* (London, 1914).
Kowner, Rotem, *Historical Dictionary of the Russo-Japanese War* (London, 2006).
Lindsay, J., *A History of the North Wales Slate Industry* (Newton Abbot, 1974).
Lloyd, L., *The Port of Caernarfon 1793–1900* (Caernarfon, 1989).
Lobo-Guerrero, L., *Insuring War: Sovereignty, Security and Risk* (London, 2012).

Lyon, P., *Merchant Seafaring through World War 1, 1914–1918* (Leicester, 2016).
Masefield, John, 'Truth', in *The Story of a Round-house and Other Poems* (New York, 1912).
Massie, R. K., *Castles of Steel: Britain, Germany, and the Winning of the Great War at Sea* (New York, 2004).
Merrigan, J. P., and I. H. Collard, *Holyhead to Ireland: Stena and its Welsh Heritage* (Stroud, 2009).
Moffat, H. Y., *From Ship's Boy to Skipper* (Paisley, 1911).
Murphy, S., *Shackleton's Photographer: The Standard Edition* (Scottsdale AZ, 2001).
Newbolt, H., *Official History of the War: Naval Operations*, vol. 5 (Uckfield, 2001).
Puddefoot, G., *Ready for Anything: The Royal Fleet Auxiliary 1905–1950* (Barnsley, 2010).
Purdy, J., *New Sailing Directions for the Mediterranean [& etc.]* (London, 1826).
Putnam, W. L., *The Kaiser's Merchant Ships in World War 1* (Jefferson NC, 2001).
Routledge, K., *The Mystery of Rapa Nui* (London, 1919).
Smyth, W. H., *Sailor's Word Book: A Dictionary of Nautical Terms* (London, 1996).
Stanley, J., *A History of the Royal Navy: Women and the Royal Navy* (London, 2017).
Stibbe, Matthew, *British Civilian Internees in Germany: The Ruhleben Camp 1914–1918* (Manchester, 2008).
Tarrant, V. E., *The U-Boat Offensive 1914–1945* (New York, 1989).
Traven, B., *The Death Ship* (New York, 1991).
Tucker, Spencer C. (ed.), *The Encyclopedia of World War I: A Political, Social and Military History*, vol. 1 (Santa Barbara CA, 2005).
Westlake, R., *British Battalions in France and Belgium, 1914* (Barnsley, 1997).
Williams, L. J., *Welsh Historical Statistics*, 2 vols (Cardiff, 1985).
Woodman, R., *More Days, More Dollars: The Universal Bucket Chain 1885–1920* (Stroud, 2010).

Articles

Barry, W. J., 'History of the Port of Cork Steam Navigation 1815–1915', *Journal of the Cork Historical and Archaeological Society*, 25 (1919).

Burton, V. C., 'A Floating Population: Vessel Enumeration Returns, 1851–1921', *Local Population Studies*, 38 (Spring 1987).

Burton, V. C. 'Counting Seafarers: The Published Records of the Registry of British Seamen, 1849–1913', *Mariner's Mirror*, 71/3 (August 1985).

Daunton, M. J., 'Jack Ashore: Seamen in Cardiff before 1914', *Welsh History Review*, 9/2 (1979).

Evans, N., 'The South Wales Race Riots of 1919', *Llafur*, 3/1 (1980).

Fisher, J., 'Neither Fish nor Fowl-Mercantile Seamen on Armed Merchant Cruisers in the Great War', *International Journal of Maritime History*, 28/3 (2016).

Hopkin, D., 'Domestic Censorship in the First World War', *Journal of Contemporary History*, 5/4 (1970).

Jenkins, D., 'Cardiff Tramps, Cardi Crews', *Journal of the Cardiganshire Antiquarian Society*, 10/1–4 (1984–7).

Jenkins, J. Geraint, 'Cardiff Shipowners', *Maritime Wales*, 5 (1980).

Kennerley, A., 'Aspirant Navigator: Training and Education at Sea During Commercial Voyages in British Ships c.1850–1950', *The Great Circle*, 30/2 (2008).

Kennerley, A., 'Nationally Recognised Qualifications for British Merchant Navy Officers, 1865–1966', *International Journal of Maritime History*, 13/1 (June 2001).

Kennerley, A., 'Stoking the Boilers: Firemen and Trimmer in British Merchant Ships 1850–1950', *International Journal of Maritime History*, 20/1 (2008).

Kennerley, A., 'The Seamen's Union, the National Maritime Board and Firemen: Labour Management in the British Mercantile Marine', *The Northern Mariner/Le marin du nord*, 7/4 (October 1997).

Killingray, D., 'A New "Imperial Disease": The Influenza Pandemic of 1918–9 and its Impact on the British Empire', *Caribbean Quarterly*, 49/4 (December 2003).

Levie, H. S., 'Submarine Warfare: With Emphasis on the 1936 London Protocol', in M. N. Schmitt and L. C. Green (eds), *Levie on the Law of War: International Law Studies Volume 70* (Newport, 1998).

Lyons, J. D., 'Churchill on Science and Civilization', *The New Atlantis*, 28 (Summer 2010).

Mäenpää, Sari, 'Comfort and Guidance for Female Passengers: The Origins of Women's Employments on British Passenger Liners 1815–1914', *Journal of Maritime Research*, 6 (2004).

Mäenpää, Sari, 'From Pea Soup to Hors d'oeuvres: The Status of the Cook on British Merchant Ships', *The Northern Mariner/Le marin du nord*, 11/2 (April 2001).
Morgan, D. Densil, 'Christianity and National Identity in Twentieth-Century Wales', *Religion, State & Society*, 27/3–4 (1999).
O'Neill, G., 'Scandal of The Baralong Incident Was Hidden in Veil of Secrecy', *Iris na Mara/Journal of the Sea*, 1/4 (Dún Laoghaire, 2006).
Owen, J. R., 'The Royal Naval Reserve and Wales: Prelude to the First World War', *Maritime Wales*, 35 (2014).
Roberts, Andrew, and Zewditu Gebreyohanes, 'The Racial Consequences of Mr Churchill: A Review', *Policy Exchange* (London, 2021).
Romero Salvadó, F. J., 'Spain and the First World War: The Logic of Neutrality', *War in History*, 26/1 (2019).
Schmitt, M. N., and L. C. Green (eds), *Levie on the Law of War: International Law Studies Volume 70* (Newport, 1998).
Smallman-Raynor, Matthew, Niall Johnson and Andrew D. Cliff, 'The Spatial Anatomy of an Epidemic: Influenza in London and the County Boroughs of England and Wales, 1918–1919', *Transactions of the Institute of British Geographers*, 27/4 (2002).
Stanley, J., 'After the Cross-Dressed Cabin Boys and Whaling Wives: Possible Futures for Women's Maritime Historiography', *Journal of Transport History*, 23/1 (2002).

Theses

Cole, Festus, 'Sierra Leone and World War One' (unpublished PhD thesis, SOAS, 1994).
Dixon, C. H., 'Seamen and the Law: An Examination of the Impact of Legislation on the British Merchant Seaman's Lot, 1558–1918' (unpublished PhD thesis, University College London, 1981).
Lilley, T. D., 'Operation of the Tenth Cruiser Squadron: A Challenge for the Royal Navy and its Reserves' (unpublished PhD thesis, University of Greenwich, 2012).
Mäenpää, Sari, 'Catering Personnel on British Passenger Liners, 1860–1935' (unpublished PhD thesis, University of Liverpool, 2002).

Index

A

Abbot, 21
Abbotsford, 166
Aberaeron, 21, 39, 40, 57, 64, 65, 114
Aberarth, 69, 116, 121
Aberavon, 49
Abercanaid, 57
Abercastle, 168
Aberdare Leader, 189
Aberdaron, 192
Aberdeen, 116, 194
Aberdovey, 12, 14, 121, 183
Aberdovey and Barmouth Steamship Company, 14
Aberffraw, 75
Abergavenny, 116
Abergavenny Chronicle, 26–7, 114–15, 195
Abergele, 142
Aberporth, 21, 28, 39, 57, 59
Abersoch, 12
Aberystwyth, 14, 59, 64, 72, 97, 121
able seamen, 5, 17, 32–6, 39, 43, 59, 65, 68, 70, 75, 84–5, 90, 93–7, 99, 100, 116, 121, 126, 130, 137, 164, 166, 187, 197–8
accidental deaths, 5, 18, 21–3
accommodation *see* crew accommodation; passenger accommodation
Adams, William, 58–9
Adelaide, 70, 90
Aden (formerly *Craigmore*), 40
Adenwen, 107, 132–3
Admiralty Naval Estimates, 4
Admiralty Transport Department, 6
Adolfsen, Daniel, 150
Adriatic, 82
Advisory Committee on Merchant Shipping, 3
Africa, HMS, 175
African Steamship Company, 20
Aguila, 133–4
Akassa, 20
Albany (Australia), 90
Albemarle, 149
Aldersgate, 50
Aldershot Barracks, 174
Alexandria, 71, 84, 86, 96, 152, 169
Algeria, 37, 67, 71, 90, 97, 106, 113

Algiers, 37, 90, 97, 106, 113
Allan, John, 75
Allan Line, 45, 83–6
Almeria, 187
Almirante Lynch, 63
Alston, 122
Amanda, 166, 167
Ambleston War Memorial, 39
American crew members, 33, 43–4, 89, 99, 106
American Ensign, 132, 133
American Line, 180
Amlwch, 57, 60, 70, 72, 158–60, 184
Anchor Line, 88
Ancona, 62
Anglesey, 12, 15, 24, 27, 40, 60, 70, 75, 83, 87, 90, 100, 116, 123, 125, 143, 184
Anglia, 16, 72–5
Anglo Saxon Petroleum Company, 95
Annie, 12
Antofagasta, 146
Antwerp, 36, 68
apprentices, 21, 33, 40, 57, 59, 85, 90, 94, 98–100, 115–16, 142–4, 168, 183
Arab crew members, 100, 106–7, 113, 132
Arabic, 62, 83, 142
Archangel, 67, 97, 115, 166
Ardrossian, 88
Argentina, 21, 31, 33, 34, 37–8, 61, 65, 89, 95, 116, 161
armed boarding steamers, 15–16, 151–2
armed merchant cruisers, 5, 6, 41, 175, 181
Armenian, 140–2
Arndale, 115
Artist, 185–6
Arvonia (formerly *Cambria*) *see Cambria*
Arvonian, 96
Ashton, Albert F., 73
Asuncion, 65
Athinai, 88
Atlantic City, 123
Auckland, 62
Aultbea, 181
Australia, 21, 24, 32, 33, 34, 35, 63, 70, 76, 90, 96
Australian Voluntary Hospital, 76
Avanti Savoia, 24

Avonmouth, 13, 71, 86, 95, 96, 107, 125, 140, 142, 145, 150
Azores, 38

B
Bagillt, 137, 183
Bagnall, George, 74, 75
Bahia Blanca, 35, 95
Bahia Rio, 37
Baker, G., 112
bakers, 70, 84; *see also* cooks
Ballater, 116–17
Baltic, 82
Baltimore, MD, 32, 37, 99
Bangladesh, 101
Bangor, 13, 23, 33, 34, 70, 71, 75, 84, 88, 126, 130
Baralong, 125, 142, 143
Barbados, 17
barbers, 84, 85
Barcelona, 95
Barents Sea, 115
Barmouth, 14, 17, 85, 130, 175, 197
Barranca, 48–9
Barry
  accidents at, 21–2
  court proceedings at, 103, 105–6, 192–3
  crew members from, 57, 59, 70, 86, 91, 115, 116, 131, 150, 168, 183, 184, 187, 188, 192
  crew members joining or leaving at, 40, 95
  port activity levels, 7, 198
  as port of departure, call or arrival, 25, 32, 34, 35, 37–8, 50, 64, 86, 91, 94, 96, 97, 112, 132, 142–5, 170, 187, 188
  protests at, 101–2, 188–9
  rescued sailors brought to, 138–9, 188
  sanitary inspections at, 41–2, 194
Barry Dock News, 22, 48, 58–9, 187
Barry Merchant Navy Memorial, 193
Barry Missions to Seamen, 50
Bassaleg, 70
Bassein, 196
Bassett, William Edward, 73
Bastian, N., 116
Beachy Head, 21
Bear Creek Oil Shipping Company, 146, 150
Beasant, L., 88
Beaumaris, 12, 13, 24
Beer, Archibald Robert, 40
Beira, 90
Belfast, 14, 16, 88, 129, 166, 181
Belfast Lough, 38, 123

Belgium, 36, 44, 64, 68, 135, 174, 196
Bellglade, 145
Béni Saf, 97, 113
Benin, 100
Benllech, 27, 63
Benoke, L. H., 144
Benue, 100, 198
Berehaven, 144
Bermuda, 20, 38
Berwindvale, 91
Bethesda, 65
Bideford, 12
Bigham, A. H., 99
Bilbao, 112
Bir Hakkim, 152
Birdoswald, 188
Birkenhead, 12, 71, 197
Birwick, W. B., 98–9
Bizerte, 96
Black Sea, 40
Blackborow, Perce, 89–90
Blaenavon, 133
Blair, D., 143
Blakewell, William, 89–90
Blowen, H. G., 116
Blue Funnel Line, 165
Blue Jacket, 161–2
Boadicea, 33
Board of Trade, 3, 5, 6, 19, 42, 47, 60, 102, 165, 188–9, 195
boarding houses, 100, 102
Bombay, 84, 86, 95, 106, 168
Bordeaux, 34, 139, 162
Boston, MA, 64, 84, 175
bosuns, 5, 15, 17, 24–8, 33, 39, 57, 59, 65, 72, 75, 90, 93–5, 97, 116, 122, 133–4, 142, 164, 183, 198
Bothnia, 133
Boulogne, 72, 76, 121
Bowness, 91
Boxer Rebellion, 135
Brake, 57
Brandenburg, 184
Brazil, 21, 32, 34, 36, 37, 64, 65, 144
Braziliana, 95
Brecon, 92
Bremen, 57
Brest, 174–5
Bretwalda, 116
Brisbane, 32, 63, 90
Bristol, 17, 43, 65, 112, 131
Bristol Channel, 13, 25, 40, 60, 69, 92, 101, 121, 145, 190
Britannic, 82
British and Foreign Sailors' Society, 189

INDEX

British Transport, 94
Briton Ferry, 89, 90
Brixham, 133
Brunswick, GA, 32, 63
Bryncroes, 39
Buenos Aires, 21, 26, 33, 34, 37–8, 61, 64, 67, 89, 116
Buenos Ayres and Pacific Railway Company, 97
Bull Bay lifeboat, 158, 159–60
Burgess, Daisy, 89
burials at sea, 4, 20, 71, 175, 186, 196
Burns, John, 18
Burns Steamship Company, 33, 88
Burry Port, 66, 99, 113, 195
Burton, V. C., 3
Butcher, A. C., 59
butchers, 20, 70, 84

C

cabin boys, 15, 36, 72–3, 75, 91, 168
Cadiz, 17, 35, 37, 197
Cadoxton, 22, 59, 86, 187, 188
Cadwalader Jones, 36
Caerleon, 131
Caernarfon, 7, 13, 17, 18, 35, 39, 57, 65, 69, 72, 73, 75, 82, 87, 90, 126, 137, 183
Cairnisla see *West Marsh* (formerly *Cairnisla*)
Cairo see *Royal Edward* (formerly *Cairo*)
Caledonia, 197
Callao, 32, 63, 65, 146
Calloway, William Henry, 73
Cambank, 158–60
Cambria, 15–16, 55, 72, 75
Cambria Daily Leader, 1, 24, 66–7, 112, 123–4, 136–7, 140, 144, 146–7, 162, 166–7, 170–1, 175–6, 180
Cambrian News, 183, 185–6, 191
Cambrian Range, 183
Cambrian Steam Navigation Company, 40
Camillo, 147
Campania, 143
Campbell, N. J., 73
Canada, 4, 17, 35, 39, 82–6, 150, 188, 197
Canadian Army Medical Corps, 75
Canadian crew members, 33
Canadian Expeditionary Force, 82–3, 85–6
Canadian Northern Steam Ship Company, 71
Canadian Pacific Railway Company, 85–6, 181
Canary Islands, 64, 133
Candidate, 137–8, 165

Cape Town, 90
Cape Verde islands, 34, 38, 92
captains, 16, 20, 22–3, 27, 61, 65, 68, 73–4, 104, 113, 119–24, 140–2, 146–7, 149, 152, 159–62, 165, 167, 170–1; see also masters
Carbonear, 17
Cardiff
  crew members from, 13, 26–8, 33–4, 39, 40, 57, 59, 60, 63, 67–8, 70, 72, 75, 85–6, 90–1, 94, 97, 99, 103, 112–13, 115–17, 123, 130, 133, 136, 139, 142–4, 148, 158, 162, 166, 168, 181–2
  crew members joining or leaving at, 21, 65, 70, 86, 91, 95, 99, 101
  deaths from Spanish flu pandemic, 174
  foreign seamen settling in, 100–3
  gunnery training courses at, 183
  'insurance jobs' at, 44
  port activity levels, 6–7, 198
  as port of departure, call or arrival, 13, 32, 37, 43, 95–9, 101, 115, 166, 172–3
  protests at, 101–2
  seamen's boarding houses, 100, 102
  shipping companies based at, 40, 57, 97
Cardiff Steam Towing Company, 13
Cardigan, 12, 28, 40, 60, 70, 99, 107, 132, 133, 144, 148, 150, 164, 168, 188, 198
Caribbean, 17, 20, 38, 61, 85, 92, 137
Caribbean crew members, 92, 100
Carlingford Lough, 16
Carmarthen, 21, 39, 65, 144
Carney, J., 72
Caroline Islands, 62–3
Caronia, 41
carpenters, 5, 15, 33–4, 39, 40, 57, 59, 65, 70, 72, 75, 100, 114, 115, 150–1, 166, 188, 193, 196
Cartagena, 40, 188
Cassis, 95
Cattaro, 151
Cayeux, 172
Celtic, 16
censorship, 2, 174, 182–3
census data, 2–3, 82, 93
Central Index Register, 3
Centurion (1891), 20–1
Centurion (1908), 165–6
Cephalonia, 99
Charente Shipping Company, 181
Charles, John, 120–1
Charleston, 105–6
Chatham Island, 147
Chepstow, 70, 99
Cherbourg, 133

211

Chester, 12
Chile, 21, 34, 35, 63, 66, 90, 144, 146
China Mutual Steam Navigation Company, 126, 197
Chinese crew members, 69–70, 100, 101–5, 107, 121, 166–7, 190, 197
Chinese Labour Corps, 174
Christiana, 23
Churchill, Winston, 105, 153, 165
Chwilog, 34
Cilgerran, 112
City of Bremen, 162–3
City of Cadiz, 57, 198
City of Khios, 59
City of Oporto, 56
City of Vienna, 27
Civilian, 96
Claremont, 96
Clarissa Radcliffe (1913) see *W. I. Radcliffe* (formerly *Clarissa Radcliffe* 1913)
Clarissa Radcliffe (1915), 41
Claymore, 133
Clayton, Richard, 121
Climo, Arthur, 22
Cloch, 91–2
Cluny Castle (1883) see *Rowena* (formerly *Cluny Castle*)
Cluny Castle (1903), 49
Clutha River, 25
Clydach Vale, 70
coal, 7, 21–2, 32, 37–8, 40, 44–7, 64–8, 106–7, 112, 147–8, 169, 170, 172, 198
coasting trade, 11–15, 17, 39, 43, 88, 91–2, 94, 171, 197
Coats, A. A., 90
Cobh *see* Queenstown
Cochin, 66
Coles, A. G., 117
Collier, William John, 75
collisions, 16, 26–7
Colon, 91
Colony, 33, 34
Colombia, 48
Colwill, George, 102
commemoration, 4–5, 26, 35, 39, 40, 72, 97, 113–14, 152, 153, 164, 193, 196
commissioned auxiliaries, 6, 135–6
Commonwealth, 97
Commonwealth War Graves Commission, 4, 196
compensation, 19, 68–9, 131, 181, 188–9, 190–3
Concord, 162
Connah's Quay, 12, 88, 144, 171, 198

Connaught, 87
Connemara, 16, 26
conscription, 36, 107
convoys, 7–8, 62, 169–76, 179
Conway Castle, 34–5
Conwy, 134
Cook, Ellen, 87
cooks, 4, 5, 12, 15, 17–18, 20–2, 33–4, 43, 50, 57, 60, 69–70, 73, 75, 84–5, 91, 99–100, 115, 125, 139, 142, 162, 171, 183–4, 187–8
Copenhagen, 18
Coppack, Tom, 171–2, 173
Coppack Brothers, 171
Coquet, 152–3
Coquimbo, 34
Cordelia, 149–50
Corinthian, 45, 85, 86
Corinto, 148
Cork, 13, 139
Cork Free Press, 89
Cork Steam Packet Company, 185
Cornish City, 64
Corsican, 84–5, 86
Corunna, 26
Cory, John, 138
Cottingham, 143–4
Cowper, Ernest S., 164
Coyle, J., 139
Craigmore see *Aden* (formerly *Craigmore*)
Craigronald see *Glyndwr* (formerly *Craigronald*)
Cranza, A., 59
Crawley, Thomas, 134
Crefeld, 64
crew accommodation, 41–2, 51, 83, 85, 147, 149, 193
crew agreements, 5, 11–18, 20–1, 24, 32–3, 35, 39, 48, 69–70, 75–7, 82–6, 93–5, 98–100, 107, 168, 170, 181–2
crew lists, 3, 5, 82, 95, 97, 168
crew shortages, 12–13, 51, 180
Criccieth, 34, 35, 61, 91, 150, 161, 166, 184
Crighton, J., 142
Crocodile, 33
Crown of Castile, 188
Crown of India, 21, 144–5
cruiser rules, 61, 67, 117, 153
Cruz Grande, 34
Cuba, 91
Cunard Line, 41, 88, 123, 164
Curtis, Ivor, 192–3
Curtiss, George, 75
Cymrian, 96
Cymric, 70, 83

D

Dakar, 96, 172, 187
Daleham, 21
Dalewood, 97
Danish crew members, 21, 33, 35, 99
Dardanelles, 150
Dartwen, 56–7
David Morris, 35
Davies, A. E., 99
Davies, Archibald, 183
Davies, D. J., 94
Davies, David (Caernarfon: master, *Ocean Ranger*), 20
Davies, David (Neath: master, *Patagonia*), 91, 168
Davies, E. (Criccieth: seaman, *Conway Castle*), 35
Davies, E. (Llangrannog: master, *Nora*), 96
Davies, F., 164
Davies, G. S., 94
Davies, Griffith, 133
Davies, H. M., 91, 168
Davies, H. O., 142
Davies, Howard, 91, 168
Davies, Hugh, 183
Davies, Iris Beryl, 91, 168
Davies, J. (Cilgerran: sailor, *Westergate*), 112
Davies, J. (Denbighshire: trimmer, *Lusitania*), 164
Davies, J. (Ebbw Vale: fireman, *Armenian*), 142
Davies, J. E. (Llangrannog: second officer, *Southwestern*), 94–5
Davies, John (Cardigan: bosun, *Lusitania*), 164, 198
Davies, John (Llangrannog: mate, *Margaret and Ann*), 94
Davies, John Thomas (Llangrannog: able seaman, *Commonwealth*), 97
Davies, Sid, 112
Davies, W. (Llangrannog: master, *King Howel*), 95
Davies, W. Evan (Burry Port: sailor, *Drummuir*), 66–7
Davies, W. J. (Cardiff: cadet, *Patagonia*), 91, 168
Davies, W. M. (port sanitary inspector), 193
Davis, Elizabeth Alice, 88
Deal, 20, 136
deck boys, 15, 21, 72–3, 85, 86, 186
deck guns, 118–19, 130; *see also* guns
Declaration of Paris, 136
decoy vessels, 5, 8, 91, 120, 123, 124, 125, 142, 153; *see also* dummy battleships
Defence of the Realm Act, 48, 51, 182

defensively armed ships, 59, 94, 96, 98, 125–6, 135–6, 150, 153, 168, 176, 183–5, 187–8, 193
Delmira, 103, 121
Dempster, John, 20
Denbigh, 70, 75
Derry, 88
desertions, 21, 33, 34, 42, 48, 70, 85, 86, 90, 94, 99, 106, 182
destroyers, 16, 38, 49, 75, 121, 133, 142, 174
Devitt & Moore, 33–4
Devonport, 86, 91, 175
Dewsland, 143
Dieppe, 39, 120
diet *see* food
Dinas Cross, 94
Dinas Powys, 40
Dinorwic, 26
discipline, 47–50, 51, 103–4, 106–7, 172, 181–2
disease, 18, 20, 42, 173, 198; *see also* illness
Distinguished Service Cross, 142
Distinguished Service Medal, 140, 142
Dixiana, 138–9
Dob, Peter, 130
Dock, Wharf, Riverside and General Workers' Union, 101
doctors, 18, 22–3, 41, 73, 151; *see also* surgeons
Dominion Line, 180
Don Arturo, 97
Don Hugo, 24–5
donkeymen, 5, 28, 39, 40, 57, 65, 112, 133–4, 158, 183
Dora, 14
Dover, 16, 72, 76
Dover Strait, 114–15
Downshire, 158
dredgers, 15
Dresden, SMS, 35, 61, 63, 65, 66
Drogheda, 47
Drumcliffe, 61
Drumfries, 101
Drumloist, 115
Drummuir, 66–7
drunkenness, 22, 47–8, 49–50
Dublin, 13, 15, 72, 88, 94
Dublin Steam Packet Company, 87, 122–3
Dudhope, 35
Dudley, Rachel Ward, Lady, 76
Duke of Connaught, 87
Duke of Rothsay see *Puma* (formerly *Duke of Rothsay*)
dummy battleships, 181; *see also* decoy vessels

Dún Laoghaire *see* Kingstown
Dundalk, 13
Dunkirk, 21
Dunraven, Windham Thomas Wyndham-Quin, 4th earl, 76
Durban, 90, 165
Dutch Red Cross, 59
Dutton, Thomas H., 20

E

Eakon, William, 188
Earl of Lathom, 144
Easter Island, 146
Ebbw Vale, 26, 142
Echo, 26
Ecuador, 147, 149
Ecuador, 149–50
Edern, 14, 36, 39, 63, 94
Edernian, 31, 36–9
Edith, 44
Edmunds, David, 113
Edmunds, H., 168
Edwards, Christmas, 185
Edwards, Helena, 88
Egan, J., 59
Egypt, 70, 71, 84, 86, 90, 94, 95, 96, 99–100, 126, 151, 152, 169, 197, 198
Elbe, river, 56, 57, 196
Elder, Alexander, 20
Elder Dempster, 20, 71, 100, 173, 175, 198
Elfrida, 112–13
Elizabeth (1858), 12
Elizabeth (1859), 13
Elizabeth Bennett, 35–6
Ellerman Lines, 97
Ellis, John, 130
Eloby, 71
Elsinore, 146–50
Emden, 61, 184
Emden, SMS, 66
Emily Millington, 60
Endcliffe, 25
Endurance, 89–90
engineers
    assistant engineers, 25, 121
    chief engineers, 27, 59, 64, 73, 103, 113, 120–1, 134, 141–2, 147, 150, 188
    first engineers, 15, 39, 57, 65, 69, 72, 91–2, 93, 99, 116, 117, 130, 133, 136, 143, 166, 183
    fourth engineers, 15, 57, 59, 72, 75, 91, 99–100, 142, 149, 168, 183, 187
    in general, 4, 5, 14, 57, 113, 123, 133, 139, 142, 149, 153

second engineers, 15, 27, 39, 40, 56, 63, 65, 70–2, 75, 90, 93, 94, 99, 106, 112, 115, 116, 130, 133, 143, 147, 150, 158, 161–3, 168, 182, 185
third engineers, 15, 27, 39, 40, 57, 63, 72–3, 90, 99, 106, 113–15, 134, 142, 158, 161, 168, 182, 183
English Channel, 38, 39, 41, 60, 114–15, 126, 131–2, 138, 145, 161–2, 172, 190
enlistment, 5, 36
Estonian crew members, 99
Euston, 40
Evan Thomas, Radcliffe, 32, 39–41, 91, 94, 95, 98–9, 143, 168
Evans, A., 83–5
Evans, Asa, 147–50
Evans, Benjamin Bruce, 166
Evans, D. J., 168
Evans, Daniel Jones, 116
Evans, E., 95
Evans, Evan O., 97
Evans, J., 121
Evans, J. C., 86
Evans, J. M., 65
Evans, J. T., 68
Evans, John (Caernarfon: sailor, *North Wales*), 65
Evans, John Raymond (Newport: apprentice, *Paddington*), 40
Evans, O., 184
Evans, R. (Holyhead: fireman, *Anglia*), 73
Evans, R. (Llangrannog: able seaman, *King Howel* and *Winnfield*), 95, 97
Evans, R. G. (Porthmadog: mate, *Elsinore*), 147
Evans, Thomas (Aberarth: master, *Therese Heymann*), 69
Evans, Thomas (Porthmadog: mate, *North Wales*), 65
Evans, Thomas John (Criccieth: Captain, *Drumcliffe*), 61
Evans, W. J. (Aberystwyth: chief officer, *Rubens*), 59
Evans, W. J. (Llangrannog: sailor, *Onwen*), 96
executions, 60
Exford, 32, 65–6

F

failures to join, 48, 85, 100, 105–6
Falaba, 134–5
Falkland Islands, 65, 66–7
Falklands, Battle of, 66
Falmouth, 37, 159, 172–3, 187

INDEX

Fastnet Rock, 39, 144
Fecamp, 172
ferries, 6, 7, 14, 15–17, 26, 86–8
Ffestiniog, 137, 142, 152
Field Line, 32, 95
fines, 47, 48, 50, 107
Finnish crew members, 33, 35
firemen, 4, 5, 14, 15, 22, 27, 32–3, 39, 41, 43–9, 56–7, 63–5, 70, 72–5, 90, 92–4, 97, 99–101, 106–7, 113, 116, 125, 130–2, 140, 142, 148, 150, 162, 168, 183, 185–6, 189, 190
Fisher, Sir John, 153
fishermen, 2, 3, 4, 5, 67, 117, 190, 195–6; *see also* trawlers
Fishguard, 7, 13–14, 15, 17, 86–7, 90, 134, 183
Fleetwood, 16, 87, 130
Flint, 142, 164
fog *see* weather conditions
food, 42–4, 51, 58–9, 63, 98, 100, 147, 149, 169, 193, 194, 199
'for the run' payments, 32, 36, 50
foreign-going vessels, 5, 11, 17–18, 28, 94, 95, 98
Fortol, 182
Foster, Bart, 137
Framfield, 195
France, 16, 37–9, 63, 70–2, 76, 84, 86, 95, 96, 116, 120–1, 131–3, 139, 143, 145, 157, 162, 168–9, 172–5, 190, 196
Francis, Rhys Edward, 40
Frau Minna Petersen, 61
Freemantle, 35
Freetown, 174–5
Freiherr von Forstner, Georg-Günther, 133
French Navy, 169
Furtenberg internment camp, 184

G

Gaelic, 60–1
Galapagos Islands, 146–9
gales *see* weather conditions
Galicia, 115–16
galley boys, 15, 73
Gallipoli, 72, 76, 197–8
Galloway, Stanley, 64
Galtee More, 16
Galveston, TX, 96, 99, 131
Gansser, Konrad, 136
Garston, 48, 159
Gatt, Dominico, 183
Geelong, 21
Geier, SMS, 63
Gem, 68–9

Genoa, 86, 95, 182
George, Gwilym, 168
George Casson, 57, 198
Georgic, 183
German crew members, 17, 33, 34, 35, 92, 99
Germany, 1, 8, 34–5, 37, 55–77, 111–26, 129–53, 157–76, 182–90, 193, 194, 198
Gertrude, 27
Ghana, 100
Gibraltar, 27, 71, 95, 100, 169, 170, 172, 188
Gill, John, 27
Glamorgan, 27–8
Glamorgan Gazette, 102–3, 173
Glanton, 65
Glasgow, 83, 84, 86, 88, 96, 99, 187
Glen, A. A., 59
Glenesk, 113
Glenholm, 144
Gloucester, HMS, 192
Glyndwr (formerly *Craigronald*), 59
Golden Cross Line, 96
Golden Gate (formerly *Lord Shaftesbury*), 89
Goodwick, 26
Goss, W. A., 142
Gower peninsula, 23–4
Grampian, 84, 86
greasers, 72, 101, 183
Great Southern, 17
Great Western, 17
Great Western Railway (GWR), 14, 15, 17, 75–6, 86–7
Greavesash, 94
Greece, 71, 72, 76, 96, 150
Greek crew members, 99, 100, 106
Green, A. S. J., 181
Greenock, 88
Greenore, 16
Greenore, 15
Greldon, 98
Grenadines, 85
Grey, Sir Edward, 143
Grianaig, 76
Griffith, William, 60–1
Griffiths, A., 63
Griffiths, Arthur, 152–3
Griffiths, G., 34
Griffiths, Griffith, 72
Griffiths, Rowland, 75
Griffiths, W., 142
Grims, J. C., 86
Grimsby, 20, 61, 67–8, 92
Guayaquil, 147, 149
gun crews, 8, 119, 153, 168, 185, 188, 193
gunnery training, 183
guns, 8, 118–19, 125–6, 130, 173, 183

215

H

Haddock, C., 139
Hague Conventions, 135–6
Hague Peace Conference, 112, 135
Hain Steam Ship Company, 57, 167
Haines, George, 183
Halifax, Nova Scotia, 40, 82–3, 84, 85
Hall, A., 56
Hallett, George, 162
Hamburg, 34–5, 55–6, 57, 58, 69
Hankey, Sir Maurice, 174
Hansen, Claus, 138
Hanson, John, 35
Harburg, 56, 57
hard labour, 48, 49, 106
Hardy, A., 142
Harland & Wolff, 63, 181
Harlech, 17
Harries, Ivor B., 168
Harris, W. E., 63
Harris, W. M., 139
Hartlepool, 25, 67, 113
Harwich, 61, 169
Haulwen, 39
Havana, 91
Haverfordwest, 12, 26, 117
Haverfordwest and Milford Haven Telegraph, 137–8, 144–5
Hawaii, 91
Headlands, 131
Heatherside, 192–3
Heke, Gwilym, 183
Herald of Wales and Monmouthshire Recorder, 55–6, 162–3
Hersing, Otto, 130
Hibernia, 16, 151–2
Hildebrand, 173
Hillsborough, 75
Hinkin, W. C., 25
Hinkin, William, 121
Hirose, 117
Holyhead
    crew members from, 15, 33, 34, 63, 72–5, 85, 87–8, 90, 116, 123, 125, 130, 164, 181, 198
    port activity levels, 12
    as port of departure, call or arrival, 15, 55, 72, 87, 122–3, 170
    rescued crew and passengers brought to, 16
Holyhead War Memorial, 152
home trade, 11, 14–15, 17, 33, 36, 88, 94
Hong Kong, 94, 103, 197
Honiton, 116
Honolulu, 91

Hood Island, 149
Hook of Holland, 169
Hopemount, 92
Hoppe, Bruno, 139, 166
Hopper, R. W., 47
hospital ships, 5, 16, 17, 66, 72–7, 88, 185, 189–90
hostages, 150–3
Houston, R. P., 165
Howth, 15
Huelva, 24, 159, 160, 172
Hugh Roberts & Sons, 65
Hughes, Arthur, 187
Hughes, E. E., 183
Hughes, Griffith, 27
Hughes, J., 73
Hughes, John (Bangor: fireman, *Linda Blanche*), 130
Hughes, John D. (Porthmadog: able seaman, *Linda Blanche*), 130
Hughes, John Thomas (Bangor: steward, *Anglia*), 75
Hughes, Lewis David, 73
Hughes, Llewellyn, 70–1
Hughes, May, 87
Hughes, Richard, 65
Hughes, Robert, 150–1
Hughes, T. L., 100
Hughes, T. O., 164
Hughes, Thomas (Bangor: engineer's boy, *Anglia*), 75
Hughes, Thomas J., (Holyhead: engineer, *Linda Blanche*), 130
Hughes, William, 75
Hughes, William Osbourne, 134
Hughes & Company, 40
Hull, 36, 38, 67, 90, 92, 94, 99–100, 116
Humber, river, 61
Humphreys, Rowland, 57
Hurd, Archibald, 4, 167
Hurstdale, 65

I

Ikbal, 198
illness, 5, 18–19, 20, 22–3, 33, 42, 94, 100, 173–6, 195; *see also* disease
imprisonment, 48, 104, 107; *see also* internment; prisoners of war
India, 66, 84, 86, 95, 101, 106, 168, 196
Indian City, 130–1
Indian crew members, 43, 101, 105, 189; *see also* lascars
Indian Merchant Service, 189
Indian Ocean, 65–6, 135

INDEX

Indrani, 64
influenza pandemic, 173–6, 198
injuries, 5, 19, 21, 141, 143, 151, 152, 181, 192, 195
Inniscarra, 185
inquests, 23, 47, 73–4, 197
insubordination, 48–9, 101, 103–4
insurance, 7, 44, 60–1
'insurance jobs', 44
international crew members, 4, 8, 21, 33, 35, 50–1, 69–70, 92, 98–107, 113, 121, 132, 166–7, 173, 189, 190, 197
international law, 62, 75, 135–6
internment, 56–60, 76–7, 184
Invincible, HMS, 181
Ipswich, 33, 34
Ireland, 3, 13, 15, 33, 38, 47, 72, 82, 86–7, 88, 94, 122, 139, 144, 163–5, 170, 185
Irish crew members, 33, 75, 87, 99, 113
Irish Sea, 16, 38, 86–7, 122–3, 139–40, 145, 158, 165, 184, 190
Iron Duke, HMS, 181
Island Magee, 33
Isle of Wight, 86, 161
Italian crew members, 92, 99
Italiana, 99
Italy, 37, 69, 86, 95, 96, 98, 99, 101, 160, 182, 188
Ivory Coast, 100

J

J. Monks and Company, 27
Jamaica, 20, 137
James Cullen, 158
Jane Radcliffe (formerly *Windsor*), 32, 98–100
Janeville quay, 13
Japan, 68, 94, 135
Java, 187
Jean, 146
Jehu, Spencer, 186
Jenkins, D. J., 96
Jenkins, Daniel, 39
Jenkins, L., 113–14
Jenkins, Thomas, 150
Jenkins Brothers, 40, 99
Jenny Jones, 17
Jersey City, 103
Jessop, Violet, 82
John, Edward William, 115
John, Percy, 193
John, Thomas E., 35
John, William, 63
John and William, 12

John Cory Sailor's Rest, 137–8, 166, 190
John Pritchard, 18
Johnson, Arthur, 106
Jones, Alfred Lewis, 20
Jones, Arthur, 64
Jones, Arthur Rowland, 165
Jones, D. A., 65
Jones, D. Hughes, 97
Jones, D. J., 96
Jones, D. Owen, 95
Jones, D. T. D., 168
Jones, David, 97–8
Jones, Elizabeth (Bangor: stewardess, *Corsican*, *Tunisian*), 84, 86
Jones, Elizabeth (Holyhead: stewardess, *Anglia*), 88
Jones, Emlyn, 183
Jones, Evan (Aberystwyth: assistant engineer, *Lizzie*), 121
Jones, Evan D. (Llangrannog: master, *Nora*), 96
Jones, G. (Llangrannog: ordinary seaman, *King Howel*), 95
Jones, G. (Pontardawe: Royal Naval Volunteer Reserve, *Artist*), 186
Jones, Griffith (Aberdaron), 192
Jones, Griffith (Porthmadog: mate, *Mary Annie*), 17
Jones, Herbert Arnold, 57
Jones, Hugh P., 27
Jones, J. (Aberaeron: mate, *Wavelet*), 114
Jones, J. (Porthmadog: bosun, *Ruel*), 142
Jones, J. O. (Pwllheli: deck boy, *Artist*), 186
Jones, J. R. (Llangrannog: master, *Arvonian*), 96
Jones, John (Holyhead: fireman, *Anglia*), 73
Jones, John (Llandudno: able seaman, *Llandovery Castle*), 75
Jones, John (Porthmadog: shipowner), 17
Jones, Kate, 63
Jones, Laura Mary, 192
Jones, Mary E., 89, 164
Jones, Owen (Anglesey: captain, *Gertrude*), 27
Jones, Owen (Holyhead: fireman, *Anglia*, age 28), 73
Jones, Owen (Holyhead: fireman, *Anglia*, age 45), 73
Jones, Richard (Holyhead: seaman, *Anglia*), 75
Jones, Richard (Pwllheli: internee), 57–8
Jones, Robert (Porthmadog: carpenter, *Conway Castle*), 34
Jones, Robert (Porthmadog: seaman, *John Pritchard*), 18

Jones, Robert John (Holyhead: fireman, *Anglia*), 75
Jones, Robert W. (Nefyn), 192
Jones, Stanley A., 24
Jones, T. (Llangrannog: second mate, *Lesbian*), 97
Jones, T. G. (Caernarfon: third engineer, *Cambrian Range*), 183
Jones, T. O. (Llangrannog: mate, *Lord Tredegar*), 96
Jones, T. O. (Moelfre: master, *Earl of Lathom*), 144
Jones, Thomas, 20
Jones, W. (Anglesey: stoker, *Cambria*), 72
Jones, W. (Holyhead: greaser, *Royal Edward*), 72
Jones, W. (Pwllheli: carpenter, *Benue*), 100
Jones, W. G. (Chwilog: sailor, *Conway Castle*), 34–5
Jones, W. John (Newcastle Emlyn: steward, *Jane Radcliffe*), 99
Jones, W. O. (Porthmadog: second officer, *Centurion*), 166
Jones, W. R. (Brynhyfryd: *Gertrude*), 27
Jones, William (Aberdovey: able seaman, *Lizzie*), 121
Jones, William (Maentwrog: cook, *John Pritchard*), 18
Jones, William (Pembroke: steward, *Conway Castle*), 34
Jones, Hallet and Company, 136
Jordan Hill, 81, 90
Jowett, F. W., 194

K

Kariba, 187
Karlsruhe, SMS, 64, 65, 160
Kate (1872), 60
Kate (1875), 12–13, 172–3, 198
Kenfig Hill, 162
Key West, FL, 38
Khartoum, 67–8
Kidwelly, 113–14
Kildalton, 146
Kindly Light, 172–3
King George, 183, 184
King Howel, 95, 97
King's Lynn, 60
Kings Lynn, 47
Kingston (Jamaica), 137
Kingstown, 15, 87, 122
Kintuck, 197
Kirwan, J., 59
Knight of the Garter, 69–70

Kophamel, Waldemar, 144
Kosrae, 62–3
Kronprinzessin Cecilie see *Princess* (formerly *Kronprinzessin Cecilie*)

L

La Goulette, 136
La Plata, 161
Ladd, W. H., 107, 132–3
Lady Plymouth, 125
Lancashire and Yorkshire Railway Company, 16, 87
Larne, 88
Las Palmas, 22
lascars, 4, 69, 100–5, 173, 189, 190
Laverick, L., 183
law of the sea, 131; *see also* international law
Le Havre, 37, 84, 96, 131, 139, 157, 188
Leeds City, 184–5
Legge, G., 190
Leghorn *see* Livorno
Leinster, 87, 122–3
Leipzig, SMS, 66–7, 147–9
Leith, 91, 114, 115
Leith of Fyvie, Alexander Forbes-Leith, 1st Baron, 189
Lemnos, 72, 76
Lesbian, 97
Lewis, J., 144
Lewis, John (Holyhead: fireman, *Anglia*), 73
Lewis, John Idwal (Porthmadog: senior third officer, *Lusitania*), 164–5
Lewis, L., 86
Lewis, W. M., 95–6, 97
Lewis, William, 73
Liberia, 92, 100
Liberty Ships, 45
Libya, 151–2
lifeboats, 24, 28, 63, 68, 73–5, 113–15, 120, 125, 129–35, 137–48, 152–3, 159, 161–8, 185–9, 194, 198
Lillie, Thomas, 130
Lilley, William, 64
Limerick, 144
Limerick, 70
Lincolnshire Yeomanry, 71
Linda Blanche, 129–30
liners, 6, 16, 27, 41, 62, 65, 70, 75, 82–6, 88, 101, 123–5, 163–5, 168–9, 172, 181
Lisbon, 43, 133
'Live Bait Squadron', 117
Liver Shipping Company, 64

Liverpool, 158–9, 163, 164, 165, 172, 180, 187
  court proceedings at, 48–9
  crew members from, 73, 75, 85, 134
  crew members joining or leaving at, 83, 85, 86, 91, 95, 165
  hospitals, 187
  as port of departure or arrival, 12, 14–15, 20–1, 32–3, 63–5, 82–6, 88, 90–1, 95–6, 115–16, 125, 133, 137, 146, 158, 163, 165
  sea scouts, 180
Liverpool and Menai Straits Steamship Company, 23
Livorno, 101, 143, 188
Lizard peninsula, 13, 38
Lizzie, 120–1
Llanarth, 57
Llanbedr, 60
Llanberis, 99
Llandaff, 28
Llandenny, 162
Llandovery Castle, 75, 185
Llandudno, 75
Llandysul, 28
Llanelli, 15, 22–3, 25, 62, 66, 106, 121, 143, 175–6
Llanelly Star, 62
Llanfair, 72
Llanfairfechan, 89, 164
Llanfair PG, 75
Llanfechan, 72
Llangorse, 99
Llangrannog, 93–7
Llangrannog War Memorial, 97
Llanishen, 39
Llanon, 26, 116
Llanrhidian, 185
Llantrisant, 97
Llongwen, 97
Lloyd, A., 181
Lloyd, Robert, 22
Lloyd George, David, 8, 42
Lloyd's List, 182
Lloyd's Register, 4, 23, 33, 182
Llŷn peninsula, 14, 36, 65
Lodorer (formerly *Sandyford*), 90–1
London, 26, 32–4, 37, 39, 40, 49, 69, 87, 91, 94, 97, 99, 112, 115–16, 126, 161, 168, 173, 180
London and American Maritime Trading Company, 161
London and North Western Railway (LNWR), 15–16, 26, 72–5, 87–8, 151
London and South Western Railway, 33, 94–5

London Naval Conference, 135
London Trader, 28
Lord Allendale, 137
Lord Shaftesbury see *Golden Gate* (formerly *Lord Shaftesbury*)
Lord Tredegar, 96
Lorton, 35
Lough Foyle, 38
Lougher, Thomas, 125
Lougher & Company, 125
Lucy (1879), 13
Lucy (1900), 15
Lugg, Herbert, 131
Lundy Island, 12, 25, 143
Lusitania, 62, 89, 142, 163–5, 198
Lutine Bell, 198
Lydney, 139
Lynrota, 64
Lynrowan, 64
Lyon, Peter, 2, 105, 130

M

McCarthy, A., 84, 86
MacDonald, Ramsay, 194
Macdonald, Thomas J., 105–6
Macedonia see *Polgowan* (formerly *Macedonia*)
McFadden, Thomas, 195
Machen, 168
McIver, James Murdoch, 75
McPherson, Emily, 92
McPherson, M. G., 92
Maddicks, W., 126
Madeira, 133
Madsen, Peter, 196–7
Madura, 106, 115
Maentwrog, 18
Magio, John, 183
Maguire, Alice, 63
mail ships, 6, 49, 83–6, 87, 88, 122–3
Malachite, 62
Malaga, 151, 182
malaria, 20, 173
Malta, 71, 86, 142, 189, 193
Maltese crew members, 86
Manchester, 39, 88, 129
Manchester Ship Canal, 88
Manipur (later *Sandhurst*), 181
Manning, L. J., 73–4, 75
Mansfield, 142
Mantua, 173, 175
Margaret and Ann, 12, 94
Margaret Ham, 13, 25
Marie, 147, 148–9

219

Mariston, 187–8
maroonings, 146–50
Marseille, 63, 86, 116, 131, 168, 196
Marshall Islands, 62
Marston, James, 188
Martin, G., 112
Mary, 13
Mary Annie, 17
Mary Edwards, 12
Mary Jane Lewis, 12
Mary Jones, 197
masters, 5, 12, 14–17, 20–1, 24–5, 28, 33–6,
 39–40, 47–50, 57, 60, 63–70, 73–5,
 89–99, 112–13, 116, 119–21, 130–3,
 137, 140–50, 153, 158–1, 168, 170–1,
 176, 184, 188, 190, 197, 198; see also
 captains
masters at arms, 165
mates
 mates/first mates, 5, 12–15, 17, 20, 21,
  24, 27, 33, 39, 40, 57, 60, 65, 90,
  93–9, 114–16, 121, 130, 133, 142–4,
  147, 150–1, 158, 168, 181, 184
 second mates, 15, 34, 39, 40, 64, 65, 70,
  93–7, 99, 100, 103, 115, 116, 122, 125,
  133, 136, 140, 142–3, 161, 166–8, 185,
  193, 195, 197
 third mates, 15, 21, 33, 40, 75, 93, 95, 96,
  100, 143, 151, 166, 168
Mathias, R. W., 94
matrons, 81, 82, 85, 88, 89, 92, 163
Matthews, Sydney, 75
Matthews, W. H., 66–7
Mauritius, 167
medals, 140, 142, 195–6
Mediterranean, 16, 17, 32, 40, 71, 125, 150,
 169
Medora, 184
Medway, 34
Melbourne, 90
Melilla, 150–1
Memel, 59
Menai Bridge, 23, 40, 70, 72, 75
Mercantile Fleet Auxiliaries, 6, 135–6
Mercantile Marine Medal, 195
Mercantile Marine Memorial, 4–5, 26, 40,
 72, 153, 164, 196
Mercantile Marine Reserve, 2, 4, 5, 6, 97,
 170, 175, 179, 180
Mercantile Marine Service Association, 195
Merchant Shipping Acts, 6, 19, 28, 42, 51, 98
Mercian, 70–1
Merevale Shipping Company, 158
Mersey, river, 13, 60
Merthyr Tydfil, 39, 40, 70

Messina, 95
Metagama, 85–6
Meteor, 115
Metropolis, 33
Mexico, 34
Meyric, 60
Middlesbrough, 39, 97, 112, 113, 136
Mikasa, 47–8
Milford Haven, 12, 84, 101, 117, 137–8,
 139–40, 145, 161, 166–7, 170, 190
Milne, 142
Milos, 96
minelayers, 111, 117
mines, 39, 55–6, 61, 67–9, 72–3, 111–17, 121,
 126, 190, 193, 195
minesweepers, 5, 113, 157, 168
minimum wage, 31
Minister Jaager, 58
Ministry of Reconstruction, 180
Ministry of Shipping, 2, 6, 7, 179, 180
Miss Morris, 182
Missanabie, 85–6
Moelfre, 27, 60, 144
Moffat, Henry, 47
Moji, 94
Mold, 25, 70, 121
Moldavia, 172
Monmouth, 72
Montenegro, 151
Montevideo, 22, 63, 89
Montezuma, 181
Montreal, 39, 84–6
Morel Brothers, 43, 126
Morfa Nefyn, 14, 65, 185
Morgan, B. J., 47
Morgan, John, 21–2
Morgan, W. H. (Cardiff: chief steward,
 Dixiana), 139
Morgan, W. H. (St Dogmaels: master,
 Ecuador), 149
Morgan, W. J., 175–6
Morocco, 150
Morris, Hugh (Barmouth: master *William
 Prichard*), 197, 198
Morris, Hugh Cynhaiarn (Barmouth: able
 seaman, *Kintuck*), 175, 197, 198
Morris, John, 197, 198
Morris, Laura Jones, 197
Morris, Richard (father of Hugh Morris), 197
Morris, Richard (son of Hugh Morris), 197
Morris, Robert D., 130
Morris, W., 100
Morris, William Edward, 197–8
mortality rates, 18, 28, 174–5
Moss Line, 165

INDEX

Mostyn, 12, 68, 144, 166, 195
Moudros, 72, 76
Möwe, SMS, 183
Mozambique, 90
Mumbles, 24
Munster, 87
Murcia, 196–7
Muslims, 100, 151–2
Myanmar, 152

N

Nantes, 162
Naples, 96, 98, 99, 187
National Insurance Act, 19
National Maritime Board, 179, 180
National Maritime Museum, 5
National Sailors' and Firemen's Union, 102, 188–9, 194
National Transport Workers' Federation, 101
Nauru, 62
Naval Discipline Act, 6
navigation, 2, 48, 153
Neath, 25, 162
Needham Brothers, 114
Nefyn, 21, 33, 34, 39, 65, 84, 86, 192, 197
Neilson, John Brustad, 114
Nelson Strait, 63
Netherlands, 68, 169
Neustrelitz internment camp, 184
New Orleans, 32, 98, 125
New Quay, 68, 97, 98, 183, 185
New Ross, 13
New York, 38, 39, 50, 61, 69, 82–3, 88, 90, 96, 103, 163
New York Times, 164
New Zealand, 62, 70
New Zealand Expeditionary Force, 70
New Zealand Shipping Company, 70
Newborough, 40, 75, 143
Newcastle (Australia), 24, 33, 34, 35, 90
Newcastle (England), 21, 47, 116
Newcastle Emlyn, 99
Newfoundland, 17, 35, 197
Newhaven, 161–2
Newport (Mon.), 6, 12, 13, 25, 26, 28, 32, 59, 63, 75, 89, 94–6, 115–16, 126, 130, 161, 164, 168, 172, 193, 196
Newport (Pembs.), 25, 40, 70, 143, 168, 187
Newport News, VA, 91, 131, 140
Newstead, 187
Neyland, 86, 99, 185
Niblick, 130
Nicaragua, 148

Nicholas, J., 147, 149–50
Nicolaieff, 91, 168
Nicosian, 125
Nigaristan, 50
Nigeria, 20, 92, 100
Ningchow, 168
nominal wages, 33, 84, 89–90, 92, 150
non-commissioned auxiliaries, 6, 135–6
Nora, 96
Nord Deutsche Line, 64
Nordenham, 37
Norfolk, VA, 64, 91, 94, 95, 99
Normanton, 188
North Sea, 61, 68, 113, 145, 190
North Shields, 94
North Shipping Company, 65
North Wales, 65
North Wales Chronicle and Advertiser, 57–8, 130, 150–1, 152, 158–60
Northlands, 136–7
Norwegian crew members, 33, 100, 184
Nova Scotia, 40, 82–3, 85
nurses, 74, 75, 76, 82; *see also* matrons

O

Oberon, 150
Ocean Coal Company, 21–2
Ocean Ranger, 20
O'Connell, B., 181
Odesa, 91, 168
officers
    chief officers, 57, 59, 73–4, 162
    first officers, 114–15, 165
    second officers, 94, 104, 142, 166
    third officers, 164
    wives and families of, 33, 58, 61, 82, 89–93, 168
Officers of Customs, 3
oil tankers, 55–6, 95, 146–50, 181, 182
Olsen, N. C., 114
Onwen, 96–7
opium, 102–3
Oran, 67, 71
Order of the White Feather, 195
ordinary seamen, 5, 17, 20–1, 34, 57, 63, 70, 75, 85, 89–90, 93, 95–7, 126, 131, 139, 142–3
Orduna, 88, 123–5
Oriana, 158
Orkney, 174, 182
Ortega, 63
O'Sullivan, Flor, 89
overtime, 31, 32, 48–9, 100
Owen, Evan, 95

Owen, G., 161
Owen, Griffith, 65
Owen, Hannah, 87
Owen, J. (Llangrannog: mate, *Onwen*), 96–7
Owen, J. H. (Llangrannog: able seaman, *Winnfield*), 97
Owen, J. L. (Llangrannog: master, *Snowdon*), 96, 97
Owen, John (Anglesey: able seaman, *Llandovery Castle*), 75
Owen, John (Benllech: mate, *Gertrude*), 27
Owen, Morris, 65
Owen, Robert (Ffestiniog: able seaman, *Candidate*), 137, 138
Owen, Robert D. (Morfa Nefyn: cadet, *Artist*), 185–6
Owen, Roger, 25
Owen, S. J., 95
Owen, Thomas H., 73
Owens, Christmas, 18
Owens, David, 95, 97
Owens, E., 59
Owens, George, 188
Owens, Hugh D., 65
Owens, Owen, 164, 198
Owens, William, 75

P

P&O Line, 168, 172
Pacific Steam Navigation Company, 63, 88, 115, 123
Paddington (formerly *Patagonia* and *Swindon*), 40
Paimpol, 173
Panama, 91, 149–50
Panama Canal, 91
Para, 65
Paraná, river, 37
Parry, A., 82
Parry, J., 83
Parry, Jane, 87
Parry, John, 21–2
Parry, Louisa, 87
Parry, R. H., 65
Parry, Thomas Richard, 73
Parry, W. W., 137
passenger accommodation, 63, 71, 83, 84
Patagonia (1906) see *Paddington* (formerly *Patagonia* and *Swindon*)
Patagonia (1913), 91, 168
Patani, 20

Patricia, 21
Patrician (later *Tarakol* and *Vineleaf*), 181
Patterson, James, 183
Patton, J. E., 148, 150
Patzig, Helmut, 185
Paul Paix, 189–90
Pauleson, E., 114
Paxton, William, 130
pay, 6, 31–6, 43, 49, 50, 51, 70, 82–6, 88–92, 94, 100, 107, 150, 165, 180, 193, 194
Pembrey, 160
Pembroke, 12, 34, 75, 144
Pen Cw, 14
Penarth, 7, 22, 28, 37, 64, 86, 96, 112, 125, 139, 166, 168, 187, 198
Penarth, 26–7
Penistone, 96
Penmaenmawr, 70
Penrhyn, 14
Penrhyn Castle, 35
Pensacola, FL, 114
pensions, 19, 181, 193
Penzance, 143, 162
Pepperell, W. M., 112–13
Pernambuco, 144
Persia, 168–9
Perts, W. H., 142
Peru, 32, 63, 65, 146
Peter Dixon and Son, 92
Peters, J. J., 183
Peterson, E. M., 116
Petroleum, 182
Philadelphia, 91
Philadelphia Public Ledger, 125
Philipps, Owen, 20
Phillips, G., 168
Phillips, Thomas, 12
Phoebe, 67
Pick Me Up, 15
Picton, 40, 94
Picton Island, 66
Pierce, Howell, 75
pilots, 38, 56, 158–9
Ping Suey, 126
piracy, 136
Plate, river, 26, 31, 38, 50
Plymouth, 13, 17, 37, 49, 60, 75, 175
Podesta, H., 114
Pointer, 88
Poland, 183
Polgowan (formerly *Macedonia*), 192
Pontardawe, 186
Pontwen, 39
Pontyclun, 183
Pontypool, 90

Pontypridd, 126
Poole, 17
Port Dinorwic, 7, 12, 20, 24, 26, 60, 75, 116, 130
Port Louis, 167
Port Natal, 90
Port of London Society, 189
Port Patrick and Wigtownshire Railway Company, 88
Port Said, 90, 94, 95, 99–100, 126
Port Talbot, 7, 24–5, 49–50, 100, 146, 157, 162
Porth, 144
Porthdinllaen, 14
Porthgain, 12, 25
Porthmadog, 13–15, 17–18, 20, 28, 34, 36, 60, 63, 65, 70, 72, 75, 100, 103, 116, 121, 130, 142, 147, 164, 166, 182
Porthmadog War Memorial, 35
Porthoustock, 13
Portland, OR, 21, 55
Portoferraio, 160
Portsmouth, 6, 91, 97
Portugal, 43, 133
Pound, A. D. R., 105
Powell, Percy B., 21
Powell, T. A., 187
Prah, 173
President Stein, 142
press coverage, 1, 2, 7, 48, 55–9, 66–7, 102–6, 113–15, 117, 122–5, 130, 132–8, 140, 144–7, 150–2, 158–64, 166–7, 170–1, 174–6, 182–7, 190
Press Bureau, 182
Prestatyn, 85
Preston, 25
Pretorian, 83–4
Price, Owen, 75
Princess (formerly *Kronprinzessin Cecilie*), 181
Princess Caroline, 116
Princess Maud, 88
Princess Victoria, 88
Prinz Eitel Friedrich, SMS, 146
prisoners of war, 17, 56–60, 64–7, 76–7, 183–4, 189
Pritchard, Hugh, 191
Pritchard, Robert, 73, 74
Pritchard, Samuel David, 16
Pritchard Brothers, 18, 20, 57
privateering, 136
prize rules, 61, 67, 117, 153
Profit, C. A., 83
propaganda, 135, 182, 183
Prosser, A., 181

provisioning, 42–4, 51, 63, 100, 193, 194
Puma (formerly *Duke of Rothsay*), 33, 88
pursers, 15, 72–3, 82, 83, 125, 141, 168
Pustkuchen, Herbert, 116
Pwllheli, 15, 39, 57, 70, 133, 185, 191–2

Q
Q-ships, 5, 8, 91, 125, 142, 153
quartermasters, 15, 70, 72–3, 142, 181
Quebec, 84–5
Queen Alexandra, 145
Queenstown, 82–3, 164–5, 172

R
R. Thomas & Company, 34–5
racism, 105–6, 194
radio equipment, 28, 61, 73, 171
Radyr, 125
Ramsay, 106
Rangoon, 58, 152
Rathmore, 16
rationing, 194
Reardon Smith & Sons, 64, 123, 131, 184
Rebecca, 14–15
Redmond, James, 73
Rees, Allen, 161
Rees, D., 95
Rees, D. A., 99
Rees, Gwilym, 40
Registry of British Seamen, 3
repatriations, 59–60, 184
requisitions, 7, 14, 15–17, 41, 69–77, 91, 151, 172, 181
Retriever, 16
Rewa, 189–90
Reynish, B., 181
Rhokotis, 65
Rhuddlan, 70, 83
Rhydlewis, 97, 116
Rhydyfelin, 161
Richards, A., 161
Richardson, James, 183
Richmond, George, 161
Riley, S., 85–6
Rio de Janeiro, 32, 37, 64, 96
Rio Grande, 37
Rio Negro, 64
Rio Parana, 160–1
Rio Tinto Copper Company, 24
Robert Adamson, 22
Roberts, David, 65
Roberts, E., 142
Roberts, Ellin R., 82–3

Roberts, Hugh (Edern: captain, *Edernian*), 36–9, 42
Roberts, Hugh (Nefyn: steward, *North Wales*), 65
Roberts, John (Menai Bridge: seaman, *Anglia*), 75
Roberts, John (St Davids: master, *Jordan Hill*), 90
Roberts, Joseph, 20
Roberts, L. W., 63
Roberts, O., 69
Roberts, Owen, 75
Roberts, R. (Edern: master, *Picton*), 94
Roberts, R. (Swansea: fireman, *Cottingham*), 144
Roberts, Richard, 73
Roberts, Robert (Caernarfon: seaman, *Anglia*), 75
Roberts, Robert (Porthmadog: cook, *Mary Annie*), 17
Roberts, William, 39
Robertson, B., 64
Romford, 193
Rosabella, 167
Rosaleen, 23–4
Rosario, 37, 65
Rosenkrantz, Baron Arild, 124
Ross, D., 192
Rosser, D. J., 113
Rosslare, 15, 17, 86–7, 170
Rosstrevor, 16
Rotterdam, 68
Rouen, 38, 132, 143, 172
Rowena (formerly *Cluny Castle*), 33
Rowlands, D., 95
Rowlands, John, 24
Rowlands, William, 39–40
Royal Army Medical Corp, 71–2
Royal Edward (formerly *Cairo*), 71–2
Royal Fleet Auxiliary, 6, 91, 181, 182
Royal Mail Steam Packet Company, 20, 37
Royal Naval Reserve, 4, 5, 12, 51, 105, 143, 180, 188
Royal Naval Volunteer Reserve, 171–2, 180, 185
Royal Navy, 4, 18, 36, 51, 82, 98, 126, 169, 170, 174, 198
Royal Oak, HMS, 36
Royal Welsh Fusiliers, 197
Ruapehu, 97
Rubens, 58–9
Rücker, Claus, 117, 152, 167
Ruel, 142–3
Ruhleben internment camp, 56–9, 61

Runcorn, 12, 13, 36, 60
Runo, 61
Russia, 57, 67, 68, 115, 135, 166
Russian crew members, 33, 35
Russo-Japanese War, 112, 135
Ruthin, 75

S

sail makers, 33, 35, 89, 144
sailing vessels, 4, 7, 11–13, 17–18, 23, 33–6, 39, 50, 56–7, 60–1, 66–7, 81, 89–90, 94, 144–6, 164–5, 172–3, 197, 198
St Andrew, 17, 76
St Asaph, 87
St Briuec, 173
St David, 17, 76
St Davids, 25, 90
St David's, 14
St Dogmaels, 12, 35, 132, 147, 149, 164, 168
Saint Egbert, 66
St George's Channel, 137, 144–5, 165–6, 190
St John's, 83–4, 85, 188
St Lucia, 38, 92
St Malo, 95
St Patrick, 17, 76
St Vincent, Cape Verde, 38
St Vincent, HMS, 105
Salmon, D. I., 59
Salonica, 71, 150
Sampson, H., 59
San Cristóbal Island, 146–7, 149
San Francisco, 33, 34, 66, 94, 149–50
San Luis, CA, 148, 150
San Wilfrido, 55–6, 196
Sandhurst see *Manipur* (later *Sandhurst*)
Sandiford, A. B., 137
Sandyford see *Loderer* (formerly *Sandyford*)
sanitary conditions, 41–2, 44–5, 193–4
Santa Cruz, 64
Santa Fe, 31, 38
Santa Marta, 48
Santos, 21, 34
Savona, 37, 69, 99, 188
Sawle, George, 183
Saxon, 57
Saxonia, 88
Scandinavian, 86
Scapa Flow, 174, 182
Scarborough, 67, 112–13
Scarsdale, 57
Schneider, Rudolf, 140, 143, 162
Schulz, Gerhard, 187
Schweidnitz internment camp, 184

INDEX

Schwieger, Walther, 137, 144, 157, 163, 166
Scilly Isles, 131, 143
Scotia, 16, 75
Scotland, 3, 15, 24, 83, 84, 86, 88, 91, 96, 99, 114, 115, 116, 187
Scottish crew members, 84, 92, 98–100, 146
Sea Scouts, 180–1
Seafarer's Joint Committee, 85
Sealey, James, 21
Seaman's Union, 56
seamen's boarding houses, 100, 102
seamen's missions, 50, 189
Seamen's National Insurance Society, 19
Seamen's Pension Fund, 19
Senegal, 96, 172, 187
Senussi, 151–2
Seville, 17
Seydlitz, 66
Shackleton, Ernest, 89–90
Shanghai, 197
shark attacks, 187–8
Sharp, C. W., 142
Sharp, W., 146
Shaw, Hugh, 12–13, 172–3
Shaw, Humphrey, 13, 198
Sheerness, 94
Shetland, 24, 146
Ship Captain's Medical Guide, 18–19
Shipping Federation, 22, 180
ship's papers, 65, 129, 135, 137, 148
Shipwrecked Mariners' Society, 158, 160, 161, 189
shipwrecks, 18, 19, 23–8, 89, 169
Sicilian, 84, 86
Sierra Leone, 92, 100, 172, 173, 174–5, 198
Silver War Badge, 195–6
Simmonds, James, 114
Simmons, W. C., 56
Sittenfeld, Erich, 187
Skewen, 99, 113–14
slate, 7, 12, 57
Slate, F., 117
Slieve Bawn, 16
Slieve Bloom, 16
Slieve Gallion, 16
Slieve More, 16
small maritime communities, 8, 93–8
Smith, Ada, 91
Smith, Florence Kate, 193
Smith, L., 142
Smyrna, 59
Smyth Channel, 63

Snowdon (1902), 16
Snowdon (1904), 95–6, 97
Socotra, 47–8
Solomon, D. R., 103
Sollum, 151
Somali crew members, 100, 106–7
Somme, Battle of the, 198
South Africa, 90, 165
South Pacific, 96
South Shields, 98, 99, 150
South Stack, 15
South Wales Weekly Post, 113–14, 184
Southampton, 71, 76, 84, 95, 161, 180
Southerndown, 76
Southport, 32, 62–3
Southwestern, 94–5
Spain, 17, 24, 26, 35, 37, 95, 112, 116, 151, 152, 159, 160, 172, 174, 182, 187, 188, 197
Spanish crew members, 106
Spanish flu, 173–6, 198
special service squadron, 181
Spezzia, 99
spies, 88, 160
Standish Hall, 96
State Insurance Office, 7
Stephens, Kate, 81, 89, 90
Stephens, Wallis, 27
Stevens, George Beynon, 21
stewardesses, 5, 15, 33, 63, 81–9, 91, 92, 133, 163, 164, 168, 195
stewards
 assistant stewards, 25, 70, 83, 85, 86, 115, 133, 188
 bath and boots stewards, 83
 bedroom stewards, 83
 cabin stewards, 83
 chief stewards, 73, 83, 91, 139
 deck stewards, 70, 83
 engineers' stewards, 59, 84, 187
 female stewards *see* stewardesses
 fourth stewards, 126
 in general, 4, 5, 15, 33–4, 41, 65, 70, 72–5, 83–6, 93, 99, 101, 116, 133, 150, 162, 175, 187
 mess room stewards, 36, 39, 57, 65, 67, 93, 95, 99, 112, 115, 116, 123, 126, 142, 158, 161, 168
 officers' stewards, 84
 saloon stewards, 83
 second stewards, 73, 83, 85, 139
 steerage stewards, 83
Stockton, USS, 16
stokers, 15, 41, 45–7, 72–3, 75, 164; *see also* firemen

storekeepers, 48, 70, 83, 164
storms *see* weather conditions
Stoss, Alfred, 160
Stöwer, Willy, 130
Strait of Magellan, 63
Stranraer, 88
Strathavon, 103–4
Strathnairn, 166–7
Streatham, 94
strikes, 31, 194
Stuart, Robert, 73
Sudan, 152
surgeons, 76, 83, 85; *see also* doctors
Swansea
    accidents at, 21
    crew members from, 33–4, 47, 57, 70, 85, 88–91, 97, 114, 126, 131, 136, 144–5, 162–3, 168, 183–4
    crew members joining or leaving at, 66
    deaths from Spanish flu at, 174, 175
    port activity levels, 6–7
    as port of departure, call or arrival, 12, 20, 66, 112–13, 131, 139, 143
    protests at, 101–2
    rescued sailors brought to, 166, 189–90
    sanitary inspections at, 193–4
    sea scouts, 181
Swansea Copper Ore Company, 20
Swansea Port Sanitary Authority, 193–4
Swedish crew members, 21, 99
Swindon (1906) *see Paddington* (formerly *Patagonia* and *Swindon*)
Swindon (1912), 95
Świnoujście, 183
Sydney, 21, 70, 90, 97
Symons, B., 91–2
Syren and Shipping Illustrated, 121–2

T

T.124 agreements, 6, 16, 51, 170, 181–2
Tacoma, WA, 95
Taganrog, 57
Talbot, E. G., 142
Talbot, E. R., 142
Talcahuano, 90
Tangistan, 113–14, 166
Tara, 16, 151–2
Tarakol see Patrician (later *Tarakol* and *Vineleaf*)
Tarragona, 188
Tatem Steam Navigation Company, 32, 65, 116, 122, 143

Taylor, E. L., 97
Tees, river, 97, 145
Tenerife, 64
Therese Heymann, 69
Thomas, Alfred, 130
Thomas, Brice, 103
Thomas, D. J., 95
Thomas, Daniel, 97
Thomas, Evan O., 96
Thomas, Hugh, 74, 75
Thomas, Idris Percy, 182–3
Thomas, J. D., 169
Thomas, J. H., 121
Thomas, Joshua, 134
Thomas, Owen, 73
Thomas, Richard, 73
Thomas, Robert, 75
Thomas, W. B., 168
Thomas, William (Amlwch: shipowner), 60–1
Thomas, William (Llanrhuddlad: shipowner), 33
Thomas and Ann (21319), 12
Thomas and Anne (74503), 15
Thomond, 166, 167
Thompson, James, 35
Thordis, 122
Times, 174
Titanic, 28
Tolin, H., 59
Tommi, 184
Torpedo Badge, 195
torpedo boats, 61, 74, 161
torpedo hits, 16, 39–41, 62, 70–2, 75, 83, 87, 89, 91, 94, 97, 121, 131, 134, 136, 138–9, 141, 151, 157–69, 173, 176, 182–9, 193, 195–8
Torrevieja, 152
Townsville, 90
trade unions, 31, 49, 101–2, 180, 188–9, 194
Trafford, 139–40
training ships, 33–4, 36, 180
tramp steamers, 7, 41–4
Traven, B., 43–4
trawlers, 2, 26–7, 67, 117, 120, 130, 137, 142–3, 162–3, 165, 180, 187, 189; *see also* fishermen
Trecastle, 183
Tredegar, 99
Treglisson, 57
Treherbert, 72
Treneglos, 167–8
Tresaith, 12
Trevider, 57

INDEX

Trickey, Captain, 140–2
trimmers, 5, 15, 21–2, 32–3, 39, 41, 43–50, 63–5, 72–5, 86, 90, 92–4, 100–1, 106–7, 117, 131, 162, 183, 189 ,190
Trinidad, 61
troopships, 5, 15–16, 69–72, 82–6, 88, 197
tropical diseases, 20, 173
Truro, 13
Truthseeker, 22–3
tugs, 11, 13, 25, 56
Tunisia, 96, 136
Tunisian, 86
Turkey, 59, 72
Turnbull Brothers, 67, 142
Turnwell, 139–40
Tuscania, 88
29th Infantry, 71–2
Tyne, river, 40, 67, 68, 69, 99, 112, 145, 160
Tyne Cot cemetery, 196

U

U-boats, 39, 40, 61–2, 70–2, 75, 83, 87, 91–7, 103, 111–12, 115–26, 129–45, 150–3, 157–69, 173, 176, 182–90, 193–4, 196
Ukraine, 91, 168
Ulster, 87
Union Castle Line, 75
United States, 21, 32, 34, 37–9, 50, 61–2, 64, 66, 69, 70, 82–4, 88, 90–1, 94–6, 98–9, 103, 114, 124–5, 131, 140, 148–50, 163, 175
unrestricted submarine warfare, 8, 62, 117, 157–76, 190
Uruguay, 22, 63, 89
US Navy, 16
Uskside, 91

V

Valencia, 116
Valentiner, Max, 71, 142, 150, 168–9
Valparaiso, 21, 35, 63
Vancouver, 150
Vandyck, 65
Varney, T. E., 187
Victoria, 117
Victory, HMS, 97
Vineleaf see *Patrician* (later *Tarakol* and *Vineleaf*)
Voltaire, 183
von Spee, Maximilian, 66
von Werner, Egon, 116

W

W. & C. T. Jones, 39, 56, 96–7, 107, 132
W. I. Radcliffe (1886), 39
W. I. Radcliffe (formerly *Clarissa Radcliffe*, 1913), 41, 99
wages *see* pay
Wahmbeck Post Bodenfelde internment camp, 184
Wallace, Alfred, 73
war bonuses, 32, 51, 70, 84–5, 86, 94, 100
war crimes, 169, 194
War Loan, 191–2
war memorials, 4–5, 26, 35, 39, 40, 72, 97, 152, 153, 164, 193, 196
War Prince, 173
War Risk Insurance Association, 7
washing facilities, 41, 44–5, 51, 149
Waterford, 15, 17, 27, 86
Waterford, 17
Watkins, B., 96
Watkins, H. V., 35
Watkins, R. J., 168
Watters, William John, 162
Watts, W., 112
Wavelet, 114–15
weather conditions, 23–7, 37, 38, 67, 115, 119, 166, 186
Weaver, Mary Jane, 86–7
Weddigen, Otto, 131, 132
Wegener, Bernd, 144
Wellington, 70
Welsh language, 49–50
Welshpool, 85
Wemyss, Sir Rosslyn, 174
Wemyss Bay, 88
Wern Mill, 168
Werner, Wilhelm, 91, 168
Wesser, river, 57
West Africa, 20, 92, 96, 100, 172, 173, 174–5, 198
West African crew members, 92, 100, 190
West Hartlepool, 25
West Indies *see* Caribbean
West Marsh (formerly *Cairnisla*), 92
West of England SS Company, 57
Westergate, 43, 112
Western Daily Press, 190
Westfield, 95
Weston Point, 13
Wexford, 13
Whitby, 67
White, Alfred, 188
White Sea, 115
White Star Line, 16, 70, 82–3, 180

227

Wicklow, 13
Wilhelm II, Kaiser, 135
William Prichard, 35, 197, 198
William Thomas & Sons, 60–1
William Williams, 12
Williams, Albert Wynn, 71
Williams, D. (Caernarfon: steward, *North Wales*), 65
Williams, D. (Skewen: second mate, *Jane Radcliffe*), 99
Williams, David, 14
Williams, David Wynn, 71
Williams, Edward, 74
Williams, Enoch, 21
Williams, Frances, 68–9
Williams, George Edward, 73
Williams, Gilbert, 187
Williams, Griffith (Nefyn: bosun, *North Wales*), 65
Williams, Griffith T. (Edern: seaman, *Ortega*), 63
Williams, Hugh (Anglesey: engineer, *Anglia*), 75
Williams, Hugh (Llanengan, shipowner), 13
Williams, J. (New Quay: master, *Jane Radcliffe*), 98
Williams, J. (Penarth: fireman, *Lynrota*), 64
Williams, J. (Swansea: master, *Hurstdale* and *Rio Parana*), 65, 160–1
Williams, J. L. (Criccieth: master *Berwindvale*), 91
Williams, J. W. (Caernarfon: able seaman, *Candidate*), 137
Williams, John (Cardiff: master, *Indian City*), 130–1
Williams, John (Harlech: cook, *Ocean Ranger*), 20
Williams, John (Porthmadog: master, *Conway Castle*), 34
Williams, John Edward (Flintshire: able seaman, *Gem*), 68–9
Williams, Joseph, 73
Williams, Lewis, 20
Williams, Mary Ellen, 91
Williams, Meredith, 73
Williams, Owen (Anglesey: master, *Rosaleen*), 24
Williams, Owen (Pwll Parc: shipowner), 36
Williams, Robert, 73
Williams, T. J., 115
Williams, Thomas (Anglesey: mate, *Paddington*), 40

Williams, Thomas (Benllech: able seaman, *Ortega*), 63
Williams, Thomas (Port Dinorwic: apprentice, *Centurion*), 20–1
Williams, Victor, 17
Williams, W. (Dinas Cross: mate, *Picton*), 94
Williams, W. (Porthmadog: sailor, *Conway Castle*), 34–5
Williams, W. J. (Monmouth: chef, *Royal Edward*), 72
Williams, Watkin, 36
Williams, William (Anglesey: able seaman, *Linda Blanche*), 130
Williams, William (Holyhead: trimmer, *Anglia*), 74–5
Williams, William (Nefyn: carpenter, *North Wales*), 65
Williams, William (Tremadog: master at arms, *Lusitania*), 165
Wilmington, NC, 37, 38
Wilson, Havelock, 102
Wilson, J. Rees, 65
Windsor (1897) see *Jane Radcliffe* (formerly *Windsor*)
Windsor (1911), 99, 143
Winifred, 60
Winnfield, 32, 97
winter lay-ups, 12
wireless operators, 15, 49, 70–1, 73, 75, 164, 184
Wirral, 183
women, 3, 6, 8, 63, 81–93, 133, 134, 163, 168
Wood, James, 166–7
Woodfield, 150–1
Woodman, Richard, 2, 4
Woodville, 113–14
working conditions, 36–51, 98, 193–4
working hours, 41, 193
Workmen's Compensation Act, 19, 68–9, 181, 192
wrecks *see* shipwrecks
Wrexham, 49, 63, 64, 83, 85, 126

Y

Yarrowdale, 183–4
Yemeni crew members, 100

Z

Zanos Sifnias, 138–9
Zasologny, J., 183